PLYMOUTH

AN ILLUSTRATED HISTORY
From Conquest to Blitz

Crispin Gill

HALSGROVE

First published in Great Britain in 2009

Originally published as *Plymouth: A New History*

British Library Cataloguing-in-Publication Data
A CIP record for this title is available from the British Library

ISBN 978 1 84114 978 3

HALSGROVE
Halsgrove House
Ryelands Industrial Estate
Bagley Road, Wellington, Somerset TA21 9PZ
T: 01823 653777   F: 01823 216796
email: sales@halsgrove.com

Part of the Halsgrove group of companies
Information on all Halsgrove titles is available at: www.halsgrove.com

Printed and bound in Great Britain by CPI Antony Rowe Ltd., Wiltshire

CONTENTS

Preface to this Edition

The City of Plymouth has undergone many changes since it's foundation as a tiny fishing port. In his book *Plymouth - A New History* the late Crispin Gill produced a standard history of Plymouth that has remained in print in various editions for over four decades. Revised and updated over time this new work is further edited in a revised format.

Starting with the Norman Conquest the book follows each major development of the city, its social and political upheavals, and the major figures who emerged to become an indelible part of Plymouth's history, and that of the nation.

The late Crispin Gill (1916-2004) was born and brought up in Plymouth where he became a well known face as a reporter on the Western Morning News, rising to become Assistant Editor for over twenty years. Few people knew the city as Crispin did, having seen it before the destruction of the Second World War, and living through its greatest period of change in the twentieth century. He later became editor of the Countryman magazine and wrote and edited many books, including *Plymouth River* and *Sutton Harbour*.

Plymouth old and new. The ruined Charles Church with the new shopping centre beyond.

CHAPTER 1

The Town is Born

When William the Conqueror died his sons fought among themselves for 20 years as to who should possess Normandy. The issue was finally resolved when King Henry I of England besieged and captured Tinchebray in 1106. Among the Cornish knights with Henry was Renaldus de Valletort. The defender of Tinchebray was the Earl of Mortain, who was imprisoned for life and forfeited all his estates.

Now Valletort was Mortain's man, and held Trematon, Lipson and Honicknowle from him. Between the battle of Tinchebray and Henry's death in 1135 the king gave to Valletort the three royal manors in Plymouth, Maker, King's Tamerton and Sutton. The gift must have been made soon after the battle and looks remarkably like a reward for supporting the king, even though Mortain, the feudal overlord of Valletort, had turned the other way.

These Valletorts, who became key figures in the early story of Plymouth, had a flair for supporting the right side. Ten years after Tinchebray, King Henry gave the Mortain title and lands to his nephew, Stephen, and when, after Henry's death in 1135, the long Barons' War between Stephen and Matilda raged for the throne of England, the Valletorts were on Stephen's side. A Valletort witnessed a grant by Reginald, Earl of Cornwall and Brittany, to St Michael's Mount in 1140, in gratitude for the safety of King Stephen.

Renaud de Vautort was at Hastings. There is a Hugo and a Reginald Valletort in Domesday Book, but as Reginald is spelt in varying ways, and may or may not be Rainaldus, and as similar confusion haunts the family down through the generations, it is as well simply to deal with the family as a whole. They were the main agents of the Count of Mortain in Devon and Cornwall, holding the honour of Trematon, 23 manors in south-east Cornwall, and land right across south Devon from Modbury to the Clyst valley. The Valletorts came from Torteval, close to Mortain itself, a strongpoint about 15 miles from the Bay of Mont St Michel, and well sited to watch the Norman frontiers with both Brittany and Maine. They can have owned little land there, for when the choice had to be made between England and Normandy, even though the Earl of Mortain most valued his Norman possessions, the Valletorts fought for England. They appear to have been adventurers who made their fortune with the English conquest. In England they multiplied, acquiring estates in Cornwall, Devon and Somerset, marrying into the best families, giving land to the abbeys at Torre and Buckfast, witnessing the foundation deeds of both Plympton and Buckland abbeys, founding Modbury Priory themselves.

Sutton Manor House

When they acquired the manor of Sutton soon after 1105 they seem to have built a new house there in which they lived from time to time. Some years they had tenants there, and from their leases and from the

Trematon Castle from the west, showing how it broods over the countryside.

eventual sale documents the site of their manor house can be precisely located. It was on the west part of Church Hill, that is the hill dominated by St Andrew's. It stood between the highways from Sutton to Sourpool, and from Sutton to Stonehouse. Sourpool was a vast saltwater lake with a narrow link to the sea in Millbay, and stretched from Stonehouse to the foot of modern Royal Parade. The foundations of the Pearl Building on Royal Parade cut through a beach that was once the shore of Sourpool, and a downpour of rain at high tide used to see Derry's Roundabout under water. For those who knew pre-war Plymouth, these roads are simple to follow. The road from Sutton came down Bedford Street and then forked. The left-hand route down George Street and along Millbay Road led to the grist mills worked by the tide rushing in and out through the narrow neck of water between Sourpool and Millbay – hence the name Millbay. The Sourpool was not 'sour' water, and most probably took its name from sorrel, the red-seeded summer plant that was called 'sure' in old English and still grows thickly round the salt estuaries of south Devon and Cornwall. The right-hand fork went down Frankfort Street and King Street and Clarence Place, to Stonehouse High Street.

Both routes skirted the edge of Sourpool, and reference in a 1370 document to 'Vautordis parke att Pole' now becomes clear; it is the park of the Vautorts at the pool. Vautort is a phonetic rendering of Valletort. A secondary title of the modern Earls of Mount Edgcumbe is Viscount Valletort, a courtesy title held by the eldest son of the earl, and the family still pronounce it 'Vautort'.

The site is very similar to those of other Valletort houses in the area. The first one, Trematon, is close to the water of Forder Creek but away from the town at Saltash. Moditonham is on a deep creek on the Cornish bank of Tamar, not far from Botus Fleming, but still isolated. Inceworth was close to the water but away from Millbrook. Empacombe still has its own little harbour, but keeps aloof from Cremyll. Houses still standing on these sites can be studied in their unchanged rural setting, and the site beside Sourpool had the same characteristics. Clearly this is Sutton Valletort.

As lords of Trematon, the Valletorts owned all the waters of Plym and Tamar, and all the fish therein. Even after centuries of over-fishing there are still a dozen different varieties of edible fish to be caught in Plymouth Sound, and in those early days they must have been even more plentiful. One cannot imagine that dwellers on this shore, even though farmers by trade, would have ignored this source of food. After all, they could not even feed their cattle throughout the winter. A few were kept for breeding, the rest were slaughtered and the meat salted down. Fresh fish must have provided a welcome change of diet. Even their church was dedicated to St Andrew, the patron saint of fishermen.

Mr Robert Pearse, the historian of the Cornish harbours, suggests that when the Valletorts moved into Sutton they also moved the manorial seine net there from Trematon. The Hamoaze may have been a rich fishing-ground but Plymouth Sound was richer, and bigger; Sutton closer and Sutton Pool a sheltered base.

There may already have been fishing boats there. A seine net is hung from a line of floats and laid in a circle, either between two boats for herrings, mackerel and pilchards, or run out from a beach for other fish, and the circle closed so that all the fish inside are trapped. Such methods are still used in the Tamar and in Cornwall. As more fish would have been caught than could have been eaten fresh, even if there had been a sale to people further inland, the surplus would have had to be salted down.

Salt was produced locally at Tamerton, Egg Buckland, Woodford and Bere Ferrers, but the method of obtaining it by evaporating sea water requires a stronger sun than ours to produce any quantity. Such salt pans are still worked on the south coast of Brittany, and in medieval days La Rochelle was a good source of supply, while further south Gascony offered a ready market for salted fish. So here was the foundation for a sound two-way trade, out with fish and home with salt. It was a pattern already established in the south Cornish ports, and soon developed in Sutton. One can imagine a fishing village growing, then becoming something more as bigger boats and larger crews were wanted for the overseas trade. An early Valletort document names the first Plymothians: Roger de Fletehenda and Reginald de Veifer (with surnames taken from the place where they lived), Gilbert Cytharista (a harper), William Pistore (a baker), John Boscher (a woodcutter); the names show the occupations of a community which was beginning to specialise.

There were other small towns already in the neighbourhood. Saltash had a market at the time of Domesday, and Richard Valletort gave the town its charter in 1190. At Tavistock, there was the great Benedictine Abbey, founded in 974, well endowed by the Saxon royal family and already the richest abbey in Devon. A small town developed outside its gates and the abbot gave the townspeople a market in 1105, adding a three-day August fair in 1116.

Plympton

Plympton had two centres of interest, priory and castle. The priory was a Saxon foundation, dating back to Alfred's reign, but Henry I closed it down in 1121 – because 'the monks would not give up their concubines' – and refounded it for the Augustinians. Ranaldus de Valletorta witnessed the deed of foundation with the queen, the archbishops and the great nobles and prelates of the day. There are undated gifts by the Valletorts to Plympton Priory which probably date from this time; the right of fishing in Sourpool (in front of the new Valletort house), and Drake's Island with its rabbits. Drake's Island was then St Nicholas's Island, named after the little chapel which stood there. There were other such chapels around Plymouth in medieval times, probably those of religious hermits, and one still stands on Rame Head. The mention of rabbits in the Valletort gifts is believed to be the earliest reference to them in England, though the early Normans are known to have set up warrens in places where they were not likely to damage their crops. There was one in the tangled Efford hills above Marsh Mills.

Plympton Castle was one of the seats of the Redvers, Earls of Devon, who also held Okehampton and Exeter castles and 159 Devon manors. In the Barons' Wars, they backed Matilda, and King Stephen himself besieged Baldwin Redvers in Exeter. I n 1136 the king sent down 100 men to deal with Plympton Castle, which surrendered without a fight. The castle was slighted, made ineffective for any further rebellion and, after three months, Baldwin had to surrender at Exeter and retired into exile. But as Earl of Devon, Lord of the Isle of Wight and a descendant of an illegitimate son of William the

Plympton St Maurice Church.

Conqueror's grandfather, Baldwin was still a powerful figure and he was back in Devon within three years, as prosperous as ever. Plympton Castle was still one of his seats and it was in the shadow of the castle, not at the priory gates, that the new town of Plympton Erle – the earl's town – grew up.

The priory stood on a damp, exposed site where the Ridgeway reached the tidewater, but at that point the creeks split, one arm going up over the Colebrook area and the other reaching up to make a small harbour right under the walls of Plympton Castle. Further down the Plym, even in Saxon times, people could wade across the Wood Ford and the Ebb Ford when the tide was low enough, and though this meant that Plymouth harbour was only accessible at high water, it was here that the medieval trade of the district began. There was the produce of a rich farming district to take out, the needs of a rich priory and a wealthy man's castle to bring in. The first cargo of which there is any record is a cargo of slates from Plympton to Southampton in 1178. The town must have grown rapidly, for the fifth earl gave it a market in 1194 and, after various other grants, Plympton Erie was made a borough in 1242, returning members of Parliament but not incorporated.

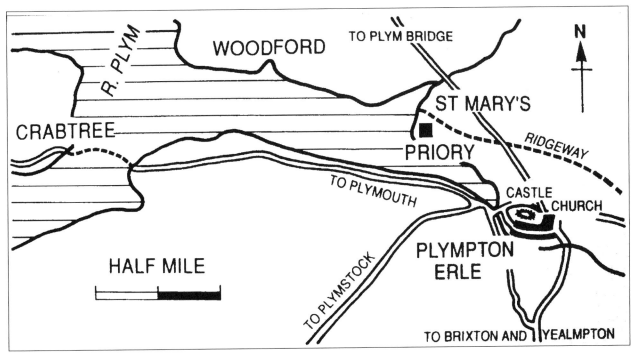

Port of Plympton. The road on the northern side of the castle to the harbour area is still called the Barbican, which means the watergate. Part of the road to Plym Bridge is now a pathfield.

Probably Plympton Erle had a church already, the Parish Church of Plympton. Another church was built outside the priory for the use of laymen, but which is the oldest foundation is a matter of dispute. The only rights the priors ever had in the church of Plympton Erle was that of appointing the priest, granted them in 1242. This church was dedicated to St Thomas à Becket and only changed to St Maurice after 1538. One would expect St Maurice to be the original Parish Church, but St Mary's has by far the bigger share of the original parish. If the priors carved out the new parish one would not be surprised at them taking all they could outside the built-up area of the little town. No town ever grew up around the priory as it did at Tavistock; until relatively recent times the parish of Plympton St Mary consisted of the hamlets of Colebrook, Underwood and Ridgeway.

Tin Mining

The real impetus to the growth of these new little Devon towns, Plympton and Tavistock, came from the discovery of tin on west Dartmoor. The earliest reference is in 1156, and almost at once Dartmoor became the largest source of the metal in Europe. There was virtually a tin rush. No mining was required, just a spade and a bucket, the patience to find alluvial deposits in the streams and the courage to endure the Dartmoor weather while washing the river sands for tin. Later, the miners dug back the banks of the streams in search of buried alluvial deposits, and worked upstream towards their original sources. Essentially it was an industry of small men, and as all the miners were under the king's protection it attracted not only small farmers and merchants from the neighbouring villages but runaway serfs and others dissatisfied with their medieval lot. It must have been a rougher and tougher business than anything Klondike or California saw in the nineteenth century. The marks of the old miners can still be seen in the south-west Dartmoor valleys, where the bottoms have been cut back to a U-shape, and where uneven heaps of stone lie just as they were thrown aside. The marks are clearly seen in the Plym just above Cadover Bridge, and, indeed, Sheepstor and Brisworthy, just north of Cadover, are the first names mentioned in tin records, as early as 1168.

From 1160 to 1190 the output of Devon tin was at its highest. It was refined into blocks, each of 160 lb, much too heavy to go far by packhorse, and shipped away, mainly to London. Three stannary (the word means tin) towns, Tavistock, Ashburton and Chagford, were named where the tin had to be taken for marketing under royal supervision. Each block was weighed, and a corner (coign) cut off so that its purity could be tested (coinage) before receiving the royal stamp. The miners had their own courts, and even their own prison at Lydford, where a castle was

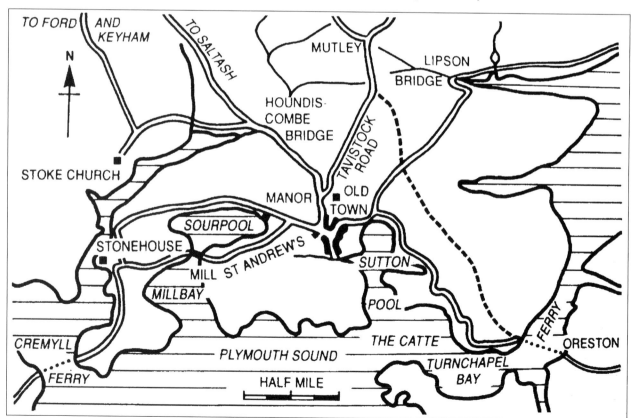

Norman Plymouth. As the village of Sutton grew, so the road pattern opened out. The Valletorts built their manor roughly just above the present Theatre Royal.

built in 1195 for that purpose. In 1198 Richard Coeur de Lion appointed a Lord Warden of the Stannaries to control the trade, with officers at each stannary town, a weigher for the Plym and Meavy valleys, and officers at the ports to see that no uncoigned tin was smuggled out.

Which were the tin ports? Tavistock almost certainly used the quays beside the Tamar at Morwellham, where the abbots of Tavistock had a hunting lodge (the building is still there, high above the river). It seems a long way upstream but it was still handling the output of mines in the nineteenth century. Whether it could handle all the west Dartmoor tin is another matter. King Richard, for instance, had 254,000 weight of tin shipped to him at La Rochelle in 1195. Was some taken downriver to Saltash and trans-shipped? Did Sutton have any of the trade? There is a record in 1313 of 129 ingots of tin being confiscated at Sutton, after having been found hidden under other cargo in the *Grace Due* of Fowey.

If tin did come down to Sutton, then the pack-horses would have jogged from Tavistock through Whitchurch, over the Walkham at Horrabridge (the boundary bridge; three parishes met there) and up to join the old ridge road to Sutton. There is evidence that a branch road to Plympton became important soon after the tin trade started. It still runs from The George at Roborough through Estover to Plym Bridge, and thence by Plym Bridge Lane to Plympton. The Plym was crossed at Plym Bridge, first mentioned in 1238. This was also an alternative route from Plymouth to Plympton when the Ebb Ford was impassable; it was necessary to go so far north because the water meadows beside the river from Plym Bridge to Marsh Mills today were in those days just mud flats in a wide creek. The route from Plymouth was through Compton and Egg Buckland to the head of the creek at Plym Bridge. The building of the bridge so early, soon after the start of the tin trade, shows the importance of the route.

Plym Bridge was also distinguished because a

Plym Bridge, the lowest bridge across the Plym. Below the bridge the water meadows were originally part of the wide estuary, and tidal.

chapel dedicated to St Mary the Virgin stood beside it. A Papal letter of 1450 directed the Prior of Plympton to depute fit priests to hear confessions there and to absolve 'the great multitude of faithful from divers parts of the world' who resorted to the chapel 'on account of the many miracles which God has wrought therein'.

When Plympton became a stannary town in 1328 its initial petition asked that the coinage should be moved there from Tavistock since it was a maritime town where the tin could be straightway put aboard ship, whereas Tavistock was so far inland that transport costs were very high. Their petition was successful (after all, the jury who made the decision was largely drawn from men living near Plympton). Tavistock was furious and protested so strongly that, in the end, it kept its stannary and Plympton was added as a fourth Devon stannary town.

Plym Mouth

But Plympton in 1328 was very worried about its maritime trade, which it was losing to Plymouth, and the reason lay in this very tin business. Tin streaming sends a lot of waste matter down the rivers to add to the silt Nature has been sending down for centuries. Protests about silt in the Plym caused by the tinners form an endless record, continuing right into Elizabethan times. The Plym, the Meavy and the Tory Brook which comes down through Plympton, were all tin-streaming valleys on Dartmoor, and were all being exploited by the middle of the twelfth century. So, from 1150 onwards, the Laira estuary and the creek up to Plympton must have been getting more and more shallow, while the fords at Ebb Ford and Woodford became bars to the passage of ships. The times when ships could get up to Plympton must have become more and more limited either side of high water and, increasingly they would have to anchor at Plym mouth and wait for high tide before going up with their cargoes. Reloaded, they would have come down from Plympton on the tide and then waited at Plym mouth for fair winds or weather to take them on their voyage. The pattern is the same today, with our bigger ships waiting at anchor in the Sound until the top of the tide will take them to the quaysides of Cattedown or Millbay or the Dockyard.

Those waiting ships could anchor safely in Turnchapel Bay whatever the weather, though they might have been a little uncomfortable with wind against tide. But on the other side of Plym mouth there was the full shelter of Sutton Pool. There, too, was the little fishing village of Sutton, with its own ships trading to western France, with carpenters, sailmakers and riggers if wanted, victuals or water available, and ale of an evening. Seamen have not changed over the centuries.

The longer tin mining went on, and the longer the waits at Plym mouth, the greater became the inducement to use Sutton at Plym mouth as a terminal port instead of Plympton. It is hard to put dates to the process, but the first record of the name Plymouth, and the first cargoes, appear in the Pipe Rolls for 1211. There was a shipload of bacon for Portsmouth, and wine for Nottingham.

So Plymouth came into being as a port at a time when events in Europe were bringing the western Channel ports into prominence. After the trouble experienced by the First Crusade, it was decided that the second should go by sea. A fleet of 164 ships was assembled and sailed from Dartmouth. When they reached northern Portugal, weary and battered, they were asked, 'Why go all the way to the Holy Land to fight the infidel? We have him here. Help us clear our land of Moors.' So the chivalrous knights agreed, Lisbon was freed, and there was born a trade in wine and fruit between Dartmouth and Portugal that continued for centuries.

In 1154 Henry of Anjou became King Henry II of England. With his own and his wife's estates, all the western Atlantic seaboard was under one rule, from Ireland through England and Brittany down to the Pyrenees. Trade was unfettered; there was La Rochelle for buying salt, Bayonne for selling salt fish and Bordeaux for buying wine. Salt fish is a thirsty business. The vineyards around Bordeaux are still the best in the world; and when Englishmen took to claret as their national wine, Plymouth built its commercial fortune on it.

Another king, John, saw Brittany become independent again and, in 1204, Normandy broke away from the English Crown. There were still vast lands in western France acknowledging English rule, but to reach them involved the long haul round Ushant and across the Bay of Biscay. And that was a voyage calling for West Country ships built for the Atlantic, and West Country seamen brought up in that trade, rather than the shallow-draught ships of the Cinque Ports, which had been the link through Normandy. Now, Dartmouth, Plymouth and Fowey had a new place on the map.

In 1244 Seville was freed from the Moors and rapidly became the entrepot where all the riches of the Mediterranean were brought into the Atlantic for purchase and reshipment by the merchants of the Channel and northern Europe. It was a simple and logical extension of the Biscay voyages. No wonder Sutton was growing in importance.

Market Grant

But to take advantage of their new opportunities the people of the little town had to be able to buy and sell, to conduct business. They had to be a market town, and the market itself would be a useful source of revenue to whoever owned it. The Valletorts were the lords of Saltash, where the market dated back to before the Conquest. At Tavistock, the Abbot had set

one up in 1105, and the Earls of Devon had been given a market at Plympton Erle in 1194. Sutton received its market in 1254, and the rights went to the Prior of Plympton. Until then, all the Priors had possessed in Plymouth was the right of fishing in Sourpool.

King Henry III was in winter quarters with his army in France when, on 27 January 1254, he signed the grant giving Sutton its market, so making it a town. He had been King of England for nearly 40 years but had little love for the English. The barons plagued him as they had his father, John, and he far preferred the French relatives of his wife. Indeed, his ambition was to win back all the French lands of his great namesake and grandfather, Henry Plantagenet. That was why he was wintering in the dusty little fortress town of Bazas, on the edge of the vineyards of Sauterne, awaiting better weather to drive out again across the sandy wastes of the Landes and clear Aquitaine of the French. Now the affairs of England were before him as he sat in council with the Bishops of Bath and Hereford, the Earl of Hereford and Essex, the Earl of Warwick and other gentlemen. Who presented the petition about Plymouth is unknown, but it was presumably the Priory. Perhaps Prior Baldwin himself had made the voyage from Plympton to Bordeaux the previous autumn, and then ridden the 40 miles out to Bazas when the Royal army had finally settled down.

One can imagine the king considering the claim, and pondering its implications. The Earl of Devon, he would recall, was lord of the hundred. True, Baldwin de Redvers was only about ten years old and a ward of the queen's uncle, but his mother's family were arrant rebels. The lord of the manor was Ralph Valletort. His wife, Joan, had been mistress of the king's brother, Richard (who had been made Earl of Cornwall and so lord of the Honour of Trematon many years earlier). The affair had gone on for ten years and there was a son. Richard's wife was the queen's sister, and even if he did not care what his brother did, had there been complaints from his sister-in-law to his queen? Plympton Priory was rich, it managed its large estates well and the Pope and the Church had always been good friends to the king – which was more than could be said for most English landowners.

So the charter was sealed, granting to the Prior and Convent of Plympton and their successors a weekly market on Thursdays at Sutton in the county of Devon, and a yearly fair there on the eve, the day and the morrow of St John the Baptist. All the lords around the table signed, as they signed State papers day after day.

Plympton Priory, an Augustine foundation, had been set up by Bishop Warelwast of Exeter, nephew and chaplain of the Conqueror, as part of the plan to bring the Saxon Church, whose priests were appointed by lay landlords, under central discipline.

The Augustines were a preaching order of canons who ministered to the people in the parishes round their priory, and whose churches came under priory control. The active interest of Warelwast brought many local parish churches into Plympton's hands but, increasingly, the canons either lived in their parishes as normal priests or resided in the priory and appointed vicars to the parishes, just like any lay holder of an advowson. In the 26 parishes to which Plympton Priory had the right to appoint priests at the Dissolution, only two of the 18 canons of Plympton were acting as vicars, Henry Luxton at Shaugh and Bernard Cole at Wembury. A thirteenth-century minstrel-turned-monk wrote of the Augustines: 'Among them one is well-shod, well-clothed and well-fed. They go out when they like, mix with the world, and talk at table.' They were not tonsured but wore a black biretta, long black cassock and hood. By 1288, Plympton Priory was the second richest religious house in Devon; by the Dissolution, it had even outstripped Tavistock in wealth.

The Prior of Plympton had upheld his right of presentment to St Andrew's against the Valletorts as early as 1159. Perhaps in those early days a canon of Plympton did officiate in the parish of Plymouth but, by 1333, the Priory was complaining to the bishop that the Vicar of St Andrew's had so increased his income (evidence of the rapid growth of the town) that the amount payable to them should be increased and the vicar's share reduced accordingly. At that time the Vicar of St Andrew's returned to Plympton as 'a professed religious' or monk, and another canon was nominated to St Andrew's as incumbent. Two years later St Andrew's was being held in plurality by Ralf de Ryngstede of Lincoln, who was also a canon and prebend of Exeter Cathedral, as well as holding offices in Bangor and Wiltshire. He declared that if he was allowed only two offices he would keep the Exeter and Plymouth posts. The Bishop of Exeter nominated the vicar in 1334 and in 1472 licensed the perpetual Vicar of St Andrew's, John Stubbes, with authority also to officiate at St Lawrence Stonehouse. It would appear that Plympton's only interest was in drawing its annual pension from the church, just as the new market town was a strictly commercial venture.

The Earl of Devon saw that he had missed an opportunity by letting the priory get a market grant for Sutton in 1254, so in 1257 he obtained one as well. But it was only a paper entry, for the earl was then actively engaged in the war with Simon de Montfort against the king, and died in 1262, poisoned, it is said, at the table of the king's uncle, Peter of Savoy, who had been his guardian. He was the last Redvers, Earl of Devon, and when his mother, Amicia, founded Buckland Abbey in 1273, it was in honour of his memory and his father's. Amicia gave to the new abbey the Redvers rights to the hundred of Roborough, but there is no mention of any market held by her family.

Ralph Valletort, the cuckold, did not argue. He gave the prior a site at Sourpool for a mill, the right of way along the old fishing-path to reach the mill, and the manorial right to grind the corn of everyone in the manor. He died soon after, and his son, Reginald, died young and without heirs. His uncle, Roger, succeeded to the Valletort estates and began to dispose of them. Richard, Earl of Cornwall, who had been defeated with the king by the barons at the battle of Lewes, was strengthening his position in the west. To Launceston he had added Lostwithiel and Restormel Castle, and in 1270 he bought Trematon Castle and all the feudal rights which went with the Honour of Trematon. Successive Earls and Dukes of Cornwall have held Trematon and all the rights it gave them over Sutton and the waters of the Sound. Roger Valletort died insane in 1275 and his two nieces began a long series of lawsuits claiming that the sale of Trematon and the rest should be set aside on the grounds that their uncle had been mad when he sold their patrimony. But it availed them nothing.

One other sale made by the mad uncle is interesting. The vital deeds are undated but, in the first, Roger de Valletort grants to Ralph, son of Richard, all Cremyll and Maker; later deeds add the Cremyll ferry rights and the fishery of Tamar. It is suggested that the Richard named is Richard, Earl of Cornwall, that his son Ralph was the result of Richard's union with Joan Valletort, and that his son's family took the name of 'de Stonehouse' after the village of west Stonehouse, which then stood at Cremyll.

The Valletorts survived, but in Plymouth they were reduced to their manor of Sutton. There long lingered in Plymouth a memory that the family had

The remains of Plympton Priory, from a sketch by Samuel Prout (1783–1852). Even this has now disappeared.

Devil's Point, seen from the rocks across the Narrows. The Gremyll Ferry had its Devon landing place where the cliff meets the Victualling Yard building.

lost its overlordship to the Crown through some villainy. The story was embroidered over the years, and in about 1540 Leland wrote: 'I hard say, that the landes of Valletorte were for a morther doone by one of them confiscate, and sins the great part of them have remaynid yn is the kinges handes.' No murder in fact, it would seem; just an unfaithful wife and a mad uncle.

Perhaps we can forgive Joan Valletort, for Richard was the king's brother and the most ambitious man in Europe; he was even elected Emperor of the Holy Roman Empire. Of the Stonehouse family, believed to be the offspring of her union with Richard, the heiress in 1369, Cecilia, married Stephen Durnford, a land speculator from Tavistock, who had already bought Stonehouse. The next year they bought the Valletort manor house in Sutton, and in 1386 Rame

was added to the estate. A century later there were no male Durnfords left; the daughter Joan married Piers Edgcumbe, whose father made his fortune in the service of Henry VII and built Cotehele. Until recent years the Earls of Mount Edgcumbe held nearly all these estates, heirs of the long Valletort story that goes back to the Conqueror.

The Valletorts may well have provided the initial stimulus which started the growth of the small fishing community between St Andrew's Church and Sutton Pool, but by 1254 they bowed out, content to remain rural landlords at Sutton Valletort. The new town became Sutton Prior, one of many such monastic boroughs created by Henry III, every one of whose histories is a long story of struggle by the townspeople against their clerkish overlords.

CHAPTER 2

The Royal Port

A market cross was the centre of Sutton Prior, and stood in a triangle at the junction of three streets: Whimple Street, leading to the Parish Church; High Street, to the waterside, and Buckwell Street to Breton Side and the road to Exeter. Around the cross every Thursday the market stalls were set up, and the Prior's steward moved through the shoppers, collecting toll from the stall-keepers, checking their weights and measures and settling any disputes between stall-holder and customer. Serious argument would be referred to a court which he would hold the following Monday morning, sitting with the leading men of the town.

But change was to follow change. In 1272 Richard, Earl of Cornwall, died. His son Edmund (by Richard's second wife, the lovely Sanchia of Provence, King Henry's sister-in-law) lacked his father's European ambitions but was concerned to pull his earldom of Cornwall into a profit-making entity. His palace was at Lostwithiel, and his secondary centres at Launceston and Trematon. By 1274 the townsmen of Plympton, their market damaged to some extent by the new rival at Sutton, complained to King Edward I that the bailiff of Trematon was using the port of Plymouth without payment or acknowledgement, had taken over the ferry from Sutton Pool to Hooe (a good route through Plymstock to Plympton), was taking sand from the estuary for agricultural purposes, and had gone into the fish business in Sutton. Edmund of Cornwall was still King Edward's cousin, and, what is more, as lord of Trematon he had undoubted rights over the waters of Plym and Sutton Pool.

By 1280, the abbot of the new monastery at Buckland had been installed and, by gift from Amicia of Devon, he was now also lord of the hundred of Roborough. As such, his court at Horrabridge was the legal authority right down into Sutton. Clearly there was a tangle of claims, and two inquiries into them were held in Exeter in 1281. At the first, John Valletort claimed that he was lord of the manor of Sutton. The Prior of Plympton declared that he owned the 'ville' of Sutton, with assize of bread and ale (the administration of mercantile law, as distinct from the civil and criminal law cases heard in the hundred courts).

The second inquiry of 1281 reached positive decisions that were of major importance to Sutton's future. To understand the decisions, one must realise that the town – that is, the built-up area – was on the north bank of an arm of Sutton Pool which reached up across the present-day Parade. Summarised, the judge's findings were that:

Sutton was on the coast of the port of Plymouth, but no part of it was on the King's soil.
Part of Sutton north of the coast was on the soil of the Prior of Plympton, where he had assize of bread and ale, and certain rents.
Part of Sutton south of the coast was on the soil of John Valletort, where he had certain rents, but the Abbot of Buckland had assize of bread and ale.
The port of Plymouth belonged to the King, and paid £4 a year to the Exchequer.
It would prejudice neither the King nor anyone else if Sutton were made a free borough and its inhabitants free burgesses.

The two vital points emerging from all this, apart from this last apparent claim for freedom by the inhabitants, was that the Prior's authority and ownership was limited to the urban area, that the Valletorts were still lords of the rest of Sutton and that the harbour belonged to the King. It would seem that this claim rested on the fact that Sutton had once been a royal manor, and that this royal authority over the water was exercised as a tenant by Edmund of Cornwall, through Trematon.

War was to make this royal claim of new importance, for when, in 1294, the French King tried to seize the English possessions in western France, Edward I, a soldier all his life, retaliated. That year, a

In this 1966 photograph of the Parade inlet of Sutton Pool, the right-hand quay is Sutton Prior, on the soil 'north of the coast', and the left-hand quay is Sutton Valletort, 'south of the coast'.

Buckland Abbey; the north transept was cut off when the building was turned into a dwelling house and the two side walls became the walls of the wings either side.

fleet sailing from Portsmouth to Gascony was scattered off the Cornish coast and reassembled in Plymouth. The following year, a fleet again assembled at Plymouth and this time the King's brother, the Earl of Lancaster, sailed with it. Corn for the Army was brought to Plymouth from all the western counties. This expedition, which was repeated in 1296 and again in 1297, was the start of Plymouth's long connection with the Crown as a naval base. As such, Plymouth rapidly outstripped its neighbouring rivals to become the pre-eminent port of the western Channel.

Dartmouth and Fowey have anchorages as sheltered as the Cattewater and Sutton Pool, and perhaps roomier. But both are approached through narrow entrances between high cliffs where the wind can play tricks, whereas the approach to Plymouth is across the wide Sound, which gives shelter in all but a southerly blow. Again, the land approaches to Dartmouth and Fowey are steep and difficult; even the railway never got to Dartmouth, and only reached Fowey with difficulty. By the time Edward I wanted a western base Plymouth had a reasonable road to Exeter, with all the rivers bridged, and so to London.

Plymouth could water the ships and the soldiers, either from the little streams flowing into Sutton Pool or from the town wells, remembered today in street names: the west well, the buck well (where clothes were bucked, or washed), the fyne well, Lady well (where a hermit had a little chapel, probably dedicated to Our Lady). Buckland Abbey was a Cistercian house and the Cistercians were the great agriculturalists of the day; with an estate of 20,000 acres stretching between Plym and Tavy they were a ready-made victualling organisation. The massive tithe barn at Buckland still bears testimony to the size of their undertaking, and it is not surprising that when the Hundred Years War started Buckland was at once given permission to fortify itself; whereas the defence of Tavistock, Plympton and Buckfast abbeys was not considered necessary until 40 years later.

Yet Plympton was a rich establishment, fit to offer hospitality to royal personages and great nobles, a place where the war chest (for it had to travel with real gold in those pre-banking days) could be guarded, away from the press of soldiers and sailors.

King Edward was himself in Plymouth for over a month in the spring of 1297. He arrived at Plympton between 6 April and 10 April, and signed a document at Sutton as late as 8 May. So long a stay shows the importance he attached to the expedition he was fitting out for Gascony, for he had just finished a campaign in Scotland, had trouble on his hands from

Wales and was planning a summer expedition through Flanders, as well as this western campaign.

He resolved to stay at 'Plemmuth' until he had seen his fleet sail. Every corner of the west was searched for ships to serve as transports and to carry food. Again, corn came in from all the western counties, and a year's output of tin was appropriated to finance the expedition.

The impetus to the growth of Plymouth in those years must have been immense. When Edward called his first Parliament in 1295, it was attended by burgesses from the older towns of Tavistock and Plympton. For the second Parliament of 1298 these two were joined for the first time by burgesses from Plymouth, William of Stoke and Nicholas the 'Rydlere'.

The Wine Ships

War, tin, fish, hides, lead, wool and cloth; these were the export trades of Plymouth. On the import side there was war again (expeditions moved both ways), wine (a little from Spain and Portugal as well as Bordeaux), iron (from Bilbao in northern Spain), fruit, woad (for dyeing cloth), onions, wheat and garlic. No customs returns are available for Plymouth but these goods appear in the records of other south Devon ports, whose trade can have been little different.

The lead was a side product of the mines of Bere Ferrers and Bere Alston, where silver had been discovered about 1290. Mines were royal property, and silver a welcome gift to a monarch with a war on his hands. Some 270 lb of silver were shipped from Maristow to London in 1294 and, between 1292 and 1297, the Devon mines yielded £4,046 in silver and £360 in lead. By 1297, the King had 284 miners from Derbyshire and 35 from Wales at work at Bere. Two years later he leased the mines to Americo Frescobaldi, one of the great Florentine bankers, the Lombards, who had replaced the Jews in England as merchant bankers to the Crown. Lombard agents were to be found all over England, and their badge of three golden balls is still the sign of the pawnbroker. They handled Cistercian wool and, quite likely, the annual crop from Buckland Abbey. Americo Frescobaldi was very close to the King, and had the wine customs of Bordeaux, making a strong financial link between west Devon and Bordeaux.

From an almost indecipherable roll in the Public Record Office emerge the names of the first Plymouth ships carrying wine from Bordeaux. The record is for 1303:

28 September La de Plenmue	*47 tuns*
30 September Navis Santi Salvatoris	
de Plemua	*49 tuns 1 pipe*
1 October Navis Sancta Michaelis de Plemua	
	79 tuns

A tun of wine was equivalent to four barrels or hogsheads of 63 gallons each. Two barrels made a pipe – half a tun. The size of a ship was calculated on the basis of how many tuns of wine she could carry, and complicated measurements were made to arrive at this figure without actually loading. So the tunnage, or tonnage, of a ship originated.

There is a gap in these Bordeaux customs records until 1308. Then, in the roll beginning 11 May and listing 44 ships, there occurs: '19 June *Navis Santi Andrei de Plomuth* portagium 124 tuns. Rector Ricardus Baykins.'

This is the first recorded name of a Plymouth sea captain, Richard Baykins, and a French clerk, using the Norman French of the day, is making as big a hash of English names as his descendents do today. Was the rector (master) really Captain Bacon, or is it an H? It would be nice to call him Haykins, or Hawkins. Fittingly, the ship (navis) was the *St Andrew*, no doubt named after Plymouth's Parish Church (30 years earlier, in the taxation of Pope Nicholas I, it was named S. Andree).

That autumn, with the wine harvest in, there were seven Plymouth ships braving the equinoctial gales round Ushant and, as like as not, fighting off French Breton and Norman pirates. All told, they carried nearly 200,000 gallons of wine. There are more records for 1310, and from them all 11 Plymouth ships emerge, eight of over 100 tons. There were other West Country ships in the trade, six from Fowey and one from Polruan, four from Looe and one from the Fal. The Cornish ships were not as big as the Plymouth ones, though there were even bigger craft sailing from Bordeaux for up-Channel ports.

Some financial returns show the rate of Plymouth's growth. The Crown, to save itself the cost of collecting dues, rented out or 'farmed' its assets to private individuals. In 1296 the farm fee for Sutton Pool was 49s.6d. a year. By 1334 it was £17.10s., a sevenfold increase in 40 years. Sutton was worth more than all the Cornish ports put together. Exeter and Dartmouth kept higher trade figures than Plymouth all through the fourteenth century. Exeter was the centre of Devon's new cloth industry and Totnes (for which Dartmouth was the outport) the second centre. Plymouth had only the coarser cloth of Tavistock, and some of the Ashburton output.

Friaries

Round the turn of the century the friars, too, were moving in; no doubt there was need of their ministration in the rapidly growing seaport whose population was liable to multiply many times over when the royal expeditions brought in soldiers and sailors by the thousand. Seaports with men of half-a-dozen different nationalities fresh in from sea, garrison towns with soldiers for whom tomorrow meant war and imminent death, and yesterday a battle they

A reconstruction of the Woolster Street Parade area in the fourteenth century, based on various excavations in the area by James Barber and Exeter Museum Archaeological Field Unit. Woolster Street (the street of the wool merchants) runs horizontally across the drawing; the merchants' houses are on the north side and their warehouses, built out into the harbour, on the south. (DRAWN BY PIRAN BISHOP OF THE EXETER FIELD UNIT)

The gin distillery; this wall, at present inside the building, was an external wall in the medieval building.

were lucky to have survived; these are never gentle places. On top of that, it was a raw new town, growing fast, with new populations moving in, mainly from the neighbouring rural areas but bringing in, too, all kinds of unsettled people.

Archaeological excavations conducted by James Barber of the City Museum staff in 1963–69, and by Exeter Museum Archaeological Field Unit in 1991, have established a great wave of new building from the late-thirteenth century to the fifteenth century. The 'digs' on either side of Vauxhall Street, roughly between the top of Southside Street and the end of the Custom House, show a succession of buildings, with merchants' houses and waterside warehouses being built out into the harbour. Tin, shipping, the support of wars, all brought an initial impetus to growth which snowballed over the decades.

No wonder the friars moved in. Since the eighteenth century a building in Southside Street has been known as the Blackfriars. Plymouth Gin, which has been distilled there since 1793 and has a black-robed friar as its trademark, does its best to perpetuate the legend. But there is no written record anywhere of the Dominicans having been in Plymouth, and Friars Lane, beside the distillery, leads to the site of the Grey Friars, the Franciscans. The building goes back to the fourteenth century and is unlikely to have been a private house. It was a gaol in 1605, owned by the Hele family later in the century, and was the Congregational meeting-house from 1689 to 1705. But there is no evidence that it ever housed any kind of friars.

The Grey Friars (Franciscans, and followers of St

Francis of Assisi) had probably built a leper house on the 'headland' (at the top of North Hill) above the town by 1300, and this Maudlyn, with its thatched roof on the healthy hilltop, was Plymouth's first hospital. 'Goddeshouse' it is called in the raw words of the Dissolution accounts of 1538, 'for the relief of impotent and lazare people'. There were 14 inmates then, though sometimes there had been 20 or more. Beside their 'mansyon house', they had funds from certain lands given them by the charitable, worth in all £4.7s. a year. In 1566, Plymouth Corporation was buying reeds for its roof, and the building seems finally to have disappeared under the Civil War defences of 1643.

The first friary proper in the town, the White Friars, was built by the Carmelites in 1314. Its site, just below Beaumont Park, is known to this day as the Friary; in the last century a railway station was built there and, more recently, a housing estate. Archaeological excavations in 1991 before the housing started revealed the foundations of a defensive wall and various other buildings.

The Grey Friars built their Friary proper on the other side of the town, on the edge of the Hoe where permission to alienate six acres of royal land was given in 1361. The site was between the top of New Street and the Hoe, bounded on one side by Castle Dyke Lane and the other by a continuation of Friars Lane – roughly the site now occupied by the ruins of Highland Cottage and the empty warehouse.

For many years it was believed that their building was on the northern side of the Parade inlet, behind the present Sutton Harbour Company office. This idea was first fostered by Harris in 1806 by the ruins of a cloistered courtyard with murals of biblical scenes. It has now been established that this was owned by the Pollard family in 1513 (when the friaries were still in business), was sold in 1544 to William Hawkins who lived there, and was being leased out in two sections by 1608. One half by the early-seventeenth century was the Golden Fleece Inn, which by 1749 had changed its name to the Mitre. The Mitre, which included the courtyard with its twisted pillars, was demolished in 1811 to make way for the Exchange.

Notice that none of these friaries was in Sutton on priory land; the established Church had no love for them and there were constant battles between the Plymouth friaries, the vicars of Plymouth and the Bishops of Exeter. Whether the friars were usurping the work of the vicar, or doing the work he was neglecting, is not clear, but certainly their friaries were as close to the town and the people they came to serve as they could get; the buildings give a fair idea of the size of Sutton. They may early have bred in Plymouth a critical view of the established church; they certainly created a taste for sermons and they were able to offer sanctuary, with freedom from arrest, for 40 days. They were outspoken to the end,

even if their friaries did eventually become as sumptuous as any buildings in the town. John of Gaunt lodged with the White Friars in 1386; it is recorded as the 'Palace of John of Gaunt, at the Carmelite Friary'. Both friaries were close to the harbour, more convenient than Plympton Priory, and one wonders how often they housed the royal persons whom the French wars brought to Plymouth.

Self-Government

These wars saw a lull in the early days of the fourteenth century, while Edward II wrestled with problems closer to home, and with the Scots. In 1302, 1308 and again in 1310, Sutton was ordered to hold ships in readiness to sail north against 'The Bruce'. But little happened and, meanwhile, the men of Plymouth were taking a close look at their own affairs.

The town's growth was being cramped by the priors, but, in 1310, a 'final concord and agreement' (which suggests a long argument) was reached in the presence and at the mediation of the Bishop of Exeter and others, between the Prior and the burgesses of the commonalty of the town of Sutton. Here is evidence that the burgesses, the chief men, were working together and forming the first local government. They had no corporate being in law, and Richard the Tanner had to affix his seal on their behalf. He is called the Prepositus, which means reeve or bailiff, but he cannot have been the prior's bailiff or he would never have signed for the townsmen. Clearly then, he was the townsmen's leader, holder of the office that in time merged into the mayoralty. A writ of 1254 to the bailiff of the port of Plymmue may refer to the King's officer, but by 1289 there was a writ to the Bailiffs and Commonalty of Plymouth, the first sign of any corporate life.

The agreement related to Sutton's market where, around the central stone cross, stalls had been set up for the sale of fish, flesh and other victuals. These stalls belonged to the Prior, and though townsmen had no right to set up any others without his permission, they had been doing so. Now it was agreed that there should be 18 stalls round the cross, for which the burgesses should pay a penny a year, this rent to be paid to the Prepositus for the time being. It was further agreed that they should not put up any more stalls, there or elsewhere in the town, without the licence of the Prior. This looks as if the Prepositus was expected to change frequently, or perhaps even to be elected annually. Certainly it indicates a body of townspeople strong enough to fight for their rights.

In 1310, Earl Edmund of Cornwall died heirless and his estates passed to the Crown, together with all the Trematon rights in Plymouth. Three years later the Crown was taking the Prior to court to prove his rights, and it was decided that he held the view of

Detail of the Henry VIII defence map of Plymouth in which all the main buildings of the town can be distinguished, including the market cross in the centre.

frankpledge (the right to try criminal cases less than felonies), of ducking-stool and pillory (for punishing minor offenders), the assize of bread and ale, the fishing of all the Cattewater, and the right to grant the lease of houses.

In 1317, the burgesses of Plymouth were themselves at court petitioning to be granted, for an annual rent, certain waste places belonging to the Crown. The Prior and two Valletorts, John of Moditon and John of Clyst (in east Devon) opposed this, claiming that the King had no land in the town, that the Prior was lord of two parts and the Valletorts of the third part. This must surely have meant that the town was growing out beyond the original land of the Prior, into Valletort land.

Plymouth's witnesses at the hearing in Exeter are interesting. Among them were John Gifforde (the Giffords were still the owners of Compton), William Kemell (from Camel's Head) and Walter Colrigg (from Coleridge). Either these nearby gentry were taking a hand in the town's trade, or else these were younger sons moving into the town to make their fortunes.

The Sheriff of Devon found that, before the foundation of the ville of Sutton, the Kings of England had a piece of waste land near the port of Plymouth, five perches long and one perch broad, and a six-acre piece of land recovered from the sea where a certain

house of the town was built. At this place, according to the Sheriff, the King's ancestors, by their bailiffs, had held their courts, and fishing-boats of the town and other places were accustomed to resort there to dry their sails and nets, and to put their fish up for sale. They had paid the King a rent of 12d., and a penny on each basket of fish, and the proceeds had amounted to £4 a year.

The oldest streets of Plymouth were built on the slopes running down from the church and the market cross. Between the foot of the hill and the water's edge today there is an area of more than six acres on which no housing development took place until Tudor times. Part of it is still called Sutton Wharf, and this must be the six acres formed 'by the withdrawal of the sea', whose royal ownership resulted from it having been part of the sea bed, and so part of the honour of Trematon. It was the base of the fishing fleet, and the site of the wholesale fish market, as distinct from the retail fish market licensed by the Prior at the market cross. There is a similar story of royal ownership, through the duchy of Cornwall, of the foreshore at Dartmouth.

Why was the court concerned with that other piece of land, five perches by one? It was not very large, just 27½ yds by 5½ yds, but it must have been important. The perch was commonly used as a measurement of stonework, and this may be the clue. Was it, perhaps, the first quay in the harbour? It would be long enough to berth a ship of the times, make loading and unloading easier than from a ship run on to the beach and unloaded into carts, or anchored off and unloaded into boats. The first sketch map ever made of Plymouth, when Henry VIII was surveying the defences, shows ships moored along Sutton Wharf and round the corner of Guy's Quay, into the Parade inlet. There is still a piece of quay wall there which fits the measurements, and it may have been that very first quay in Sutton Harbour.

What becomes very clear from all this is that the influence of the Prior of Plympton was confined to the town, and his powers to appointing the vicar, holding the minor law-court, and collecting rents and market dues. Otherwise, he was limited to the position of any other landlord and, moreover, had to contend with a strong body of townspeople already developing their own form of self-government.

In shape, Plymouth was similar to many little towns which grew up in the days of Edward I, with parallel streets at right-angles to one another, the church and the market-place standing apart, the market-place the rallying place from which streets ran out to the perimeters of the town. But in the case of Plymouth, Edward I was there to see it taking shape and, through the port so firmly established as belonging to the Crown, he built up its prosperity.

An army assembled again in 1324, when Edward II, having made a truce with the Scots, could turn to the perpetual nibblings of the French kings at

Gascony. A fleet was assembled in Plymouth, 200 foot soldiers were sent from south Wales, and 800 archers came from south and south-east England. But royal troubles at home kept the fleet from sailing, and it must have meant a rowdy summer for the town to have 1,000 idle soldiers and the crews of an idle fleet kicking their heels in the port. The ships were private vessels pressed into the King's service, and while they waited they earned no money. Small wonder that many slipped off to their normal business; trade never yet stopped for war.

The Hundred Years War

With Edward III on the throne, a soldier like his grandfather, he resumed the French wars in real earnest in 1336. This was the start of the Hundred Years War and Plymouth was many times to pay the price of being a royal port; regularly were the townsmen to see the red glow of their burning houses and each time it was part of the major design of the war.

In 1337, the French King assembled a fleet at Marseilles for a Crusade; instead, he brought it north to the Channel to help his Scottish allies. Edward invaded the Low Countries; the French fleet attacked Hastings, Dover and Folkestone; Southampton was burnt; 18 French galleys and pinnaces were sent down-Channel and descended upon Plymouth.

'They brent certain great ships and a great part of the town,' says Stowe. The French were driven back by the Devon militia under the 80-year-old earl, and it is claimed that 500 were drowned. This seems a large number, but those Mediterranean galleys ranged up to 1,200 tons and carried 180 rowers each, paid men, not slaves. The cost to the defenders was 89 men killed. It must have been a considerable battle but whether it took place in Sutton Pool or the Cattewater is impossible to say; we are not even sure whether there was just one raid, or a second in 1339, for the chroniclers all give different dates.

The battle of Sluys in 1340 brought a respite after this first raid and for the next 20 years the English were to be masters of the Channel. England had learnt the importance of sea power. In 1344, the bailiff of Plymouth, in common with those of Bristol, Hull, the Cinque Ports, Exeter and Dartmouth, had been ordered to send two men with a knowledge of shipping to London, to advise the King. Portsmouth sent only one. In 1345, for the Duke of Lancaster's expedition, Plymouth sent 15 ships compared with Dartmouth's nine, and the Plymouth crews totalled 300 men. For the siege of Calais in 1347, for which the Channel ports were scoured for ships and men, Fowey found 47 ships and 770 men, Dartmouth 31 ships and 757 men, and Plymouth 26 ships and 603 men. Seven of the Plymouth ships had more than 50 men in the crew and the biggest had 80; the size of Plymouth ships was growing considerably.

The year after Calais, 1348, a fleet of 40 western ships assembled in Plymouth to take the King's daughter, Joan, to Bordeaux. It was hoped to marry her to the King of Castile and so attract him away from his friendship with France. The large fleet was probably meant to impress him. It was also a necessary defence. After 50 years of war and legitimate commerce-raiding, there was a vast amount of piracy going on. In 1342, Plymouth men captured a Breton ship carrying salt for England, brought it into their home port and sold the cargo. Even a ship carrying royal envoys from Spain was boarded in the port and the cargo stolen. The *Trinity* of Fowey, carrying wheat and victuals for Bordeaux, was plundered off the Lizard by Plymouth men and, four years later, a ship loaded with wine and salt from La Rochelle for Bristol was attacked by a Plymouth ship in a Cornish harbour and its cargo stolen. This piracy was by no means confined to Plymouth men, but had become so widespread that a law was passed in 1353 to deal with it, after which conditions began to improve.

In the year that Princess Joan sailed from Plymouth, her brother was also in the port. The Black Prince, although just 20, had won his spurs at Crecy two years before, and been made Duke of Cornwall. As such, the honour of Trematon and the royal claims in Plymouth were his, and the duchy of Cornwall was established as the property of the sovereign's eldest son, as it has remained ever since. In 1348, the Prince was returning from Gascony, where there was temporary peace. He dined at Plympton with the Prior before journeying on. He was to come again.

Two years later Plymouth was raided by the French, but the town was so well defended that the invaders were only able to destroy 'some farms and fair places around', possibly the hamlet of West Stonehouse at Cremyll. Plymouth had learnt the lesson of that first raid.

In 1355, the Black Prince was appointed Lieutenant of Gascony and mounted an expedition designed to put an end to the constant nibbling by the French King. All through that summer the Prince's forces were assembling at Southampton and Plymouth. The first orders went out on 24 April and the ships began to gather in May. The sheriffs of Devon and Cornwall were ordered to send hurdles and gangways to Plymouth by 14 June, the hurdles to corral the horses ashore, and the gangways to get the baggage trains aboard the ships

Trade was at a standstill. No ship was permitted to go to sea unless well armed. Ships in harbour had to anchor close inshore. Local men had to be armed in case of attack. Fire-beacons were set up to warn of the approach of any invader. Fighting men came in from all over England, archers from Wales in green and white uniforms, archers from Cheshire who were given 21 days' pay before they started the 275 mile march to Plymouth. The Prince's retinue comprised

Sutton Harbour in 1978; the medieval town was sandwiched between the Parade inlet, the left-hand part of the harbour beyond the old fish market and the modern city centre above. South of the inlet is really a later suburb.

433 men-at-arms and 700 archers. All told, his force totalled about 3,000, including 1,000 men-at-arms, 1,000 horse archers, 300–400 foot archers and 170 Welshmen. They came from all corners of the kingdom, among them a fair sprinkling of gaol-birds hoping to win their pardon. Theft, rape, abduction and prison-breaking were among their crimes; there were even 120 murderers.

What a summer Plymouth must have seen, even if only half the army was there. How did a population of under 2,000 cope with all those stores, horses and men? Devon, Cornwall and Somerset were scoured for wheat, wine and firewood. Did the men who could not be billeted in the town camp out on the neighbouring hillsides, setting the slopes above the town a-flicker with their camp-fires at night? Could any hen or sheep within miles have survived their cooking-fires? Were there no fights of a night-time outside the alehouses between locals armed against invasion and the soldiery, or between the Englishmen, the Welshmen and even the Germans who made up the army?

The ships were supposed to be assembled by 11 June, but more were still being sought in July. The Prince was due in Plymouth on 1 July, but did not arrive until 26 July. Problems of supply, and of assembling the army, caused yet more delays. Strong winds held back the up-Channel ships, and it was not until 9 September that the fleet finally sailed and Plymouth could breathe again.

During those 45 days of his stay the Prince lodged at Plympton Priory, attended by four veterans of Crecy, the Earls of Suffolk, Warwick, Oxford and Salisbury. With him, too, were other distinguished soldiers and Crecy knights, such as Audley, Stafford and Chandos; and his chamberlain, Sir Nigel Loring. It must have been an expensive visit for the Prior, and some local merchants, like one who was instructed to buy gold for the Prince, would have done well. But many who sold stores to the army had to wait a long time for payment.

The Prince and his officers would have done much of the planning for the campaign at Plympton, and he must frequently have ridden into Plymouth to

An old drawing of Plympton St Mary Church.

inspect ships, men and stores, to meet local merchants and to confer with the bailiff and chief citizens about the problems of so large an influx into their town. Not since the days of his great-grandfather, Edward I, could Plymouth have seen so much excitement.

Even greater must have been the excitement two years later when the Black Prince sailed into the Sound again. He went as the hero of Crecy; he came back with Poitiers added to his laurels, and for this first and last time a king of France was brought captive to England. The English army had marched to the Mediterranean coast and back to Bordeaux, then north to the Loire. Then the French King cut them off, and the English choice was literally victory or death. The French were sure of themselves, the English hardened veterans. They stood firm and, one after another, the French divisions broke upon their ranks. King John of France led the last desperate charge, only to fall prisoner with his younger son, Philip. The Constable of France and 16 nobles lay dead upon the field, 2,000 Frenchmen around them. The rest were scattered.

All that winter the Black Prince rested at Bordeaux, and Plymouth sent out to him hay, oats, corn and even gold. In March 1357 a truce was signed; in April, the Prince sailed for home. His royal prisoner was in another ship, and both reached Plymouth about 1 May. Three weeks later they were in London amid tremendous rejoicings and excitement, such as there must have been in Plymouth for the few days the Prince rested there while his ships were unloaded and men and horses recovered from the voyage.

In the resulting treaty, King Edward III renounced his claim to the French throne but was established in Gascony. The French King was ransomed for three million gold crowns. Most of the English leaders did well in ransom money, but there were other rewards. Sir Nigel Loring was given the manor of Trematon, and the Black Prince gave his porter, William Lenche, who lost an eye at Poitiers, the rights of Saltash ferry. The Prince was in Plymouth again in 1362 and again in 1364, when he made the award to Lenche, and there is a legend that he was rowed across to Saltash by the women of that town, whose fame as boatwomen has come down through the ages. A room in the gatehouse at Trematon is shown as the chamber in which he slept.

During all these Plymouth visits in the course of his travels to and from Bordeaux, the Prince busied himself with the affairs of the duchy. In 1358, he ordered a warship to be built in Plymouth, the first written evidence of local shipbuilding, though it must have already been a well-established trade. Old enough, too, to have labour troubles, for the men struck for more wages. The Sheriff of Cornwall was ordered to send in men to finish the job and the contractor, William le Vennour, was told to pay them reasonable wages.

At one time, a complaint was brought to the Black Prince by the master of a Hamburg ship. The Saltash ferry-boat was under repair and the Cremyll ferry was being used in its place. The German captain was incensed when his boat, in turn, was taken to serve as the Cremyll ferry, and he was not even given a share of the fares. In the same document the Prince is recorded as making a grant to some 'poor brothers', friars perhaps, at Plymouth.

The town was now growing steadily, and Professor Hoskins calculates that by 1344, when Bristol was the biggest provincial town, Exeter ranked twenty-third and Plymouth twenty-fifth. By 1377, Plymouth moved up to the twenty-second place, one above Exeter, and had a population estimated at 1,700; a fair-sized village today.

Trade

Trade flourished in spite of the brief halts called by war. Wine from Bordeaux and La Rochelle was transhipped at Plymouth for Calais and North Sea ports. In 1362, the town was licensed to trade with Portugal, and, two years later, it received further licences to export 2,000 coloured cloths and 2,000 packs of cloth from Devon and Cornwall to Gascony and Spain. One merchant alone exported ten packs of cloth, 20 coloured woollen cloths and ten tons of hake. This fish, caught by fast trawler round the Eddystone, was always a Plymouth speciality. There was another licence in 1364 for 30,000 hake from Plymouth and Mousehole for Gascony. Tavistock and Ashburton were the nearest wool towns, and no doubt Plymouth was shipping their tin as well. Worth calculates from a customs scale of Richard II that the goods passing in and out of Plymouth included wine, honey and mead, coloured, russet and close cloths, canvas, hides, hake, herrings, pilchards and other fish, salt, coal, iron, cheese, soap, hemp, cords, wax, cornboards, pitch, tar and slate. Wheat and malt were brought from Weymouth in 1375.

In 1373 there were four large merchant ships at Plymouth valued at 70,000 livres, an immense sum. This may have been the first appearance of the Genoese carracks, big ships which carried not only the rich cargoes of the Mediterranean but the spices of the East as well. Certainly there was a carrack in Plymouth in 1376 and another in 1387. As a rule, they sailed from Italy right through to the German ports. Sometimes they waited for fair winds in the virtually deserted mouth of the Fal (hence the Carrick Roads as the name for the Falmouth anchorage), preferring to avoid busier ports where they offered too much temptation. One at Dartmouth in 1373 was described as being 'under arrest', and in 1403 the burgomaster of Bruges complained to the Bishop of Lincoln, who was passing through, that goods belonging to his town had been seized on board a Genoese carrack at Plymouth. One sheltering in Plymouth in 1433 was plundered 'by certain evil-doers'. At sea, they were more than a match for our smaller craft; 'orrible grete and stout' runs an English description of these new ships in the Channel. But we could learn from these fast, two-masted ships; the steeply-raked bowsprit of our cogs became a foremast and, by the mid-fifteenth century, we had three-masted ships, with a fore-and-aft rig on the mizzen that enabled them to sail closer to the wind.

When the carracks first appeared in Plymouth they joined shipping from half Europe. Baltic ships brought in linseed oil, rosin, tar and masts for shipbuilding, and took away wine from the south. After 1386, the wine ships ran in convoys to beat the Breton pirates, and Plymouth was the starting and finishing point for the convoys. Hides were going from Plymouth to Holland, and salt came back from Zeeland. Ships were plying to Spain and Portugal; the *Trinity* of Plymouth, for instance, regularly traded as far south as Lisbon.

The trans-shipment of cargoes was so important that special facilities were given in 1393 for merchants, local seamen and foreigners to land goods at Convers (or Conyers) on St Nicholas's Island without payment of customs duty, provided that the goods were not put up for sale. The reason given was that, in past times, the town's greatest aid and chief advantage came from merchants who entered the port for 'safety, refreshment and victuals', and that they were now ceasing to call because customs officers were demanding duty. The beach on the north side of the island is well sheltered and isolated enough to stop pilfering; it must have been useful, too, for storm-damaged vessels who could lighten ship and make temporary repairs on the beach.

Pilgrims

There was a two-way trade in pilgrims. Inward-bound, they were going to the shrine of St Thomas à Becket at Canterbury. The shipman from the west whom Chaucer met at Southwark with the Canterbury Pilgrims might have been William Hawley of Dartmouth, with a personally conducted tour of foreigners he had brought over in one of his ships and for whom he provided horses and guidance. The church at Kingswear is dedicated to St Thomas à Becket, as originally was the church of Plympton Erle.

Outward bound were English pilgrims going to Santiago (the Spanish form of Saint James) de Compostello, where the bones of the Apostle were miraculously discovered in the ninth century and inspired the war against the Moors. Edward I had made this a fashionable pilgrimage for the English. In 1361 a party of 24 men and women, with their horses, left Plymouth for Bordeaux and the long journey overland. In 1384, Plymouth was named as a place where passports to leave England could be obtained, and in 1389 it was decreed that no one, save merchants and known soldiers, should leave the country other than by Dover or Plymouth. These were the only legal routes for pilgrims and, as they had to be rich to make such a journey, it was a lucrative business. A man from Landulph had ships engaged in it and, in 1395 alone, there was one party of 80 pilgrims and two of 60, one party sailing in the *Margaret* of Plymouth.

All this went on against the routine background of war, and it took the fitting-out of the Poitiers campaign in 1355 to put a stop to the pilgrim trade. There were also regular calls from the Crown for ships and services, and a request from the King in 1369 for mercantile officers was addressed for the first time to the 'mayor' and bailiffs of Plymouth. A document of the previous year carries Plymouth's first seal, with the device of a single-masted cog on the sea, rounded to fit the circular shape, and the legend round the border 'Si Commumtatis ville de Suttun super Plymouth'. In 1370 there appears the name of the first mayor so addressed, Maurice Berd, and in the same year the Black Prince's youngest brother, John of Gaunt, led a fleet from Plymouth to Bordeaux.

It was from Bordeaux that the Prince had, since 1362, ruled Gascony, virtually as a sovereign with a lavish court, but suffering constant French raids on his frontiers. In 1371, he came home through Plymouth with his wife, the 'Fair Maid of Kent', and his son, Richard. He was a dying man. He rested a few days in Exeter on his way to London, and Plymouth saw him no more.

Protecting the Town

Times were changing. The command of the sea, which England had won by smashing the French fleet at Sluys in 1340 and kept by defeating the Castillian navy in the Channel in 1350, was lost when the English fleet was beaten by the King of Castile in 1372. Calais, and a narrow coastal strip from Bordeaux to Bayonne, were all that remained of English possessions in France. Once again, the English coast was open to the raiders.

In 1374, the aged King Edward gave orders for the defence of Plymouth. Letters patent were sent to William Cole, Stephen Durneford, John Sampson, Roger Boswines, Robert Possebury, Geoffrey Couch, John Weston, William Trevys, William Gille, Maurice Berd, William Bourewe junr and Humphrey Passour, burgesses of the borough of Sutton. They were to survey all the weaknesses of the town's defences and put them right; they were to see that there were arms for all the men of the town, and do all they thought expedient for the safety of the town. 'Moreover the mayor and bailiffs and all and singular the inhabitants of the town were to be obedient and aiding in the performance and execution of these premises.' The abbeys at Tavistock, Buckfast and Plympton were ordered to raise men to guard their estates.

Hardly was Edward dead in 1377 than the French fleet was off the English coast. Dover, Rye, Hastings, Portsmouth, and Plymouth were all attacked with fire and pillage. The new King, Richard II, who had visited Plymouth with his father, the Black Prince, in 1371, realised that while defences could be ordered, they had also to be paid for. So, in 1378, and because Plymouth was in great danger and neither enclosed nor fortified, he made a grant for its defence of six years' customs duty to the 'mayor, bailiffs, honest men and commonalty'. He also granted 100 marks a year for 20 years, to be spent on walling under the direction of the Prior.

He launched a roundabout offensive against France, and in 1381, and again in 1385, expeditions fitted out in Plymouth for Portugal. These set that country free, enlisted new support for England against the Kings of Castile and resulted in the foundation of England's oldest alliance when John of Gaunt's daughter married the King of Portugal. But basically, these expeditions to Lisbon were designed to keep Castillian galleys out of the Channel. They were also the background to a bitter dispute among the men of Plymouth as to who ruled the town.

King Edward's defence order had been addressed to the men of the port, and the mayor and bailiffs were to be obedient to them in matters of defence. These port men can, in some cases, be identified from ship records, but there is another clue to their authority in the port. Three of them, Thomas Cole, Geoffrey Couche and Humphrey Passour, together with Thomas Fishacre (is this a significant name?) were licensed by Richard II in 1384 to alienate six acres of land held of the King in chief to the Grey Friars.

King Richard's order had gone to the mayor. Since the 1311 market agreement, the Prior's steward had ridden into Plymouth on the first Monday after the feast of St Michael, 29 September, to swear in 12 of the Prior's tenants, who had then elected a reeve or Prepositus. He was presented to the Prior's steward and, if acceptable, took the oath. Thereafter, he was head of the court which sat in Plymouth every Monday, exercising for the Prior the assize of bread and ale, authority over weights and measures, millers, bakers, butchers, sellers of wine and those who brought bread in from outside the town; and with jurisdiction over transgressors. He collected all debts due to the Prior, rents, dues to the Sourpool manorial mill, and market stall rents, and he rendered an account of all this to the Prior's agent at the end of the year. He was the chief magistrate of the town, and was known as the mayor from 1369 onwards. But, though elected by his fellow townsmen,

Left: *First seal of the town of Sutton.*

he was still acting on the Prior's authority, exercising the Prior's rights, and subject to the approval of the Prior.

In September 1384, John Sampson was so elected. He had been to Westminster in 1369 with Thomas Fishacre as one of the King's shipping advisers, and was one of the port men to whom the defence order of 1374 had been addressed. Clearly he was in the shipping business (there had been a Sampson who was master of a wine ship in the 1310 fleet), and the 1369 service shows that he was not a young man. He was in for a stormy year.

A number of the burgesses of Plymouth elected a rival, Humphrey Passour, who not only set himself up as mayor without the approval of the Prior but, from January onwards, prevented John Sampson from sitting at the Monday court by force of arms. The authority he and his friends quoted was that 1374 writ which ordered the burgesses to see to the defences, and the mayor and burgesses and all and singular to be obedient to them.

Passour's name had been the last on the list in the 1374 writ, and it was his first appearance in the town records. It appears to have been a case of youth versus age, of young Passour anxious to shake off the Prior's domination and old Sampson (who was also in that 1374 list) content to accept it. These were times of rebellion; the Lollards were preaching equality, and the voice of John Ball had not gone unheeded in the west. When the peasants of Kent marched to Blackheath in 1381 the first John of Gaunt expedition to Portugal had been fitting out at Plymouth. When news came that Wat Tyler had been stabbed to death in front of the boy King, Richard II, the noblemen and gentlemen at Plymouth had hurriedly embarked in their ships and anchored well off the land, in spite of stormy weather, for fear of West Country uprisings. There must have been local rumblings then; now there was a real challenge to authority.

The Prior protested to the King, who ordered an inquiry. The King's officers, Walter Cornu and Richard Gripston, swore-in their jury at Egg Buckland one Wednesday early in June 1385. If one takes the Plym Bridge route, then Egg Buckland is halfway between Plympton Priory and Sutton Prior, and so might be considered as neutral ground. The jury consisted of 12 local men, independent, in theory, of both parties but close enough to the scene of conflict to be able to bring their local knowledge to bear. But their names suggest that they were all country gentlemen who could be expected to find for the landowner. This they did but, on the evidence, they could hardly have done otherwise. They found the Prior proved in all his claims to authority in Plymouth, and that there had never been a mayor there before the previous January, only the Prepositus of the Prior.

Passour tried again to uphold his claim, in the courts the following year, quoting all the documents of Edward III and Richard II addressed to the mayor of Sutton Plymouth, and claiming that such forms of address were appointing the people of Plymouth to have their own mayor. But the address on a letter meant nothing against the sealed charters of the Prior. Passour's blow for independence failed, but it was not forgotten.

There was still the money granted in 1378 for defence. Richard's reign ended in turmoil and the grant may soon have dried up, though there is evidence that the mouth of the harbour, at least, had been made impregnable by 1403. It is most likely that during those 25 years a chain was stretched across the harbour mouth at the narrows where the entrance piers now are, that a windlass to raise and lower it was set up on the Sutton side and two towers built at the cliff to prevent an enemy attacking the windlass or cutting the chain.

Over a shop window at the bottom of New Street there is still to be seen an ancient stone into which has been cut the words 'HE SAMPSON'. It is not on its original site and, as a rule, only stones of importance were preserved. There was a Henry Sampson in the town in 1395, and may it have been that the two towers, the start of Plymouth's medieval castle quadrate, were built at this time? Was Henry a son of John Sampson and the man entrusted with the building, and was his name placed over the main entrance? One can only surmise. There may have been a start on a town wall, possibly no more than a ditch with the earth thrown out to form a bank on the inner side, and surmounted by a wooden palisade.

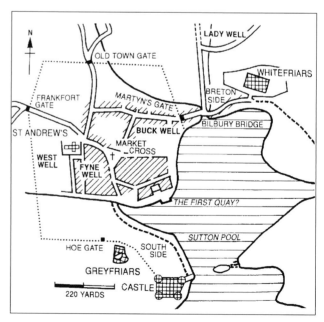

Plymouth, 1400. The built-up area is uncertain. The two friaries are outside the town proper. The town gates are marked in their known positions but the dotted line of the wall in between, if it existed, is conjectural.

Plymouth Burnt

With weak government in England, the French were at our gates and there were two or possibly three major attacks on Plymouth at the turn of the century. The 1399 raid is described as an attempt to fire the town, and was repulsed with the loss of 500 men. How these optimistic round figures of enemy losses echo down the centuries!

There are two versions of the 1400 raid. One is that James de Bourbon, Count de la Marche, coming into Plymouth on his way to help Owen Glendower in Wales, set fire to the town but lost 12 of his largest ships in a gale. The other is that Bourbon was coming back from Wales and chased seven trading ships into the Sound, where their crews abandoned them and escaped into Plymouth. It is said that the people in the countryside around crowded into Plymouth in wild alarm but were forced out again when the town shopkeepers doubled the price of provisions for outsiders.

The raid of 1403 is clearer in the records. A strong force, 30 ships and 1,200 men-at-arms led by Le Sieur du Chastel, came into the Sound on Wednesday, 10 August, from St Malo. They sailed into the Cattewater and landed their soldiers within a mile of the town. This suggests that the entrance to Sutton Harbour was strongly defended, but that the guns covering the chain could not be trained to cover the Cattewater. Probably, the soldiers landed on the Cattedown ferry beach opposite Oreston and marched along the road to Plymouth, looking down on the little town and laughing at the guns that could not reach them.

They entered at the 'bak haf of the town, under the White Friars convent (now Friary Park housing estate) and ravaged, burnt and plundered throughout the night. An attempt to storm Old Town was beaten off, and many of the Bretons were killed or captured there. One can imagine the hand-to-hand fighting in the narrow streets leading up the hill; for towns are still hard nuts to crack even in modern warfare. The invaders spent the night in the lower half of the town and withdrew at ten o'clock on the Thursday morning, taking their dead and wounded with them.

Bretonside; part of a prehistoric British village, medieval town gate, famous battle with Bretons, leading eighteenth-century hotel and the office of the first American consul, Colonel Hawker. The two tablets (above and inset) *are on the left-hand building.*

The old town that clearly was never taken must be the original town round the market cross, not the old farm. Until 1789 Martyn's Gate stood on this side of the town at the foot of the hill, the medieval main road from Exeter (it was Exeter Street until relatively recently and is now Bretonside: the gate was outside the Plaza snooker club). There was evidence of a wall running at right-angles to the main road. If this wall had been started by 1403, even if only a bank and palisade, it may explain why the old town held out. In the raid, 600 houses are reported to have been destroyed, but so many would have housed the whole town. Fire will travel fast along narrow streets of wooden dwellings, and it may be that the Bretons found fire was invading where they could not, and so left it to finish their work. It must have been a grim Thursday morning for Plymouth.

The part the Bretons did occupy, outside Martyn's Gate, has been called Breton Side ever since (though a modern council has moved the name uphill into old Plymouth to a bus-station, and so confused the issue). It is believed to be a memory of this Breton raid, though the earliest spelling was Britayne Side, and it is also the site of Bilbury, that Celtic fort whose name survives today. John Harris, in his 1810 history of the town, suggests the name implies that there had been a colony of descendants of the ancient Britons living outside the town proper. Similarly, Professor Hoskins thinks that the Bartholomew Street corner of Exeter, once also called Britayne, was the British quarter where they survived until they were expelled by Athelstan in the tenth century.

King Henry IV (he was Henry Bolingbroke, John of Gaunt's son, and had ousted Richard II in 1399) at once ordered a reprisal. It was mounted from Dartmouth the same autumn (which shows that Plymouth had not recovered sufficiently to play its usual role) and did much damage around Quimper. Next year, the Normans attacked Portland and the Bretons Dartmouth, but both were defeated; du Chastel, who had led the Plymouth attack, died in Dartmouth itself. A Te Deum was ordered in Westminster Abbey to celebrate this success and 20 famous Breton knights were English prisoners. Clearly, these were not just cross-Channel rivalries, but part of the national war.

In 1404, King Henry ordered a wall of stone to be built round Plymouth; the wording of the order suggests that there were already perimeter defences but, clearly, these had not been enough. To sharpen the need, there was another minor raid in 1406 by ships from Castile.

In the Channel there was complete anarchy. In the 1370s the Dartmouth ships under John Hawley, and the Plymouth ships under Roger Boswines, formed a western squadron that virtually ran the war in their own waters. John Hawley certainly had the King's licence which permitted him and his captains 'at their own charges, under the King's protection to attack

and destroy his enemies'. This letter of marque was common up to Napoleonic times; the holder was a privateer to his own side and a pirate to the other, for in the heat of a sea battle it is hardly possible to examine the other man's papers before firing the first cannon. Ships mixed legitimate trade with privateering and, at times, straight piracy; King's officers could turn pirates and vice-versa. Harry Pay, the great Poole pirate at the turn of the century, finished up as the water bailiff at Calais. John Hawley, leading a fleet of Bristol, Dartmouth, and Plymouth ships in 1403, took seven vessels carrying goods of Genoa, Navarre, and Castille, and refused to make any restitution.

Richard Spicer of Plymouth had been on the King's service in Portugal, but he twice captured galleys belonging to the Florentine Society of the Albertine. He was probably the principal pirate out of Plymouth at this time. When the *Trinity* of Plymouth was captured by the French off the Isle of Wight in 1403, it was Spicer who rescued her. In that year John Kyghley was named as a banned sea-robber. In 1404 he sailed into Weymouth and cut out the *Marie of Bordeaux* as she lay at anchor, and he was in command of one of Spicer's ships. Spicer was not alone. In 1403 Henry Don of Plymouth was summoned to appear before the Privy Council on a charge of piracy.

The Castle Built

Ordinary trade was going forward. Plymouth had ten ships in the 1409 wine convoy. The seamen were willing to fight their ships through their legitimate business but they wanted to be sure that they would not come home to find their houses burnt down and their wives ravaged in a ruined town. But first, they had to get unity in the town; the division between the seafarers in the King's port and the traders in the Prior's town had to end, and each must learn to live with the other. In particular, the nonsense of the two mayors of 1384 had to be done with.

So in 1411 a petition went to Parliament. The inhabitants of Sutton Prior and Sutton Vautort, commonly known as Plymouth, asked that in future they might elect a mayor each year and that they might be a body corporate, capable of purchasing lands without licence from the Crown. The town, it was explained, was close to a large port which was liable to attack in time of war. Being unwalled, the town was exposed to great danger. To build the wall, they wanted to be able to levy tolls on cargoes discharged in the port.

Here were two problems. Until they became a body corporate, they could not own property, nor buy land. No one would want a town wall built across his land unless someone would pay him for the land. Thus the land and the wall had to be paid for, and it seemed reasonable that ships seeking the

The one surviving fragment of the Castle Quadrate, at the bottom of Lambhay Hill. This 1966 photograph shows the two 1812 piers and the coal wharf still working on the far shore. In 1993 the new fish market was started on this site.

protection and the facilities of the port should contribute.

But the port customs were royal prerogatives, and the right to collect them was farmed out at a fat fee. The King was a chronic invalid, sick and suspicious. 'Let the petitioners compound with the lords having franchises,' came back the answer, 'before the next Parliament, and report having made an agreement.' The pigeonholes of government are ageless. There was no agreement by the next Parliament, nor by the next quarter-century. It would seem that the townsmen got on with the wall as best they could; they had acted in the past as if they were an incorporated borough, and they could do so again.

They may well have found more unofficial support from Henry V, who came to the throne in 1413. His Lord Chancellor, Bishop Stafford of Exeter, granted indulgences in 1416 which helped them to

repair the causey at the entrance to Sutton Harbour, and to build two towers of the castle. They put Bishop Stafford's arms on one tower and it was long known as the Bishop's Tower. Probably, it completed the castle quadrate. In 1449 Bishop Lacy granted another indulgence for the new castle and ditch, but this looks more like a maintenance appeal for something already built.

So in all likelihood the castle and the wall – of stone in the most vulnerable points, wood elsewhere, and with mound and ditch – were completed in Henry V's time. The castle and wall were all on Valletort land, which explains the later story that they built it all. Certainly it would not have been built without their consent, and the limestone quarries which furnished the stone were on their land, too.

Henry V also helped in other ways. He built up

The King of France is brought to Plymouth a prisoner; in this painting by Hamilton Smith (1776–1849) the Mayor is being presented to him by the Black Prince.

the naval forces and passed another anti-piracy law in 1414. It is significant that, after the record of Henry Quental of Plymouth capturing three Breton ships in 1412, there is no further piracy suggestion against Plymouth until 1419, when certain Bristol merchants brought into Plymouth carracks and other ships loaded with merchandise from Genoa. Thomas ap Reece, the leader of the Bristol men, asked that certain of these goods should be sold to him, for which he most certainly would pay – which rather looks as if the Welshman was talking his way out of detected crime. But piracy was not entirely stopped, and in 1422 three Bristol ships, with one from Plymouth, plundered a carrack in Milford Haven.

That year, Henry V died and weak government was back. The King's ships were sold up and privateers licensed in their place to give naval defence. The argument that the anti-piracy laws hurt legitimate trade became so persuasive that they were suspended in 1435. The rogues were in full gallop again. The notorious William Kydd of Exmouth cut

a Breton ship out of St Pol de Leon harbour in 1436 and brought it into Plymouth. That year, John Zeelander of Fowey captured the *Mighell* of Dartmouth in the very entrance to Plymouth Harbour. Zeelander was one of the Flemings who had settled at Fowey and made that port's name a by-word. The 'Fowey gallants' were cock of the Channel, and had even fought a pitched battle with the men of the Cinque Ports. There were Cornishmen in the business at Fowey along with the polyglot settlers; John Mixtow once brought in a carrack he had captured off Cape St Vincent, even though English merchants were actually aboard at the time.

Out of this desperate world, while the dissensions of York and Lancaster were raging around the monkish King, and Joan of Arc was driving the English out of France, Plymouth finally won its independence and its self-government. The struggle for freedom, which started with Humphrey Passour in 1384, saw final success in the charter of 1439.

CHAPTER 3

The Young Borough

Plymouth obtained its charter largely through the exertions of William Venour. A Walter de Venour received royal orders to detain ships in 1358, and had been mayor of Sutton Prior in 1377. It was an old family, and of some substance. William Venour had married Thomasine, sister of Richard Trenode, Sheriff of Bristol in 1422, mayor in 1432, and three times Member of Parliament for the town. Venour sought his brother-in-law's aid in securing the Plymouth charter and the two men acted as the town's agents. Neither were young men; indeed, Venour died in the middle of the charter negotiations and one of Plymouth's first acts as a borough was to set up a chantry priest in St Andrew's Church to say daily prayers for the souls of the Trenode and Venour families 'in consideration of the labour and charges sustained' by them in securing the charter.

Bristol had been subject both to the counties of Somerset and Gloucester, as Plymouth had been subject to the courts of the Prior of Plympton and the hundred courts of the Abbot of Buckland. So the charter that Bristol had obtained in 1373 was used as a pattern for Plymouth's request in 1439. In accordance with the 1411 command, the petition was addressed to Parliament – a sign that, with the weak boy King Henry VI, on the throne, Parliament was fast growing in strength.

Plymouth, said the petition, was made up of the town of Sutton Prior, the tithing of Sutton Raf and the hamlet of Sutton Valletort. It was an important port and had often been burnt 'by reason of a defect in the enclosure or walling of the same', the inhabitants despoiled of their goods and 'many carried away to foreign parts by the said enemies, and cruelly imprisoned until they have made fines and ransoms'. And, the petition added, 'all these things might happen again'.

The 'proper remedy' which Plymouth asked for the relief, fortification and bettering of the town, was five-fold; that they should be a free borough, with one mayor, a perpetual commonalty and a common seal; that they should be capable of owning land, and capable of suing and being sued in the courts. These five points were held to be the essential points of incorporation.

The petition set out the boundaries and asked for the fee farm of the borough at 40s. a year (other boroughs had to pay up to £50). It asked for authority to fortify the town, that William Kethrich, one of the more honest and discreet men living in the town (an ambiguous compliment) should be their

first mayor, and that certain rules should govern the annual election of a mayor thereafter on the feast of St Lambert (17 September). There are full details of how Plympton and Buckland were to be compensated (Plympton with a fee farm rent of £41 a year), and the town was to buy the advowson of Bampton from the Prior of Bath and give it to Buckland.

The assent to this petition declared that it should not affect the manor of Trematon, the borough of Saltash, the water of Tamar or the Crown land. The next step should have been to obtain the letters patent, but they were never entered on the Patent Roll; either the Chancery clerks were lax, Plymouth did not pay the necessary fees or the death of Venour may have introduced complications. But there must have been letters patent, for they were copied into the town's 'Black Book' in 1534.

The 1439 charter was amateurishly drafted and, though it might have sufficed for towns with long-established government, it was not enough for Plymouth. A new professional charter of 1440 added the right of Plymouth to have its own quarter sessions.

This kept the county magistrates, the hundred power of Buckland, out of the town. The mayor also became a justice and the town was given a recorder and a coroner. There was authority for a merchant

The Mayor's seal of 1439.

29

guild, for weekly markets on Mondays and Thursdays, and for two four-day fairs, in September and January.

William Kethrich remained mayor until September 1442, when Walter Clovelly was elected, and was probably in office until the whole transition was complete. But:

... between 12 November 1439 and 25 July 1440 Plymouth obtained the powers and privileges which, with some very minor changes, were to last it until 1835, and which still to some extent affect its constitution. In the course of nine months an unprivileged and divided market town had become a borough with powerful rights and privileges.

It was the first town in Devon to be incorporated. Totnes followed in 1505, and Exeter in 1537. Plymouth also was the first town in England to be incorporated by Act of Parliament.

How close to the heart of Plymouth was the need for defence set out in the petition for incorporation, and how proud the people were of their new castle, is shown in the mayor's first seal. In place of the old ship design there now appeared the cross of St Andrew and, between the arms, four castles, representing the castle quadrate. It is still the centre of

Plymouth's coat of arms. Around the seal was the legend *S'officiz maioratus burgi ville dni regis de Plymouth* ('The King's burgess town'); here was the final shaking off of the Prior's town label and the victory of the King's port.

The boundaries set out in the charter used the Stonehouse and Lipson creeks on the landward side, so that the new borough had only a narrow land link with the rest of Devon. It took in just two Domesday manors, Sutton and Lipson, both Valletort holdings. The petition said that Plymouth was made up of the town of Sutton Prior (which was just the built-up area by the harbour), the hamlet of Sutton Valletort (the rural area centred in the manor house by Sourpool, and the few cottages which had probably grown up beside it), and the tithing of Sutton Raf. The word 'tithing' survived (in the tithing of Compton Giffard, for example) into the nineteenth century to mean a self-governing part of a parish, and probably has the same meaning here. Raf, or Ralph, was a common Valletort Christian name, and Sutton Raf looks like the old Lipson manor, which was originally between the Lipson and the Tothill creeks, extended southwards to take in Cattedown when that part was cut off from Sutton Valletort by the growth of Sutton Prior.

There turns up in the seventeenth century a new

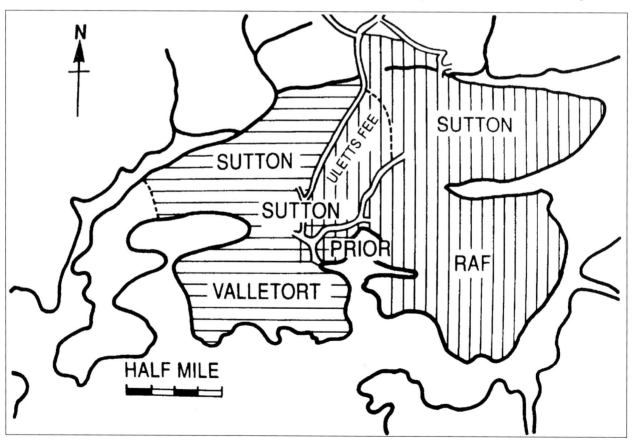

The Borough of Plymouth, 1439. The landward boundary ran from the head of Stonehouse Creek, up the brook now under Central Park Avenue, then by Dale Road and Ermington Terrace to Mutley Plain, on the old ridge road. From Hyde Park Corner (boundary stone still there) it ran behind Connaught Avenue and then Elm Road to the tidal head at Lipson Vale. Shaded areas indicate the locations of the three Suttons which made up the town.

The Old Passage House Inn at Cattedown, until modern times the Plymouth end of a ferry to Oreston. It was replaced in 1902 by the present building.

manor, 'Uletts fee, als Lulytts Sparke als Luletts fee.' From the evidence of property deeds it was clearly between Sutton Valletort and Sutton Raf, stretching from the northern edge of Sutton Prior up to the headlands, the slope still remembered by old people as Vinegar Hill. The Sparke family in the seventeenth century had acquired the Whitefriars, and Vinegar Hill is believed to recall the vineyards of the friars (it would be quite possible to grow vines on this south-facing slope). Perhaps this is the estate of the White Friary, a further wedge between Sutton Valletort and Sutton Raf.

From early references to street names and from old maps, the shape of the town can be established. The southern edge was Notte Street, or Nut Street, in all likelihood looking across a little stream running down to Sutton Harbour, with hazel bushes on the far bank. On this bank, the south side, a path ran to the four-towered castle dominating the harbour entrance. The western edge was Catherine Street, St Andrew's churchyard, and Old Town Street, with the backs of the houses looking across open ground to the town wall. Only the St Andrew's end of Old Town Street was built up, and a line from the present top of New George Street east to the junction of Bretonside and Exeter Street would mark the northern edge of the houses. Between them and the wall on that side were still the fields of Old Town. The wall turned south to Sutton Harbour on the line of the modern Bilbury Street, with Bilbury Bridge outside, then the strange suburb outside the wall of Britayne Side, and then the White Friary. An imposing building this, with a spire to its church, its own gateways and a wall round the conventual buildings. Between the town and the Hoe was the Grey Friary, with its domestic buildings looking across a cloister garth to the church and a crenellated wall enclosing the whole.

The town had four gates which, in time, became impressive stone structures, reflecting local pride as much as defence, for they always seem to have been more substantial than the walls that linked them. The Barbican, or watergate, was really part of the castle. Hoe Gate, in the south wall, led to the Hoe. Frankfort Gate was in the west wall; outside, the roads forked to Stonehouse and to the manor mills on Sourpool. Old Town Gate in the north wall was the dividing point of the roads to Tavistock and Saltash;

Tavistock road up the old ridge way and the Saltash road across the heads of Stonehouse Creek at Pennycomequick, Keyham Creek at the junction of St Levan Road and Wolseley Road, and then Camel's Head Creek at Weston Mill Bridge. In the east wall there was Martyn's Gate, with the Exeter road climbing up Lipson Hill, winding down the steep slope beyond to the head of Lipson Creek, and then following its northern shore to the Ebb Ford and so to Plympton. Looking across the long-disused Ebb Ford was a lonely public house called the 'Crabtree Inn'. It probably marks the oldest inn site in Plymouth, where people must have waited for the tide to fall enough to let them cross, and where shelter and refreshment were no doubt provided. One can remember the channels in these muddy rivers being marked by branches of trees stuck upright and irreverently called 'winkle-trees'; were there even earlier such branches to mark the line of the ford and were these the 'crab-trees'? From Martyn's Gate, another road ran out over Cattedown to the Oreston ferry, and an inn there is still called the 'Passage House Inn'. It must share the antiquity of Crabtree and of the inns at Saltash Passage.

Between the town centre and the waterfront one area was not developed until late. The main streets there are now Looe Street and Vauxhall Street. Looe means pigs (as at Looseleigh, which means the pig-clearing in the forest), and Vauxhall is a polite spelling of Foxhole; direct references to the rural state of early Plymouth.

Local Government

Plymouth was basically a commercial centre, and the merchants very much its rulers. They were given a guild in the charter of 1440, and very soon the usual form of government of a guild, the 12 and the 24, was the form of the town council. The 12 were aldermen – itself, originally, a guild term – and the 24 were councillors. The Plymouth merchant guild was that of 'Our Lady and St George', and in the early days everyone who ran a business or traded in the town was a member. A guild meeting was a meeting of all the townsmen. The guild enforced trading regulations, saw fair business done, made sure that there was no unfair competition. The town council were the senior members of the guild, acting as the executive committee of the guild and of the town.

As the town grew, as some men became richer and others poorer, as the number of apprentices becoming masters grew fewer and the number becoming employees grew more, so the merchants' guild became more exclusively the club of the big men. So, in turn, trade guilds developed, for men of certain crafts. In Plymouth, a tailors' guild was set up in 1496, the only one of which there is record, though no doubt there were others.

Only freemen could hold office in the borough and, to tighten the circle, the council decreed in 1471 that every freeman had to be a brother of the merchants' guild. Half-brothers paid sixpence a year to the guild, full brothers a shilling, councillors an extra eight pence and aldermen another shilling. Discipline was strong. In 1516 it was resolved that anyone disobeying the mayor should be punished by him, and freemen would be imprisoned in the guildhall. Anyone betraying council secrets could be put out of the council and disenfranchised for ever, and so could anyone who sought outside help from any lord to oppose the mayor. In 1520 it was laid down that no freeman should leave the town without special licence during the 28 days prior to mayor-choosing, unless he could be back in time, and that every freeman should be at the guildhall for mayor-choosing.

How tight this governing clique grew over the years is shown by a council resolution of 1683, when the mayor and seven of the town's 12 magistrates (magistrate and alderman appear to be synonymous by this time) decreed that for the next five years they would select the townsmen to serve on the council and councillors would have no say in the matter. The trouble was that when the councillors had been invited to elect into their ranks people nominated by the mayor and magistrates, they had persisted in electing people of meaner condition, to the neglect of people of quality and known loyalty. There is a memorandum under this entry declaring that this was contrary to the practice of the town, where it was customary for the whole 12 and 24 to elect burgesses to fill any vacancy. Patently, the town council was a self-renewing body.

The council met in the guildhall. Originally, this was the meeting-place of the whole guild, and as the council comprised the elders of the guild they met there, too. Not until 1873 did the council attain a chamber separate from the guildhall, and, to the present day, Plymouth has retained the feeling that the guildhall is the meeting-place for all the people of the town, and the council chamber a place apart.

There is no written evidence of the location of the first guildhall, but when a new one was built in the market triangle in 1606 the old one had first to be demolished, so fairly clearly it was on the same site, and it is the most logical position. It must have been built beside the market cross soon after the charter of 1439 for, in the town accounts of 1480, there is a note of eightpence having been paid to Watkyn, the mason, for work at the guildhall (the first written reference). It must have been repair work; there was more done in 1494, and in 1501 it is referred to as 'the old geld hall'. Next year, it was 'made fine' with plaster of Paris, a glass window was mentioned in 1503 and a clock installed in 1526.

The ward boundaries of the town met in the market-place, running north, south, east and west along street lines as far as they would serve. Old

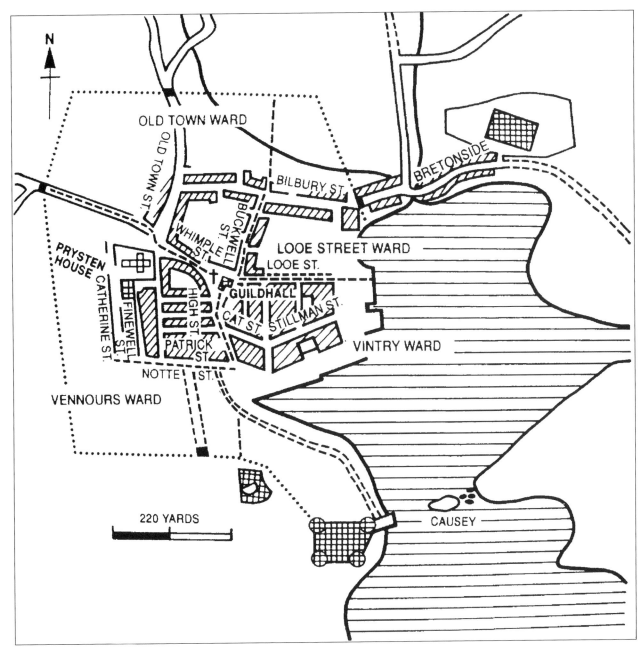

Plymouth, 1500. By this date 13 street names appear in various documents. By mapping them and the known buildings, as has been done above, the shape of the town becomes clear. One or two unnamed streets have been drawn in, although they are no more than 'probable'.

Town was to the north-west, Venours to the south-west (named in honour of the man who won the charter and who had a house in this area), Vintry to the south-east (note that the port area is given a name meaning 'the gathering place of wine merchants'), and Looe Street to the north-east. The first three wards are named by 1480; Looe Street, the last area to be built up, does not appear until 1500.

The mayor was chosen on the first Monday after St Lambert's Day, as in Priory times, but did not take the oath and office until Michaelmas Day. One custom prevailed right up until the Reform Acts changed the council composition; on Michaelmas Day the council would assemble at ten in the morning and wait until 11 before the mayor took the oath. It was a legacy of the old days, when the burgesses had to wait for the Prior's officer to arrive before their choice could take office. After the oath, the mayor and corporation went in procession through the town; they had two standards (coloured or 'stayned' in Totnes) and a great banner by 1486. By 1572 the alderman had to have red robes, and in 1580 (Drake's mayoralty) the councillors had them as well.

Between St Lambert's Day and Michaelmas Day the town boundaries were beaten, a significant choice of date whereby the new mayor was reminded by his predecessor of the town's extent. It was a day's holiday, and in 1496 there were two gallons of wine 'for ye mayer and his bretheren when they sawe ye franchyse abut'. In 1516 there were pears, apples and nuts for the children on this holiday, and ale for their elders. Granite boundary stones began to be set up in 1518, 'ffredome stones', the old records call them.

This Freedom Day gradually developed into one of the chief holidays of the year, with a battle between the Old Town Boys and the Breton Boys to finish it off. Old Town by now is the town within the walls, while the Breton Boys came from the suburb east of Martyn's Gate. It seems an odd way to remember the Breton raid of 1403, and could have been a remnant of the old animosity between the town and the 'Britayns' outside their gate. History became more confused when the Freedom Day fights became too much for the town and were moved up the hill to the open spaces of what became known as Freedom Fields, because it was also the site of the vital Civil War battle. The Freedom Day fights eventually became drunken brawls, the Breton Boys' name degenerated into Burton Boys (until recently remembered in a public house name), and the whole affair was finally suppressed after a number of bones were broken in 1792.

Corpus Christi

The other great holiday of medieval times was Corpus Christi, the Catholic festival in honour of the Sacred Host, in early June. On this day, a church-ale was held in aid of St Andrew's Church funds, and everyone in the town would gather up their friends and acquaintances, men and women, and go to St Andrew's churchyard. It was an all-day party, for they could take with them whatever food they liked for dinner and supper, except bread and ale. These they had to buy, and this made the money for the church. To ensure a good profit, no tavern in the town was permitted to sell wine or ale on that day.

The great event of the day was the procession. The rules of the Tailors' Guild ordained that they should 'make a pageant yearly into Corpus Christi', just as it was earlier ordained that each ward should 'make an ale' on that day. There were rules, too, about the men who 'carried the ship'. One imagines that the mayor went in procession with his gilded maces and his officers and his banners, that each ward and each trade guild followed with a tableau, and that the ship was a massive model of canvas and wood carried shoulder high by the Corpus Christi guild – a symbol of the town's main interest and the source of its prosperity. The parading of a model ship on May Day continued until quite late in Cawsand and Stonehouse (it has been revived in Millbrook). In some Breton churches such ship models are still stored in the church from one feast day to the next, together with giant figures of St George and the Dragon, the Virgin, and so on, mounted on carrying poles. No doubt the Plymouth Guild of Our Lady and St George had its gaudily-coloured models, too.

What the old records variously call the 'Corpus Christi Ilde' and the *Fraternitat corpis xpi* must have been a religious brotherhood formed to run this great church day, and not a trade or craft guild. People left money and property to it as they did to other religious bodies, and the guild was a tenant of the town in 1490. By 1645, the town had acquired certain property and fields which were called 'Corpus Christi', and there was a Corpus Christi House in Bedford Street as late as 1874.

There were other feasts, too, unconnected with the church. May Day and Midsummer's Night were

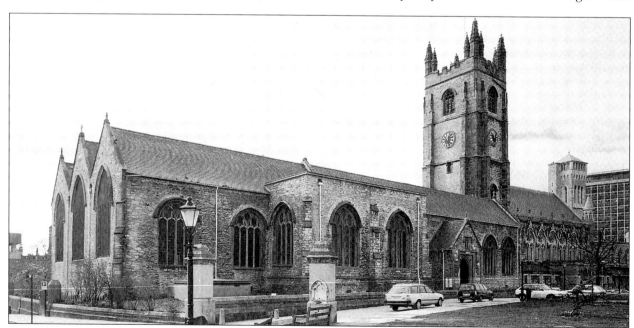

St Andrew's, mother church of Plymouth, fittingly dedicated to the patron saint of fishermen. The greensward in the foreground is the old churchyard.

celebrated with Morris dancing, and visits by teams from Bodmin, Stonehouse, St Budeaux and Tavistock are recorded. One year, there was a hobby horse; on another, a maypole was painted. There were waits on Midsummer's Night (singing men were not limited to Christmas carols), and wine for the mayor and his bretheren that night at 'High Cross'. This must have been a cross upon the Hoe, near the little chapel of St Katherine, and the figures of Gog and Magog, which were fresh cut each year. It was an odd survival of pre-Christian dances beside pagan images, and perhaps there may still have been undertones of witchcraft, of pagan abandon which chapel and cross had been set up to combat.

Christmas was the winter feast; in 1566 there were 10s. for the schoolmaster and children from Totnes 'whiche played in Christmas', and there had been minstrels in 1495. Six players gave an interlude in the mayor's house on the Saturday before Twelfth Night in 1539, and the mayor and his brethren watched a juggler on St John's Day. Strolling players and minstrels began to appear, often under royal or noble patronage, the 'King's Joculars', for example, in 1523. In 1529 the servant of the Duke of Suffolk appeared with a dancing bear and a dancing wife, perhaps a more refined entertainment than straight bear-baiting. A 1516 entry reads 'Reward to luskum for his dogge at the Bere baytinge, iiijd'. Bull-baiting was an everyday entertainment; it was thought to make the meat more tender and butchers were fined for not having their animals 'bayted'. There was a bullring on the Hoe and another just below the guild-hall in High Street. That was right in the heart of the town, and if a bull broke away he might well finish up in a china shop.

Crime and Punishment

There were strict rules of business for butchers, bakers, brewers and the shopkeepers. No strangers were to be in the town for more than two days unless their business was known. No man was to walk up and down on working days to ale and wine unless he was a man of substance, or a merchant waiting on a gentleman. No innkeeper was to give shelter to any suspicious person, or let any man and woman lodge together unless he knew they were man and wife. Nor was he to keep in his house any harlot or strumpet.

People were no better than they are now. In 1502 a coroner's inquest found that John Croste, a groom of Lipson, had stabbed and killed Robert Matthews in his house at Stonehouse, and that the dead man's wife, Elizabeth, had been an accomplice. Murders and death in brawls were not unknown; men were not to carry arms

High Street as it was towards the end of the nineteenth century; it has since been widened and called Buckwell Street. In medieval days bulls were baited at the top.

without the mayor's consent and everyone was to be indoors by eight o'clock, when the town gates were closed. Not that this stopped crime, for there are records of theft, false pretences, breach of covenant, even stealing a man's wife as well as his goods, and breach of promise.

John Meyow of Plympton was arrested to 'answer' Joan Collins, the daughter of a Bickleigh man. She was an honest maid, said her counsel, replete with many honest and womanly qualities, but that had not stopped John Meyow on 4 August in the Vintry ward:

Blinded by inordinate concupience he did with force of arms with knives and daggers, and false promises of marriage, provoke her to consent to his filthy lust of the flesh and so with her did execute the act of carnal copulation, abusing her body so that he hath begotten her with child.

He had then declined to marry her, and Miss Collins was suing for £100, which was more than the whole town's expenditure in some of these years.

Punishments were hard. In 1486 there was a pennyworth of straw for prisoners in the clink, which was probably in the basement of the guildhall.

Left: *The ducking stool, still preserved in the City Museum.*

Iron bars closed its windows. A gallows was set up in 1498 to hang a thief, and the town accounts, as they so often do, set out all the grisly details: fourpence for timber, a shilling for building, tenpence for a ladder, fivepence for a halter and a rope to bind the arms, a penny each for six men to be guards at the hanging, and fourpence for their ale. Another man was set in fetters and a blacksmith was paid to smite on the gyves. There were stocks, and a pillory set up beside the market was regularly used. Down by the harbour there was a ducking or scold's stool; this was a seat on the end of a long pole which pivoted so that an offending woman could be tied on and dipped into the sea. All these ranked as public amusements in those rough and hardy times, when death was commonplace, plague was ever present and war never far away.

Even the 12 and the 24 had to be ready to stand to arms. The mayor was also commander-in-chief and, when danger threatened, he took charge of the north-east tower of the castle quadrate, the key point over-looking the harbour. The rest of the council were divided among the four towers, the three aldermen and six councillors of each ward to their own tower. These wards were strictly for administrative and not electoral purposes. Town finances were collected on a ward basis, each ward had its own rules for keeping the streets clean and in each ward the aldermen appointed constables who kept the peace. No doubt they also organised archery practice at the butts on the Hoe.

Trade Depression

Though they were warring days when Plymouth won its charter, trade was still going on. In 1437, two years before the town's incorporation, there are records of cargoes reaching Plymouth from Guienne, Landerneau, Brest, Guerrade, Oporto, Lisbon, Norway, Denmark, Genoa, Dusant (or Fusant), Spruce, London, Dartmouth, Guernsey, Exmouth, Fowey and Exeter. Fish was being sent to Bristol and there was a trade with southern Ireland. It was the old pattern, but it was changing. In 1420 men from the east coast ports and Bristol began to fish off Iceland, and the wealth of cod they found there cut deeply into the dried and salted fish trade of the west Channel. The wine trade with France, too, took a mortal blow when the English were finally driven out of Bordeaux in 1451. It had survived the tramp of armies through the vineyards, the depredations of pirates, the discipline of convoys and the doubling of prices. And, because the Bordelais, living 60 miles up the Garonne, were never seamen, the English had taken over their export business, set themselves up as factors in the port, married and settled down – no doubt with Plymouth men amongst them. But after 1451 no Englishman was permitted to live in Bordeaux, and the wine trade fell into the hands of

the Hanseatic League and the Flemings, those merchants of the Baltic, of Bruges and Ghent, who had no love for the west Channel men. The wine trade gone, the Plymouth business in pilgrims went as well, and even the salt trade fell into the hands of the 'Eastlanders'.

The first 25 years of the new borough must have been difficult times. With failing trade and weak government, it is no wonder either that piracy was abroad again. In 1449 Robert Wennington was ordered to 'cleanse the sea of pirates' and assembled a West Country fleet at Dartmouth. He met a convoy of about 100 Hanseatic and Flemish ships carrying salt off Portland, and set about it to such effect that all the ships surrendered. All the government could do was to pay compensation, and then only the Flemings got any of it. That same year Fowey men (still the arch pirates) came out of the Cattewater and took a Barcelona galley anchored in the Sound off to their home port, together with a cargo worth £12,000. Not only were half the gentry and lawyers of Cornwall named in successive court actions as owners of pirate ships and as receivers, but James Durnford and Thomas Tregarthen, distinguished Plymouth men, were also accused. Some of the booty was even in Tregarthen's house, but he claimed that it had been put there while he was away in London.

The Wars of the Roses

With the final eviction of the English from France, the Wars of the Roses, long smouldering, turned into open civil war. Devon had been generally Lancastrian in sympathy, with the Earl of Devon and his Courtenay relations the chief supporters, but the Bonvilles, a powerful family in east Devon, were Yorkist, and the two families conducted virtually a private war in the 1440s and 1450s. This anarchy on land, and the weak rule of the Lancastrian King at sea, which left the Channel a playground for pirates, began to produce a strong Yorkist faction among the merchants and in the seaports. In Plymouth, Vincent Patilysden, mayor of 1453, 1454 and 1456, wore the red rose of Lancaster in his hat when he went to church and the aldermen and burgesses followed his example, 'but which, as they saw the York faction arising [writes an old diarist] they afterwards did prudently decline'.

In the vital year 1461, when the young Duke of York, although beaten at the second battle of St Albans, seized London, was proclaimed King Edward IV and then crushed the Lancastrians on Towton Moor, the French King sent a force into Plymouth to try and help the Lancastrian cause. There is reason to believe that the local Lancastrians knew what was afoot, for when William Champernowne of Modbury, a Yorkist (and a relation by marriage of the Bonvilles), sent his men towards Plymouth to repel the French, he was intercepted by

Courtenay men (the Earls of Devon still held Plympton) at Yealmpton and kept out of the town.

Plymouth must have suffered from that French 'visit', for a merchant, William Savage, went to law with a complaint that, when the Frenchmen were at Plymouth 'and spoiled the town', he had been robbed of his goods, save some jewels which he sent away by a servant, and they were taken by a servant of Thomas Carewe. After York's triumph, Baldwin Fulford tried to raise Devon to rebellion in support of Lancaster but he was quickly taken and beheaded.

That autumn John Page succeeded William Yogge as mayor of Plymouth; he wanted the vicar to offer prayers for the success of Lancaster but the vicar prudently declined. Then the new King's brother, the Duke of Clarence, came to Plymouth and the mayor quickly changed his tune:

> ... this very mayor in the same year [to quote the diarist again] feasteth the Duke of Clarence... right royally, here in Plymouth, and drinketh long life and a prosperous reign to King Edward IV.

It looks like a disciplinary visit, and a new regime which was taking no chances. John Rowland was mayor for the next three years: 'a man of great interest and sway, and closely attached to the house of York. He was chosen mayor more from fear and awe, than reverence and love...' He was also a member of Parliament in a Yorkist-packed Commons.

But Plymouth was clearly impoverished by the falling off of its old trades and the anarchy that reigned by land and sea. When Edward IV renewed the town's charter the annual rent to the Prior of Plympton was reduced from £41 to £29.6s.8d. because of the town's poverty.

William Yogge was mayor again in 1470, when the Lancastrians once more used Plymouth in an effort to regain power. Warwick the Kingmaker, who had put Edward IV on the throne, had now turned against him and seduced his brother, Clarence, from his loyalty. The two landed at Plymouth with the Earls of Pembroke and Oxford, and were dined by William Yogge in the guildhall, where Henry VI was proclaimed king again. They marched away and were briefly successful, until Warwick was defeated and killed in the battle of Barnet; Clarence, who had twice dined in Plymouth Guildhall, returned to his brother's side, only to become suspect again eight years later and be drowned in a butt of malmsey.

William Yogge, who had been four times mayor, disappears from the records in 1470, and in the following year the town council resolves that no 'foreyn' man shall be a freeman – which means a foreigner's exclusion from all office. The next entry in the town's records is 'John Yogge, John Shipper, and other foreyns putte owte of theyre ffreedom'. It may all be coincidence, but it does rather look as if

Known for decades as the Prysten House, this building was originally the private house of Thomas Yogge, which he built at the time he was giving the stone for the building of St Andrew's tower, c.1487.

the Yorkist element in Plymouth was in control again, that old Yogge – who had been in office during each of the Lancastrian landings at Plymouth – was now dead, and they were determined to have no more trouble with a Lancastrian family. So Yogge's Cornish origin was being used as an excuse to put Yogge's son out of reach of any possible future authority.

Edward IV proved a strong king who restored the mercantile life of the country and brought discipline back into the Channel. He captured the pirate leaders of Fowey by a trick, hanged them and got the men of Dartmouth to take away their ships and their harbour defence chain. Piracy still lingered on but the changed conditions can be seen in a 1474 report. Raulyn Pape, of Dieppe, was anchored in Falmouth when Henry Hornebroke, of Plymouth, cut out his ship. Pape says that he and his crew were 'bete and wounded' by the attackers, and then cast adrift in an open boat without a compass. Rescued by a French vessel, Pape had no hesitation in going to Plymouth, where he bearded the mayor, Nicholas Heyncott:

> ... and in the presence of many and divers notable persons then all being in the chirche of Plymouth shewed unto him his hurtes and damages and required him to put under arrest the goodes of the said persons...

This is the last fifteenth-century reference to a pirate from Plymouth. Thereafter strong central government not only made punishment more certain but, by restoring trade, made an honest life more profitable. But with Edward's death, uncertainty and unrest returned. His brother, Richard Crouchback, made himself King, declared his brother's sons illegitimate and imprisoned them in the Tower, where they were later put to death. The true line of Lancaster had disappeared but a new claimant arose in Henry Tudor, Earl of Richmond. From Brittany, he organised a rising in the west to synchronise with the Duke of Buckingham's revolt in Wales.

For the third time Plymouth was chosen for a Lancastrian landing; evidence of Plymouth's sympathies and of the fact that the only out-and-out Yorkist mayor had been forced on the town. But a great storm upset the Lancastrian plans; Buckingham was defeated and executed, and by the time Henry Tudor appeared in Plymouth Sound the western rebels had fallen back into Cornwall. Henry waited in Cawsand Bay while he took stock; a royal proclamation against him said he had 'a greate Navye and Armye of Straungiers'. Writing about Cawsand a century later, Richard Carew states:

I have heard the inhabitants thereabouts to report that the earl of Richmond (afterwards Henry the Seventh), while he hovered upon the coast, here by stealth refreshed himself; by being advertised of a straight watch kept for his surprising at Plymouth, hied speedily a shipboard and escaped happily to a better fortune.

King Richard III came down to Exeter and beheaded three of the western leaders. Others fled. The Courtenays and the Bonvilles had wiped each other out. The Lancastrians predominated now in Devon and Cornwall, and many western gentlemen spent that Christmas in exile with Henry Tudor in Brittany. In 1485 they landed with him at Milford Haven, crushed Richard on Bosworth field, and set the Tudors on the throne of England. After a century of warring dynasties, it was to be many years before the Tudors were to feel secure on the throne and Henry ruled as firmly as Edward IV had before him.

St Andrew's Church

This restored prosperity is seen in the wave of church rebuilding throughout the west. Plymouth had probably rebuilt the nave of St Andrew's in the early-fourteenth century with the money brought in by the naval activity of Edward III. In 1481 there was a fresh spurt. The town's oldest surviving account book, called 'Thomas Tregarthen's Book' after the mayor of 1480–81, has a Latin inscription on the fly-leaf which declares that the book was started by the decision of Thomas Tresawell, mayor, and his predecessor, Tregarthen. The book, it is written:

... appertaineth to the church of St Andrew in Plymouth, started on 24 August 1481, to put in writing all the ornaments of the church as well as all monies belonging to the 'reparacion' of the church.

First, is the list of such money as is 'assigned and granted by diverse persons to the making of the south aisle'. The legacies and gifts recorded easily meet the bill from John Dawe, mason, for £44.14s.6d. for the materials and labour of building the south aisle between 1481 and 1485. But, after three pages, the format of the entries changes into what are fairly obviously the churchwarden's accounts.

After 1485 the town's audit book contains entries for money spent on the church; stained-glass windows (such windows of this period can still be seen in the churches of Bere Ferrers and St Neot), stones for the north aisle and the tower, and for paving the street by the church stile. Leland, who visited Plymouth in the next reign, writes that 'of late' a merchant of the town, Thomas Yogge, paid for the building of the steeple (steeple, a spire or tower) and the north aisle of the church, and that the town supplied the material. Here is the church starting to rebuild, completing the south aisle, and then in 1485, when Henry Tudor overthrows the House of York, a

St Andrew's Church tower.

Yogge comes forward and takes upon his shoulders the main burden of rebuilding the church. His family had long been enemies of the House of York and seem to have suffered at their hands; is this an act of thanksgiving? Yogge's tower still stands, surviving nearly five centuries and a war that destroyed nearly all around it; was it built originally as a monument to celebrate the Tudor accession?

The town was proud of its church and, at the mayor's command, John Gill preached a special Christmas sermon there in 1486. Soon the mayor's pew was carpeted and two goatskins were stuffed with flock to make cushions for his pew, gold paint being used to pick out the town's arms on the cushion covers. A man from Looe was paid to make a cross and weather vane, with iron obtained from Plympton. There was music, too; in 1487 a shilling was paid 'to the old man the singer' to go to Plympton to fetch songs for the mass.

Probably the merchant's Guild of Our Lady and St George had always had a Lady Chapel. Now the new south aisle was dedicated to St George, and the north aisle to St John the Baptist. Apart from the vicar – who had his vicarage just under the east window, in the corner between St Andrew Street and Whimple Street – there were three or four chantry priests licensed to the church. Chantries were common enough, and were priests maintained by endowment to pray for the souls of certain people. It was the middle-class equivalent to the rich man's piety in founding abbeys. At Plympton Erle John Brackley dedicated a chantry to St Maurice which eventually became the dedication of the church and altered the town's name to Plympton St Maurice. At Tamerton Foliot, a chantry was set up for the souls of the Copplestones of Warleigh. In St Andrew's there was the Venour chantry, to pray for the family of the man who won the town's first charter, the Dabernon and Paynter chantry founded by two merchants to pray for their families, and the Jaybyn chantry, for which land was given to the corporation on condition that the revenue was used to pay the stipend of a priest to say masses at the altar of St John the Baptist, in the church of St Andrew, for the soul of John Jaybyn.

Just south of St Andrew's Church there is still a house which architectural evidence dates as late-fourteenth century, the period when St Andrew's was being enlarged and beautified. It is still called the Prysten House, but in fact was a new house which Thomas Yogge built for himself. For several centuries past it was called 'the Abbey'. The first

Yogge's house, north elevation.

Stonehouse from the Henry VIII defence map. The fortified manor house stands above the village with Buckland Abbey's grange on the other side: note the deer in the manor's deer park.

suggestion was that canons coming from Plympton to conduct services in the church lodged there. When it became clear that canons had stopped rendering this service long before the house was built, it was believed to have been built for the chantry priests.

In fact the 'prysten house' of the chantry priests was much further down St Andrew Street. In 1538, the year of the Dissolution of the monasteries, the mayor and council of Plymouth made a grant to Sir Thomas Flyte, chantry priest of Jaybyn's chantry of the 'prysten house, together with the chamber that he now hath both under and above, during his lifetime, without disturbance of any of his fellow-priests there'. The grant was made in consideration of Flyte having paid for the repair of the prysten house kitchen.

Flyte seems to have been long in office, and his name appears in the only two surviving lists of Plymouth chantry priests. In one, he is joined by Sir Keysar and Sir John Nicholas; in another by Sir John Crofts and Thomas Washington. 'Sir' merely marks a priest who had not been at a university. Since Sir Thomas and his brothers moved out, the building has served many purposes, from wine store to provision merchant's warehouse, and when the church regained possession the interior was smoke-blackened by long years of bacon-curing. The real Prysten House, long vanished, may well have been Plymouth's earliest school. At Ashburton, the keeping of a free school was a duty specifically laid upon the chantry priest, and though the merchants of Plymouth, who must have been men of considerable education, may have received it as a friary school, a chantry school is much more likely. It is significant, too that, within 23 years of the dissolution of the chantries and the friaries, Plymouth found it necessary to establish a Corporation grammar school.

Another social work conducted beside the church, and possibly a joint enterprise by church and corporation, were the almshouses just north of St Andrew's tower. Their age is uncertain, but the wardens were paying rates in the earliest surviving records of the late-fifteenth century. A Norman-type archway was preserved when the building was removed in 1868, but it was then thought not to date the building itself but to have been originally part of the church fabric. It may have been a side door of the fourteenth century nave, removed in the 1485 reconstruction and used to embellish the almshouses; in which case it seems that the reconstruction covered the entire group of church, priests' houses and almshouses.

Edgcumbe and Broke

Among the western men who came home with Henry Tudor was Sir Richard Edgcumbe, whose family had sprung from yeoman stock at Milton Damerel and, by marriage, had acquired Cotehele, beside the Tamar. Sir Richard's loyalty to Henry in exile and on Bosworth field was rewarded with high office as Controller of the Royal Household, which made him a rich man. He also became Sheriff of Devon in 1494, and Plymouth made him presents of two sugar loaves, wine, pomegranates and oranges. In the previous year his son Piers had married the last of the Durnford family, the heiress Joan, who brought him all the old Valletort lands at Stonehouse and Maker. Piers may have lived part of the time at the old Valletort house at Church Hill, in Plymouth, and certainly lived at the Stonehouse manor house off Durnford Street. When Piers brought home his bride, Plymouth welcomed them with gifts, and he is constantly referred to in town records of the time. In 1530 their son Richard was born at Stonehouse. Piers later turned Maker into a park, and built the great house that he called Mount Edgcumbe. A descendant still lives in the park as the Earl of Mount Edgcumbe, Viscount Valletort and Baron Edgcumbe.

Another returning soldier was Sir Robert Willoughby de Broke, who became Plymouth's first Lord High Steward. A soldier of fortune, he made himself a landed gentleman by marrying Blanche Champernowne. The Champernownes, originally of Dartington, had acquired the Valletort lands at Modbury by marriage, and Blanche's grandmother was a Ferrers, a family descended from William the Conqueror's chief farrier, whose badge was a horse-hoe. Sir Robert was very fond of his new houses at Newton Ferrers, near Callington (his tomb is in the parish church there), and at Bere Ferrers. His arms are still in Bere Ferrers church, bearing the horseshoe of the Ferrers and a rudder, said to signify his appointment as England's first Lord High Admiral.

In 1486 Plymouth officers met their new Lord High Steward at Plympton 'when we made owre benevolence', and gave him two sugar loaves. That December, the mayor, Thomas Tresawell, went to see him in London 'for ye benevolence'. No doubt this was all concerned with the renewal of the town's charter, for Henry's title to the throne depended on the House of Lancaster; he would not recognise the two Yorkist kings who had preceded him or the confirmations they had given to the charters of the boroughs. So Plymouth had to go back to its original charter of Henry VI, who was fortunately a Lancastrian and who had even been proclaimed king in Plymouth Guildhall during William Yogge's mayoralty of 1470.

Two Rebellions

Plymouth's charter was renewed 15 months after Henry VII came to the throne, but the new king soon showed himself to be a hard man, extorting every penny he could in taxation. Exchequer pressure was such that, in 1495, the town treasurer rode off to see Thomas Yogge at Ashburton 'when he was seke', and next we find Yogge in London on the town's busi-

Palace Court, home of the rich merchant Paynter, where Katherine of Aragon was entertained on her arrival from Spain. It was demolished in 1880.

ness. The very next entry in the town accounts is a payment for 'Rollying of the Chartour', which all suggests that Yogge's influence was used to get the charter entered on the patent rolls as a defence against the Treasury.

Cornwall, too, felt the weight of the tax collectors, but, as a royal duchy, could seek no such legal protection. In 1497 taxes levied to defend the Scottish border proved the last straw, and the Cornishmen rose in revolt. The rebels marched as far as Blackheath before being defeated, and there was at least one Plymouth man, Robert Warwick, among them. The Warwick family owned 'a certain mansion, lands, meadow and pasture' in Plymouth.

Perkin Warbeck, the imposter who claimed to be one of the princes murdered in the Tower by Richard III, decided that Cornishmen were of greater valour than the Scots he had been trying to stir up. So that same summer he landed at Sennen Cove and again the Cornish rose. The rebel army marched through Launceston to Exeter, and though it bypassed Plymouth, the town was much alarmed. A man was sent to Exeter to 'spy tydyngs' and a boat went out to Penlee to speak to Mr Treffry. This second revolt met a bloody end in the villages of east Devon. The King

himself spent a month in Exeter to ensure that Cornwall was disciplined and the Mayor of Plymouth, Thomas Tresawell again, went up to Exeter while the King was there. The Earl of Devon, Lord Willoughby de Broke, and Lord Daubenny were appointed commissioners to receive the submission of Cornwall, and no doubt they were the 'Lord Prince's Council' for whom Plymouth supplied 15d. worth of wine at the mayor's house. The town dressed eight men in uniforms of green and white, the Tudor colours, to join Lord Devon's escort in Cornwall.

A more serious danger to Plymouth at this time were the French again, for Henry was supporting Brittany's efforts to keep her freedom. Twice Willoughby de Broke commanded armies in Brittany, and Plymouth strengthened her defences against possible attack. Gunpowder had brought a vital change into warfare; the castle quadrate now covered too limited a field to be effective, and bulwarks and gun-platforms were built along the edge of the Hoe cliffs to command the entrance into the Cattewater. In the town's oldest surviving accounts, for 1486, there is mention of a watchman at Rame beside a fire beacon, another beacon and a bulwark, on the Hoe,

Mill Bridge, the tidal mill built in 1525, seen here before being demolished.

and candles bought for the night watch. Moulds were made from which cannonballs of lead and iron were cast; shot was also made from stone. In the first few years of the sixteenth century the bulwarks were extended and more guns bought, including two from the Spanish, then the best gunsmiths in Europe. Henry VII sought a link with Spain to counter the Franco-Scottish alliance, and to this end there landed on the Barbican in 1501 a slight, weary girl – Princess Katherine of Aragon. She came to marry Henry's eldest son, Arthur, and, when he died, she married the second son, Henry. Perhaps the English temperament made the break with Rome and the Dissolution of the Monasteries inevitable, but this sad and serious little girl was to provide the spark that set it all off. No one could have foreseen this when the gentlemen of Devon and Cornwall assembled to welcome Katherine; indeed, she was in the care of the Abbot of Compostello, whose cathedral church had been the goal of that pilgrim trade from the town up to half century earlier. The town had its address of welcome translated into Spanish and Latin, gave the royal household sheep and oxen and wine (Thomas Yogge supplied the claret), and paid minstrels to entertain the guests.

Tradition says that the Princess and her household gave thanks for their safe arrival at St Andrew's and spent a fortnight recovering from their journey at the house of John Paynter, a merchant who had been mayor in 1487. His house was in the angle between High Street and Catte Street, and one wall survives in the garden of a school which is still called Palace Court, the name that ever after attached itself to Paynter's house. The house itself stood four-square about its courtyard until 1880, when it came down to make way for the school; in its last days it was rack-rented and verminous. It was never a thieves' kitchen such as the Whitefriars, once the palace of John of Gaunt, became, but both the royal residences of Plymouth came to shabby ends. The fine houses of the Paynter and Yogge families, and the rebuilding of St Andrew's, show that Plymouth was at last recovering from its mid-century depression. In Henry VII's reign, the Plymouth-Fowey customs returns doubled, from £327 to £647, though depreciation in the value of money, and Henry's more efficient tax collection, must be allowed for. The Exeter-Totnes customs returns trebled, from £515 to £1,615. Plymouth fell from being the twenty-second town in England in 1377 to the thirty-third in the 1520s, while Exeter had gone up from the twenty-third place to fifth. Even Totnes, though smaller than Plymouth, had richer merchants. The wool trade was making these towns, whereas Plymouth handled only the coarse cloth from Tavistock and some from Ashburton. Even in fish, Torbay was yielding more than the old grounds off Plymouth. Tin-mining on Dartmoor had a boom in the early-sixteenth century, but as the miners had to dig further for the metal so the waste in the rivers increased. Once again, there were constant complaints about the state of the Plym and the way the miners were silting it up.

The Breton raids of 1403, the cost of rebuilding and strengthening defences afterwards, the loss of ancient trades and the anarchy of the Wars of the Roses had all combined to give Plymouth a bad time for the first half of the fifteenth century, even though the town had become independent. There was some recovery in the second half; the town was able to improve its guildhall and nearly renew its Parish Church, to support merchants whose houses were fit for a princess and to create the new Looe Street ward, but clearly the recovery did not keep up with that of the rest of the country, or even the rest of Devon.

Stonehouse by now had grown into a sizeable village. The Durnfords had a manor house at Stone Hall which they had been licensed to fortify. One crenellated wall still remains, though the last 'big house' on the site came down in 1963. Houses lined both sides of Stonehouse High Street and Buckland Abbey had a house where the Naval Hospital now stands. In all probability, the monks built it and turned to Stonehouse as a port from which to ship their products when they lost their rights in Plymouth on its incorporation. The new borough seems to have aroused James Durnford's ambitions, for in 1442 he set up his own court and a pillory in Stonehouse. But Stonehouse, as part of the hundred of Roborough, was still controlled by the abbot of Buckland, who made Durnford close the court, remove the pillory and pay him £20 in compensation. In 1472 Stonehouse, which had been part of the parish of St Andrew's, had its own chapel of St Lawrence licensed for divine worship. This church was removed in the nineteenth century to make way for the Royal William Victualling Yard, though part of its tower is the folly in Mount Edgecumbe Park, visible from the Hoe.

The Wise family acquired Stoke by 1428 but they continued to live in their big house at Sydenham, near Lifton, letting the Keyham manor house remain as a farm. In 1525 they relinquished their rights on the northern bank of Stonehouse Creek to allow the new owner of Stonehouse, Sir Piers Edgcumbe, to build a tidal mill at Millbridge. This bridge opened up a new route from Stonehouse up Molesworth Road and down the hill to a ford over the Keyham Creek (which in time gave its name to the modern district of Ford), and so to St Budeaux.

Here the Budockside family was prospering, and by 1482 the population had increased sufficiently for them to complain to the Bishop of Exeter that it was unreasonable for them to have to go all the way to St Andrew's for baptisms and funerals, when they could celebrate the other services of the church in their own chapel. The Bishop agreed and gave them the licence they wanted, on condition that they provided a priest's house and a graveyard. Successful yeomen and merchants of Plymouth moving out into the country were building houses big enough to have private chapels licensed, such as for the Haisendes at Kinterbury and for Roger Boswynes, the seaman.

It was all very pastoral. Leland came over the Saltash ferry and rode over Weston Mill Bridge, down Swilly Road to Pennycomequick and so into Plymouth. 'The ground between the passage of Asche and Plymmouth', he wrote 'hath good corn but little wod.' Shipbuilding had long since bitten into the big timber; the unproductive coppices had made way for golden barley and oats to feed the new town. The new Mill Bridge was evidence of agricultural prosperity. Was anyone aware, in all this quiet pastoral of waving cornfields, that the world was opening up? Certainly on the Plymouth quayside they must have known that Columbus had opened for Spain a new way to what he thought were the Indies, and that Cabot had sailed from Bristol to a New Found Land. But they could little have foreseen that this opening up of the Atlantic was in time to cover all their fields with close-packed houses.

CHAPTER 4

The New World

When Turkish wars closed the Mediterranean, western Europe cast around for other routes by which to reach the spices of the East. A Portuguese ship had rounded the Cape of Good Hope by 1487, and Columbus crossed the Atlantic for Spain in 1492. The Atlantic islands, Madeira, the Cape Verdes, the Azores and the Canaries, had already been colonised. Henry VII, who often talked of war with France but wasted little money on it, encouraged Cabot and the Bristol men to cross the Atlantic, but their New Found Land was a cold place and it was some time before its wealth of cod was realised. Henry VIII, however, was no sooner on the throne in 1509 than he was at war with France, and Plymouth, on the edge of the ocean that was exciting men's attention, was soon rebuilding its bulwarks under the Hoe and buying more guns, for fear that the French would come.

Plymouth escaped being burnt by the French, as Fowey was in 1511, but saw no profit from the war, even though it was being waged in its old stamping-ground of Gascony. The mayor hired a fishing-boat and took 12s.6d. worth of chickens out to the Lord Admiral when he came home to Plymouth that year with an unsuccessful army. By the end of the war in 1515, there were formidable defences facing the Sound, set up at considerable expense and named after the alderman or wards who were responsible for manning them, like Thykpeny's bulwark and the Looe Street gun.

A new man moved into Plymouth about this time, William Hawkins. His father was a rich merchant of Tavistock, and his mother an Amadas of Launceston. William was exporting tin and wool (clearly acting as a shipping agent for his father), and importing salt from La Rochelle, wine from Bordeaux, Portugal and Spain, pepper from Portugal, olive oil and soap from Spain and fish from Newfoundland. Not until 1543 is there a payment to the watchman at Rame 'for his comyng hither by nyght when the newfoundland men came yn', but Plymouth ships must have been in the business much earlier. The Bristol links were strong. By 1523 William Hawkins was worth £150 a year, one of the five richest men in Plymouth. Next year he was treasurer of the town (a post then held annually by a member of the council, and a stepping-stone to mayoralty). The town's income which he handled in the year was £63, less than half his personal wealth. Of the £150, £140 was ventured in trade with Spain. He helped man the bulwarks when French pirates chased an Italian ship into the Sound

in 1527. The French captains were brought ashore and detained until they agreed to sail in peace; their ships, meanwhile, being menaced by the guns on the Hoe. When they did go, the Hoe gunners were given a shilling's worth of wine, and the Italian 'argosy' paid Plymouth £26.13s.4d. in gratitude. That year, too, William Hawkins was accused with other leaders of the town of beating and wounding John Jurdon – 'so as to endanger his life' – but no one seems to have been very upset about it.

All this time Hawkins was hearing stories from west European ports, especially Lisbon and Seville, of the riches being brought home from the Guinea coast of Africa, and from the Americas. Plymouth had been trading with Spain and Portugal for a century and more; in fact, so many Englishmen had settled in San Lucar, the outport of Seville, that they had their own church of St George there. No doubt there were Plymouth men among them, and Hawkins himself had probably visited his agents in Lisbon and Seville.

In 1530 Hawkins decided to make the venture himself, the first Englishman to trade across the Atlantic. He was between 35 and 40, but Richard Hakluyt, setting down the story years later, recorded:

Olde M. William Haukins of Plimmouth, a man for his wisedome, valure, experience and skill in sea causes much esteemed, and beloved of K. Henry the 8, and being one the principall sea-captaines in the West parts of England in his time, not contented with the short voyages commonly then made onely to the knowne coasts of Europe, armed out a tall and goodly shippe of his owne, of the burthen of 250 tunnes, called the Paule *of Plimmouth, wherewith he made three long and famous voyages unto the coast of Brasil...*

It was not a difficult voyage for seamen accustomed to running down the coast of Spain. There they could pick up the north-east trade winds down the African coast, fair winds and currents across the narrowest part of the Atlantic to Brazil and fair winds up to the westerlies for the straight run home. Hakluyt records that Hawkins loaded ivory on the Guinea coast, but as it was also the centre of the 'Guinea grains' trade, as the local pepper was called, he probably added some to his cargo. In America, he took on the Brazil wood much needed in Europe for dyeing cloth (and which gave the country its name). Politically, the voyage was safe enough, for it touched only the coasts claimed by Portugal, which the French were

The present retaining wall of Madeira Road, in front of the Citadel, is built on the lines of the Tudor bulwarks.

already raiding, and did not involve any Spanish lands, which would have upset King Henry's fostering of his Spanish alliance.

It must have been a profitable voyage, for Hawkins went again in 1531 and again in 1532, and became so friendly with the natives in Brazil that one chief returned with him, a member of the crew, Martin Cockeram being left as a guarantee of the chief's safe return. Hawkins took the chief to London 'at the sight of whom the King and all the Nobilitie did not a little marvaile'; not surprisingly, as he had bones fitted into holes in each cheek which stood out an inch and another hole in his lower lip in which was set a precious stone the size of a pea. One hopes that he was an honoured if incongruous guest on St Lambert's Day in Plymouth that autumn, when William Hawkins was chosen mayor. Next spring Hawkins stayed at home, but his ship made the voyage back. The chief died on the way, but such was the word of the English, that Martin Cockeram was allowed to return to his native Plymouth, to live on for 50 odd years.

Hawkins seems never to have made the voyage again himself but continued to develop the trade, re-exporting the Brazil wood even to Italy. A Bristol exporter shared a ship with Thomas Cromwell, MP for Taunton and already in the Privy Council. Hawkins was writing to Cromwell seeking royal loans with which to arm his ships; he had three or four in the trade and lost at least one. A clue to the profit of these voyages, which other ports were now

emulating, comes from the accounts of the *Paul*, master John Landy, in 1540. She sailed in February with 940 hatchets, 940 combs, 375 knives, 10cwt of copper and lead arm bands, 10cwt of lead in the lump, three pieces of woollen cloth and 19 dozen nightcaps. The cargo was worth £23.15s.0d. and paid export duty of £1.7s.3d. (the manufactured goods seem to have been described merely as metal, an early example of customs evasion). The sole shipper was William Hawkins.

The *Paul* was back on 20 October with a dozen tusks of ivory and 92 tons of Brazil wood, valued at £615 and paying duty of £30.15s.0d. For a 250-ton ship, it was a light cargo and there may well have been peppers passed off as ship's supply and other disguised goods. But the profit for a six-month voyage is fantastic; allowing for the cost of wages and victualling, and forgetting what else may have come home, it must have been over 1,000 per cent. No wonder Hawkins in 1536 could buy a new house and garden in Kinterbury Street, just below Old Town Street, and eight years later an even bigger house down by the harbour. No wonder either that he was in trouble with the customs. Peter Grisling, who had been indicted with Hawkins in the 'affray' of 1527, was the 'searcher' or customs officer. Soon after Hawkins's mayoralty, he and two other merchants, James Horsewell and John Eliot (who had previously been in business at Ashburton, like the Yogges), complained that Grisling was exercising his office with rapacity and extortion, and making it his main source of income. The battle raged for years, and in 1536, when Horsewell was mayor, Grisling called him 'a naughty heretic knave'.

The Dissolution

It was a dangerous charge, for 'heresy' then meant opposition to the King's desire to divorce Katherine of Aragon, the dispute that led to the break with Rome. The friars in Plymouth were particularly outspoken against this, and Horsewell had given proof in April 1533 that he was no 'heretic' when he warned Cromwell that 'there be knave friars here that play their part'. The Grey Friars, in particular, were protesting, and Sir Piers Edgcumbe was sent into town to examine them. He sent the warden, Friar Gawen, to Launceston Castle and put others who spoke ill of Queen Anne Boleyn into the pillory or the stocks. Thomas Mychelson, 'the clerke', was sent to the Bishop of Exeter's prison.

It was abundantly clear that the religious houses were doomed, and up and down the country the abbots and their friends were making anticipatory dispositions. At Stonehouse, the Abbot of Buckland made over all his manorial rights, and probably the abbey building as well, to the Edgcumbes. In 1534 Plymouth was finally relieved of its annual payment to Plympton Priory, which was given instead to the advowsons of Blackawton and Ipplepen. The excuse was Plymouth's 'ruen and decay', and though Leland the antiquarian, who was in the town about this time, writes of decay in the Old Town Ward, it is

far more likely that the Prior of Plympton cancelled Plymouth's pension rather than see it bought up like an annuity by some speculator.

The small houses went first. In the autumn of 1538 the 'Lord Visitor in the West', the Bishop of Dover, rode down through Somerset, Devon and Cornwall closing down the friaries. Plymouth took him two days; he dealt with Whitefriars on 18 September and Greyfriars on the 19th. Local officers assisting him were the mayor, Thomas Clowteynge; the mayor-elect, William Hawkins; and the town clerk, James Horsewell. Six brothers signed the surrender of Whitefriars. There was not much in the house, but 211ozs of silver which had been purloined were turned over to the Visitor. How much had gone and was never returned was another matter. At the Greyfriars next day there was even less; John Morys (who signed as 'Warden of Plymouth') and his seven brothers had been left with what remained in the church, together with the bells and clock in the steeple; the rest had been 'brybeyd away'. There is no record of any of the other friaries in the west clearing out their possessions like this, before the Visitor's arrival and, considering that all the local dignitaries at the time were fighting High Court actions over customs, it suggests a tough and independent town.

The alabaster table which the Visitor found at the high altar in Greyfriars Church indicates its wealth, for English alabaster of the time was famous throughout Europe. Table may mean retable, a long shelf behind the altar with richly carved panels;

The rood screen of Blackawton Church (top), which is said to have come from the Greyfriars in Plymouth. In the panels are the initials of Henry VIII and (far right) Katherine of Aragon. The bosses in the fan vaulting (above) are Tudor roses and in the panels is carved the pomegranate badge of Aragon.

Friary Court, 1830; all that remained of the mighty medieval Whitefriars. (A DRAWING BY C. ELDRED)

Artillery tower in Firestone Bay, made into a restaurant.

possibly the altar itself, movable, had also been 'brybeyd away'. What is said to have been the rood-screen of the Greyfriars is today in the Parish Church of Blackawton, between Totnes and Dartmouth. It is carved with the initials of Henry VIII and Katherine of Aragon, and the Aragon badge of the pomegranate. Katherine must have landed on the Parade not far from the Greyfriars, and the rood-screen would have been a fitting memorial. Some of the friars who risked prison by speaking up for her at the end may even have remembered the tired young girl of all those years before, and perhaps the Abbot of Compostello had been their guest.

Hawkins and his friends took delivery of the buildings for the King, and Horsewell acquired a lease of the Whitefriars. It was a splendid building at Coxside standing inside its own walls and with an imposing gate; a spire on the church dominated the head of the harbour. In 1546 Gregory and Charles Isham, London speculators in monastic property, bought both the Plymouth friaries, later selling the Whitefriars to William Amadas, a Hawkins cousin. Through marriage, it passed on to the Sparkes in 1600 and they were there until 1714. Then decay set in; during the Napoleonic Wars the Whitefriars was a military hospital, and by 1830 it had become a common lodging house, as low a den as one could find, with its thieves and beggars gathering of an evening for a communal meal. The last vestiges of the building were swept away with the building of Friary Station and the Roman Catholic Church of the Holy Cross.

The great monasteries followed the friaries within six months. The buildings at Tavistock and Plympton became quarries; the lead was stripped from their roofs and the structures soon disappeared. The Tavistock estates were acquired by the Russell family who, ennobled eventually as Dukes of Bedford, became a new power in Devon. The Champernownes had Plympton for a time, but the

estates broke up. They also bought St Germans in 1541, but sold it in 1565 to John Eliot, the Plymouth merchant. The family are still there, in their house beside the priory church called Port Eliot, and their head is now the Earl of St Germans.

Buckland was bought by Sir Richard Grenville of Bideford, who had been Marshal of Calais. His wife was a Whitleigh, one of a family of landowners who took their name from the manor north of Plymouth, and she brought to him half of Compton and Efford. He settled Buckland Abbey on their son, Roger.

In the years after the Dissolution, William Hawkins was accounting to Plymouth for church silver he had sold on the town's behalf; the King did not get it all. Much came from the Greyfriars, but there was a chalice from St Katherine's upon the Hoe and another from Our Lady's Chapel at Quarrywell, the site of which is marked by the side turning off Regent Street still known as Ladywell. There must have been a little chapel over a holy well of the kind that still survives in some Cornish villages. The rest of the church silver included silver candlesticks and figures of saints which may have come from St Andrew's; a little ship of silver 'hangying apon Seynt Clers cloth' and a bigger ship of silver gilt, weighing 18oz, both reminiscent of the Corpus Christi ship.

The money from the sale was spent on gunpowder and bows and arrows. Much attention was still being given to defence; the butts on the Hoe were in regular use and wine barrels were moored in the Sound for gunnery practice. Henry VIII mapped the defences of the South Coast and, in 1539, built round guard towers at Fisher's Nose to protect the mouth of the Plym, at the entrance to Millbay, and on Devil's Point to cover the mouth of the Tamar. The Fisher's Nose tower and the bulwarks that ran along the Hoe cliffs are now the base of the pavement that runs along from the point to the Royal Plymouth Corinthian Yacht Club house; the irregular pattern of the sea wall still shows the angles of the gun platforms and can be seen by peering over the wall. The towers at Devil's Point also remain, even if the best survivor was converted by Stonehouse Urban Council into a public lavatory. It is now a restaurant.

The 1549 'Commotion'

These defences were wise precautions, for in 1544 France made peace with Spain and turned her energies against England. Horsewell was Mayor of Plymouth that year and, together with Hawkins and Eliot, he received the King's commission to 'annoy the King's enemies'. It was privateering again, with the problems of enemy cargoes in neutral ships, and a fine line between legality and piracy. The line proved too fine for William Hawkins, who was called before the Privy Council when the King was at Portsmouth with the fleet, and sent to prison. Sir George Carew of Antony and Roger Grenville of Buckland Abbey were also there as captain and second-in-command of the *Mary Rose*; when she sank at anchor both were among the 500 men drowned. Eight Plymouth ships, and two from Saltash, were in the fleet. The spell in prison did not mend Hawkins's ways. He was in more trouble when his *Mary Figge* captured some Flemish goods, and again in 1546 when he captured a Breton ship after peace had been signed. No one seems to have thought any the worse of him, and a naval officer, Thomas Wyndham, became his partner after the war and reopened the Brazil trade. Hawkins himself was summoned to the first Parliament of Edward VI as member for Plymouth, he and Horsewell having previously sat several times in Henry's day.

Plymouth washed the town flag and had a 'triumph' for the coronation of the boy king. The following year the town was celebrating the victory of the Scots at Pinkie with a banquet for which oysters were fetched from Saltash, and meat and drink 'for them which played the antic'. But the reformers about the new king were at work again; they ordered the removal of all images from the churches and stopped what they regarded as superstition in the services. In that spring of 1547 it moved the men of Cornwall to rebellion for the third time in half a century.

Plymouth paid 26s.8d. to Henry Blase and his company 'when they rode with Sir Richard Edgcumbe into Cornwall against the rebels there', and bought a dozen bowstrings for them. The country was 'pacified by the gentlemen of the country with small trouble', says the Black Book, 'but yet certain of the chief of the commons were hanged drawn and quartered'. One execution took place on Plymouth Hoe. In the 1547 accounts are the grisly entries: the faggots and the 'quart of rhede' for the fire, the cost of the gallows, payment to the executioner and to the man who led the horse which dragged the 'Traytor of Cornwall' to his death. His name is unknown, but his head and one quarter were raised on poles over Plymouth Guildhall, and another quarter exhibited in Tavistock.

These dreadful displays were a warning to Cornwall and the border town. Plymouth set about defending St Nicholas's Island (Hawkins, Eliot, John Thomas and Richard Hooper going to London about it) and the town settled down. A priest rode to London about the sale of chantry land. The King's fiddler was paid 5s. and English songs were bought for the choir; Latin may have gone but not music. The Act of Uniformity of 1549, which made the English prayer-book compulsory, launched another rebellion in Cornwall, and in Devon, too.

There was considerable alarm. Old Sir Richard Grenville shut himself up in Trematon Castle with the gentry of east Cornwall; his daughter-in-law had married an Arundell and was living at Clifton, now just a farm beside the Tamar, and she probably brought her son, Richard Grenville, into the castle too. A yeoman farmer from Crowndale beside Tavistock, Edmund Drake, who was a relative of the Hawkins, fled to Plymouth and took refuge on St Nicholas's Island; his small son, Francis Drake, with him. The aldermen and councillors of Plymouth stood to their posts in the castle quadrate.

Trematon was captured, the gentlewomen stripped and robbed, old Sir Richard flung into Launceston gaol. The Cornish army moved on to Plymouth, where, says the Black Book, 'The castle was valiantly defended and kept from the rebels'. Efforts were made to defend the town, and guns were dragged from their store at the Guildhall up to the Hoe and to the Maudlyn, some to St Nicholas's Island. But the town was taken. 'Then was our stepell burnt with alle the townes evydence in the same by Rebelles', records the Black Book.

This was all the town records, stored in the tower of the Guildhall. No doubt the relics of the traitor of Cornwall, still on poles over the Guildhall from the year before, infuriated the Cornishmen and led them to set fire to the Guildhall; 15 years later the town was to spend £120 on a 'newe gildhall'.

Only four books survive from before this destruction of the town records: Thomas Tregarthen's book, which was probably in the church vestry, the Black Book (bought in 1535 as the town's ledger), the current account book (which, like the Black Book, was in everyday use and not with the archives), and Simon Carsewell's book, the records of a lawyer who had been the town coroner and who probably had the book in his office. Fortunately, all the vital decisions of the town's earlier history had been copied into the Black Book; without that Plymouth's medieval history would be even more difficult to unravel.

Lord Russell came down with an army to subdue the 'commotion' and took the leaders off to swing at Tyburn. They and their fellow defenders of the old religion had been too impatient, for with Mary Tudor on the throne in 1553 the Catholic religion was restored. Next year, she married King Philip of Spain, after the Earl of Bedford had sailed from Plymouth to wait upon him, and the Lord High Admiral, Lord William Howard, had been in Plymouth to receive the Spanish envoys. Philip himself landed at Southampton but the Hawkins family is thought to have been busy with ships and escorts in the business and the younger Hawkins son, John, seems to have won King Philip's favour and even a Spanish knighthood. King Philip landed at Plymouth in 1557. Old William sat in Mary's first Parliament but died soon afterwards, and the family business was then divided between his two sons, William and John.

The Slave Trade

William seems to have managed affairs at home, while John went to sea and had made several voyages to the Canaries before 1560. The old Hawkins partner, Wyndham, was pushing further down the African coast to the Gold Coast and Philip and Mary, sensitive to Portuguese feelings, ordered this trading to stop. But it continued nevertheless, and when Elizabeth came to the throne in 1558 she regarded the Portuguese occupation as so ineffective (as indeed it was) that she refused to recognise it. The French, notably the Huguenots, were raiding this territory, as they were the Spanish mainland round the Caribbean, and these Protestant Frenchmen, seamen of Normandy and La Rochelle, were so beyond their country's control that, when France and Spain made peace in 1559, it was agreed that it should not apply south of the Tropic of Cancer or west of the longitude of the Canaries. There was no peace beyond the lines.

This was the world into which John Hawkins launched himself. He took a house in London in 1559, married Katherine Gonson, daughter of the Treasurer of the Navy, and formed a syndicate of wealthy London merchants to back a new ambitious venture, direct trade with the Spanish colonies. Hawkins was presuming on his favour with the King of Spain and on the fact that

he would be providing a service that the colonies badly needed, to overcome the Spanish law that only Spanish ships could trade with their settlements. They were sadly short of labour and Hawkins aimed to take Negro slaves from Africa and exchange them for the produce of Spanish America, so gaining the advantages of a double turnover in one voyage. It was also a natural use of the Atlantic winds, for coming home from the south Atlantic it was easier to move into the Caribbean and pick up the westerlies than to struggle through the capricious wind belt north of the south-east trades.

Hawkins sailed from Plymouth in 1562 with three ships, *Salomon*, *Swallow*, and *Jonas*, picked up a pilot in the Canaries, loaded 300 or 400 slaves in Guinea and traded them in the smaller Spanish American ports for pearls, ginger, sugar and hides. To demonstrate his good faith, he sent a Portuguese prize under her own captain to Seville, and two cargoes to San Lucar under his second-in-command, Thomas Hampton. But the Portuguese took his ship to Lisbon and the Spanish confiscated the cargoes that reached San Lucar. Hampton narrowly escaped arrest and met Hawkins in Plymouth with the story in August 1563. Hawkins went straight off to Queen Elizabeth, who took up his case; he may even have gone to Spain himself to claim his cargoes. But to King Philip, Queen Elizabeth was a heretic, and the privateers she had licensed in a new war against France were also harming Spanish neutrals.

Undeterred, Hawkins fitted out a new expedition, and this time there were Navy Board officers and men of the Privy Council in his syndicate as well. The Queen herself chartered a royal ship to Hawkins, the *Jesus of Lubeck*, and told him to sail under Royal colours. Now an extra service was being offered to the Spanish colonies; defence against the French raiders. King Philip had entered into similar arrangements with Catholic Italy in the Mediterranean; perhaps he would do the same in the Atlantic with England. The *Jesus* was an impressive ship of 700 tons, with a massive poop and forecastle, towering above Hawkins's own three little ships. Henry VIII had bought her from the Hanseatic League 20 years before, and long neglect under Edward and Mary had left her so rotten that she had already been condemned once before

John Hawkins (top left) *and the* Jesus of Lubeck (below left).

Hawkins took her. The fleet sailed from the Cattewater in October 1564 and Hawkins demonstrated his honesty towards Spain by sheltering for five days in Ferrol, in northern Spain itself.

He had to do some fighting to collect his 400 or 500 slaves in Guinea, and on reaching the Spanish Main found that the colonies had been told not to trade with him. But they needed his slaves, and at port after port the pretext was that they traded with him under threat of violence. On his way home, Hawkins called at the first French colony in America, in Florida. He found the colonists close to starvation, and they would have been well advised to accept his offer of a passage home, for, a year later the Spaniards massacred them all. Hawkins reached Padstow in September 1565, with the *Jesus* in such bad shape that she could not sail round to Plymouth until the following spring. But Hawkins showed a profit of 60 per cent and the Queen gave him a coat of arms with a bound slave as the crest. John Hawkins was the first Englishman to enter the slave trade, but in those days no shame was attached to slavers. One age must not be judged by the morals of another.

John Sparke

Among Hawkins's officers on that voyage was Anthony Parkhurst, who later moved into the Newfoundland trade and, in 1578, was arguing that England should found a settlement there to support the fisheries. Another was John Sparke, whose father had moved from Cheshire to Plympton, and who wrote a graphic account of the voyage. He tells us that an officer was killed at the very start of the voyage, by a falling pulley in Plymouth Sound, and records the renowned order that John Hawkins made to his fleet off Ferrol: 'Serve God daily, love one another, preserve your victuals, beware of fire, and keep good company.'

John Sparke is the first Englishman ever to mention either the potato or tobacco. Of their first watering-point on the Spanish Main, he says:

Certain Indians... came down to us presenting mill and cakes of bread, which they had made of a kind of corn called maisce... also they brought down to us which we bought for beads, pewter whistles, glasses, knives, and other trifles; hens, potatoes and pines [pineapples?]. These potatoes be the most delicate roots that may be eaten, and do far exceed their parsnips or carrots.

So here, in the very dawn of English exploration, is the traditional picture of bartering on the beach with the naked Indians 'tawny like an olive'. It was not until they were at the French settlement that Sparke saw tobacco for the first time.

The Floridians when they travel have a kind of herb dried, which with a cane, and an earthen cup in the end,

with fire, and the dried herbs put together do suck through the cane the smoke thereof, which smoke satisfieth their hunger, and therewith they live four or five days without meat or drink, and this all the Frenchmen used for this purpose; yet they do hold opinion withall, that it causeth water and fleme to void from their stomachs.

What stories for a boy to bring back to Plymouth. 'The commodities of this land are more than are yet known to any man... gold and silver they want not...' He told, too, of a Frenchman who traded a hatchet for two pounds of gold.

There was a John Sparke a year or two later in the Russian trade ventures of the day, but he is not now thought to be our man. It seems that after his one Caribbean adventure he came home to settle in Plymouth as a merchant and town councillor.

Fighting Begins

Hawkins kept plugging away at his Atlantic dreams. Of three ships that sailed (not very successfully) for Guinea in 1566, the leader was the *Castle of Comfort*, jointly owned by Hawkins and Richard Grenville. A squadron of four ships was also sent out by Hawkins under the command of a relative, John Lovell. Another member of this expedition was Hawkins's cousin, young Francis Drake. After the 1549 rebellion, his father had gone to the Medway as chaplain to the fleet, and become vicar of Upchurch there. Around the mudflats and in the tides of the Thames estuary young Drake had learnt to be a seaman and, by legend, had been so good a mate that his first master left him a small coaster. True or not, he was back in Plymouth in 1566, about 23 years old and sailing in his cousin's ship. He was already a man of determined ideas, for long afterwards a Welshman, under the pressure of the Inquisition, confessed that during this voyage Francis Drake had made him a heretic. The expedition made the usual round trip, Guinea and the Caribbean, but with no success, and Hawkins never again employed Lovell. Two other captains, Thomas Hampton and James Ranse, together with Drake, were transferred to a new expedition which Hawkins was already gathering when they returned.

It was an expedition for which John Hawkins had made careful preparations, dining with the Spanish ambassador in London, offering to fight the Turks in the Mediterranean for King Philip, and assuring the ambassador that neither he nor his ships would go to the Indies that year. There was even a story about a fabulous goldmine in Africa, and two Portuguese renegades joined the fleet in Plymouth as pilots. There were four Plymouth ships and two Queen's vessels, the *Jesus of Lubeck* again, and the *Minion*. The *Minion* was only half the size of the *Jesus*, but just as rotten; she had been built in 1536.

Drake's Island showing the different periods of fortification: on the left *medieval crenellations,* on the right *Victorian casemates and* on top *Second World War gun emplacements.*

What Hawkins was really planning is unknown, but whatever it was, Spain was not trusting him. In August 1567, seven ships from the Spanish Netherlands came bowling into the Sound and headed straight for the Cattewater. They made no salute: neither their Spanish flags nor their topsails were dipped. Fearing an attack, Hawkins opened fire from the *Jesus* and *Minion* right there in the Cattewater:

He 'commanded his gunner to shoot at the flag of the admiral which, notwithstanding, they persevered arrogantly to keep displayed, whereupon the gunner at the next shot raked the admiral through and through.

The Flemings then went about sharply, and sailed out of the Cattewater to anchor under St Nicholas's Island. The admiral sent protests to the Mayor of Plymouth and was referred to Hawkins, who received him on the quarter-deck of the Jesus with an armed guard. Hawkins said bluntly that he was the general of the Queen's ships in the Cattewater and must enforce the respect that was her due. He mollified the Dutchman with presents of beer and poultry, but the squadron remained in the port until the end of September; watching Hawkins, protesting to the Spanish ambassador, and eventually securing a diplomatic reprimand from the Queen to John Hawkins.

Altogether, it was a worrying autumn for Hawkins. A Spanish ship came into the Cattewater with Flemish prisoners aboard, and when some masked men set the

prisoners free, the Dutch admiral accused Hawkins of the deed. Hawkins's retort was that it had probably been done by the admiral's own Flemish sailors. Then his Portuguese pilots escaped in a ship to Spain. The Queen again censured Hawkins, but eventually agreed that he should make the usual Africa–West Indies voyage. So, after a service in St Andrew's Church attended by the 400 men of his crews and all his officers, Hawkins sailed at last, on 2 October, the customary time of year for these Guineamen.

A gale scattered the ships and nearly sank the *Jesus*. There was fighting on the Guinea coast, and more trouble when they eventually arrived in the Caribbean with 500 slaves. Real force had to be used, and trade was unsatisfactory. Then a hurricane battered the ships, the old *Jesus* needed repairs and all the ships food and water for the voyage home. Hawkins put in to San Juan de Ulloa, the outport of Mexico City and the terminal point of the *flota*, the fleet that each year took the treasure home to Spain. It was not due for a fortnight, by which time Hawkins hoped to be away again. It arrived the next morning.

Hawkins was so positioned that he could have denied the *flota* entry. But he had been in trouble the year before for shooting at the Spanish flag in Plymouth and here he was in a Spanish port claiming to be serving the King of Spain. He decided to make terms with the *flota*, and offered to let the Spanish ships in if they would allow him to complete his repairs and leave. A

Left: *An English ship, c.1580.*

new Viceroy was in the flota; he agreed that Hawkins had been trading honestly in the Indies, and accepted his bargain. But once inside, the Spanish attacked the English.

Only John Hawkins in the *Minion*, and young Drake, who had been given the command of the little *Judith* during the voyage, brought their ships out. Drake reached Plymouth in January 1569. Hawkins limped into Mount's Bay at the end of that month. William Hawkins had to send a fresh crew down from Plymouth to sail the *Minion*, her own men could go no further. Of 400 men who sailed from Plymouth in October 1567, only 70 came home again. Apart from the lost ships, £3,100 in treasure had been left behind in San Juan.

Robert Barrett of Saltash, a cousin of Drake's, had been Hawkins's flag-captain in the *Jesus*, a man who had been entrusted with all the dangerous jobs, who might well have become the greatest sea captain of the age. With the other prisoners, he was shipped back to Spain and the Inquisition. He was burned at the stake in the market-place of Seville. Some of his companions rotted and died in prison there. Six were sent to the galleys, from which Job Hortop escaped after 20 years to come home to his native Plymouth. Paul Horsewell, the 11-year-old son of John Hawkins's sister, was kept in Mexico more less as a house slave, settled there and raised a family.

About 100 men who had been set ashore on the North American seaboard rather than face the voyage home in the *Minion*, were nearly all captured. Anthony Goddard, their leader, was set free in 1571 and got home to Plymouth; three men apparently walked the length of North America to be picked up by a French ship off Cape Breton. Miles Phillips, a boy, escaped to England in 1583. Many who were taken, either at San Juan or from Goddard's party, went to the stake. The Inquisition was more merciful in Mexico than in Seville; these men were strangled first. Others ended in the galleys. The sentences are in the Spanish records: John Moon of Looe, 26, seaman, 200 lashes and six years in the galleys; John Williams of Cornwall, 28, 200 lashes and eight years in the galleys; Robert Plinton of Plymouth, 30, 200 lashes and eight years in the galleys. As the report leaked home to Plymouth, so the bitterness grew. San Juan de Ulloa was the turning point; it was war from thenceforward.

The Protestant Fleet

Times had changed while John Hawkins was away on that 'troublesome voyage'. The Prince of Orange had launched a Protestant rebellion against Spain in the Netherlands. Mary, Queen of Scots, had fled to England and was a prisoner, but still a threat to the English throne as a Catholic alternative to Elizabeth. The Duke of Alva was leading a Spanish army in the Netherlands, and a squadron laden with treasure to

pay his soldiers had been dispatched from Spain. Huguenot privateers from La Rochelle chased these treasure ships into Fowey, Plymouth and Southampton in the autumn of 1568. William Hawkins, who was then Mayor of Plymouth, had a ship sailing with the Huguenot privateers under licence from the Prince of Condé, their leader; while another privateer was Henry Champernowne of Modbury, nephew of Sir Arthur Champernowne of Dartington, Vice-Admiral of Devon. The ship that came into Plymouth Sound anchored off Saltash, as far from the privateers waiting in the Channel as she could get, and her captain was persuaded to unload her cargo for greater safety. William Hawkins and Sir Arthur Champernowne supervised the unloading, and 64 cases of silver coins were taken to Plymouth Guildhall for safe keeping.

Spain accused the English of seizing her treasure ships, and retaliated by seizing all English ships and goods in the Low Countries. Elizabeth ordered the seizure of all Spanish ships in her harbours. William Hawkins heard that his brother had been killed in Mexico, and sent anxious inquiries to London. Elizabeth, discovering that the money for the Spanish troops had actually been borrowed by Spain from Genoese bankers, treated with them and had the loan transferred to herself. The day after John Hawkins crept into Mount's Bay, Sir Arthur Champernowne set off for the Tower of London with the treasure from Plymouth Guildhall, riding away up Lipson Hill with an escort of 50 horses, 50 foot soldiers and artillery.

Denying Alva his pay-chests was a major victory for the Protestant fleet in the Channel. It was becoming a religious battleground, with the Huguenots in rebellion against the Catholic monarchs of France, the Calvinist Dutch fighting the overlordship of Spain in the Low Countries and Protestant England on their side yet not wishing openly to antagonise France or Spain. Elizabeth was very conscious that they could in turn organise religious rebellion against her.

When that Spanish treasure ship was chased into Plymouth there were believed to be 50 Huguenot privateers in the Channel, 30 of them English. William Hawkins had the biggest stake in the fleet; he was virtually the commander-in-chief and Plymouth the main base of their operations. Helping the French Protestants had an honourable background; Devon men had helped to defend Le Havre in the first French war of religion, Humphrey Gilbert of Dartmouth had been wounded there, the twin brothers, Nicholas and Andrew Tremayne of Collacombe, near Tavistock, killed.

Four young cousins who had sought adventure by helping defend Vienna when the Turks overran Europe – Richard Grenville, Henry Champernowne, Philip Budockside of St Budeaux and his brother-in-law, William Gorges, from Somerset – now joined

Above: *Budshead House being demolished in 1964; all that remains on the site is a few doorways.* Below: *The Budshead ruins.*

forces with William Hawkins. The Budocksides were coming up in the world. Apart from marrying Sir Arthur Champernowne's sister, Roger Budockside had rebuilt his house at Budshead early in 1560, and largely rebuilt (or at least provided the land) for the rebuilding of St Budeaux Parish Church on its present site. Perhaps the old church, with its tower and three bells, was too near his manor house, or he disliked the parishioners invading his privacy. Some of the stones of the old church seem to have been used in the new; it was planned for the new prayer-book with no chancel, and no doubt the altar was well out in the nave. Roger's son Philip became his uncle's partner in the *New Bark*.

Philip Budockside held letters of marque from the Prince of Condé. In 1569 the privateers chased a squadron of Flemish ships into Plymouth Sound. They were sailing under the Spanish flag and carrying goods from Morocco; sugar, molasses and ostrich feathers. 'Barbary hulks', the records call them. Flying the Queen's flag, Philip Budockside sailed out to tell them that there was a general stay of shipping, that the Queen's ships were outside and they could not escape. He placed four men aboard each and brought them up off Saltash. That night his men descended upon them and stripped them; three

he actually sailed right over to La Rochelle. Richard Grenville was in the business, too, and in the late 1560s (after he had sold his grandmother's land at Compton) he shared the *Castle of Comfort* with William Hawkins. It was a ship that managed to get into more scrapes and more Admiralty Court wrangles than any of the western privateers.

Another name now turned up, one that was later to stand in the first rank of Elizabethans; Martin Frobisher. An orphan from Yorkshire, he had first gone to sea with Wyndham when that partner of old William Hawkins had reopened the Guinea trade in 1540. By 1563 Frobisher was in Plymouth, a Hawkins captain. That year he brought in five Frenchmen; the next year he took a ship which was carrying tapestry for King Philip himself, and that landed him in Launceston gaol. But he married a Launceston girl, and thereafter was as much West Countryman as Yorkshireman. He was privateering in the *Mary Flower* in 1565, and at sea under a Huguenot commission the next year. In 1569 he held the Prince of Orange's commission, but again had a spell in prison, which does not appear to have harmed his career as, by 1572, he was in the Queen's service in Irish waters.

The State papers are full of the screams of those who suffered from these marauders. In November 1568 the 'Rochellers' brought 16 French prizes into Plymouth to sell their cargoes. In December, the *Marseilles*, obviously a Frenchman, was stripped in the harbour, and in January 1569 certain English pirates brought three Flemish and one Spanish vessel into Plymouth, divided their rich cargoes, and sold them. The Spanish ambassador complained that the marauders in the haven of Plymouth were being favoured by friendship at the Court. In March another Plymouth pirate with a crew of 200 took a Flemish ship into the Cattewater, stripped it, and put the crew ashore on the Barbican. They were left to beg at the door of St Andrew's, and would have starved had not a countryman living in the town kept them for several days. One of the men heard an Englishman say what a fine ship the *Brielle* would make for Admiral Hawkins.

John Granger plundered the *Pelican* of Normandy in the Cattewater, and three of the crew were slain. Bernard Grave of St Malo was imprisoned in his own ship by a Plymouth pirate and William Hawkins, who was ordered to rescue him, kept the ship for himself. They were pirates to Spain, privateers to the Huguenots and very welcome in the eyes of the Queen. Plymouth was fighting her war for her.

In 1569 the Prince of Orange brought the Catholic Flemings and the Calvinist Dutch together to fight the Spanish, and began issuing letters of marque to his own people and to the English. When driven out of the Low Countries, these Dutch Sea Beggars made Dover their base. There was another Huguenot force operating from the Solent under Pourtault de Latour; he was killed in the spring of 1569 and Jacques de Sores, who had been in command of a Hawkins ship, took over the Solent leadership. The three Protestant squadrons became international, each a mixture of English, French and Dutch in ownership, leadership, and crewing. Plymouth must have been a more polyglot port than ever, and with so many Dutchmen in harbour (and there had been Dutch residents since 1436) it is no wonder that Plymouth became the traditional English home of gin.

No wonder either that Plymouth needed more quay space. In 1572, says the Black Book:

... the kaye on southesyde, whereof the southe ende adjoneth to the Barbygan ynderneath the Castell, was Builded by the towne vnder full sea marke, and Contayneth in lengethe one hundred and Thurtie Foot and in Bredthe fourtie and fower foot.

It is still there, although it has doubled in length.

This was the far-from-peaceful England to which the men of San Juan de Ulloa returned. For them there was little peace either side of the lines now. Drake, for instance, was packed straight off to London to tell his story, and that spring of 1569 was probably an officer in a naval squadron, escorting a convoy of English ships past the Spanish Netherlands to a new trading point in Europe, Hamburg. He was back that summer and married Mary Newman in the new church at St Budeaux.

Legend makes her a Saltash girl, but there are many Newmans in the St Budeaux registers and one would expect a girl to marry in her own Parish Church.

The Newmans had strong links with the sea; a Harry Newman had served in the San Juan de Ulloa voyage, and in 1560 Mary's elder sister, Margaret, had married a John Bodenham, whose son, Jonas, later became Drake's right-hand man. Probably John Bodenham, now Francis Drake's brother-in-law, was related to the Roger Bodenham who called at Plymouth in 1550 on a Levant voyage. Marrying and settling in Seville, he traded from there to Barbary and made one voyage to Mexico, and was still living in San Lucar in 1580. It gave Drake an odd but close link with those Anglo-Spanish merchants, and a valuable source of information.

While Drake was getting married, John Hawkins seems to have been leading an English fleet to restock La Rochelle and bring home all the Huguenot plunder they could not sell in France. Among it, there were even French church bells, whose bronze may well have gone into the new guns for the defence of Plymouth. Of the sixty ships that made up the convoy, eight were owned by

Top centre: *Martin Frobisher.* Above: *A Victorian view of the Barbican with the quay on the line of John Hawkins's 1573 quay and before the old fish market was built. In the distance is the eighteenth-century Watch House, demolished in the 1930s, on the site of the original barbican, or watergate.*

William Hawkins. Later that year, Henry Champernowne and Philip Budockside took a company of local gentlemen down to aid the 'Rochellers', and their jaunt gave a first taste of war to another Devon youngster, Walter Ralegh. Budockside never came home. Philip's father, Roger, died four years later and the St Budeaux estates passed to William Gorges.

In 1569 there were rumours in Spain that one or both of the Hawkins were at sea, and in the following year John Hawkins was putting up to the Council in London a plan to capture the Spanish *flota* on its way home from San Juan de Ulloa. It would have been the perfect revenge, but he wanted royal ships with him to avenge the insult of 1568 to the Queen's ships. He had his own strong fleet at Plymouth, and a Spanish spy in Plymouth reported its numbers, strength and arms in detail to the Spanish ambassador. All told, it amounted to 3,170 tons, 1,585 men, and 406 guns.

But the Queen preferred to keep all her ships in home waters; there were too many threats from Scotland and Alva. John Hawkins heard news of some of his men being in prison in Seville, and set to work to secure their release. He began to bargain with the Spanish ambassador, and even entered into a plot with him whereby, in return for his men, he would aid an English rising in favour of Mary, Queen of Scots. By early 1571 he was offering to turn his Plymouth fleet over to Alva and leave the Channel mouth open to invasion. His intermediary was George Fitzwilliam. He had been captured at San Juan; now he had won his release and through the Hawkins plot – he was even professing to be a secret Catholic – he gained the release of a score or so of Hawkins's men.

John Hawkins had won his main objective, at the same time he had wormed himself into the full Spanish plan and was telling Burghley all about it. The leader of the English plotters, the Earl of Norfolk, was arrested and executed, but the Spanish still did not discover John Hawkins's double game. Even when the Spanish ambassador was told he was *persona non grata* and sent packing, Hawkins went with him to the coast. It is a strange business for a Plymouth MP, as John was in 1571, to be engaged in – real cloak and dagger, complete with invisible ink and all the trimmings.

After this Ridolfi plot something had to be done to smooth relations with Spain, superficially at any rate, and to mollify France. Both were complaining bitterly about the Channel privateers. So, in 1572, John Hawkins was commanded, together with William Winter, an officer of the Navy Board, to order out all the privateers from the harbours of the eastern

Left: *Sir Humphrey Gilbert.*

Channel, and to warn the English of those ports to give them no further aid. It seems a strange order to give to a man whose brother was the privateer admiral of the other half of the Channel. The Sea Beggars made no argument. The Solent squadron sailed up to join the Dover force, and the two squadrons sailed east to capture Brill, on the Dutch coast itself. A little later they took Flushing, and were never turned out. Their war against Spain was now being run from their home country. Did John Hawkins just order them out, or did he, on the Queen's behalf, plan just this very move with the Dutch commanders? After all, Sir Humphrey Gilbert, who had sat with John Hawkins as Members of Parliament for Plymouth in 1571, was in the Low Countries in 1573, fighting with the Dutch Protestants against the French and Spanish Catholics.

The French massacre of the Huguenots on St Bartholomew's Day 1572 cut their strength to nearly nothing. They were reduced to La Rochelle, and a Plymouth expedition under Henry Champernowne failed to help them. Nevertheless, they hung on, and patched up a kind of peace with the Catholics. Elizabeth made a second gesture of friendship towards France and Spain, and her Navy cleared the Channel of such privateers as were left. The *Castle of Comfort* stayed in the privateering business with a French captain, which brought both William Hawkins and Richard Grenville into trouble. William and John went on buying cargoes in Plymouth from privateers, and lost ships about their legitimate business to privateers elsewhere. But privateering in the Channel was fading out as a respectable business. The Hawkins ships were in a more legitimate trade, reaching even down to Genoa in Italy. John continued as MP for Plymouth and was more and more concerned in national affairs, finally succeeding his father-in-law as Treasurer of the Navy in 1577. His fellow MP for the town was Edmund Tremayne of Collacombe, whose younger brothers had died at Le Havre. Tremayne eventually became Clerk of the Privy Council, an important link at Court. William remained in Plymouth, mayor in 1578 and again ten years later. The two brothers ran the town mills at Millbay and built a new weigh-house.

But the war with Spain was not over. The privateering moved away from the Channel to the Atlantic, and Plymouth continued to be its base. The Hawkins brothers were still deeply involved, but the leadership passed to their young cousin, Francis Drake.

CHAPTER 5

War With Spain

Neither Plymouth nor the Hawkins brothers forgot San Juan de Ulloa. Nor did young Francis Drake. He had seen John Hawkins's attempts at peaceful trade come to naught on the Spanish Main, and was resolved to try different ideas. Late in 1570 he sailed in a Hawkins ship, the little 25-ton *Swan*, probably under Huguenot letters of marque. It was a voyage of reconnaissance, on which only one or two merchantmen were captured to feed his men and pay his way.

Drake wanted more than commerce-raiding. His goal was the main treasure route. The treasure came up from Lima, the capital of Peru, through a peaceful Pacific where only Spanish ships sailed, was transferred by land across the narrow isthmus of Panama and, heavily guarded, was shipped again from Nombre de Dios for Spain. In that winter of 1570/71 Drake established a secret base in the Gulf of Darien, between Panama and South America proper, where he buried some stores and made friends with the Cimaroons – escaped Negro slaves who lived in their thousands in the jungle of Panama – before returning home.

At Whitsun 1572 he sailed again in a Hawkins ship, the 72-ton *Pasco*, with his younger brother, John, in command of the *Swan*. Another brother, Joseph, was with them. Only one man, John Oxenham of Plymouth, was over 30. At his Darien base he found pinned to a tree a note from another Plymouth captain, John Garrett, warning him that the Spanish knew of his base. Drake fortified it, and stayed on. A little later, Captain James Ranse of Plymouth, a friend of earlier voyages, arrived and agreed to join him. They nearly captured Nombre de Dios itself, but such a raid was too much for Ranse, and he went home.

Drake stayed on in a new base, raiding towns and ships. John Drake died while attacking a ship, Joseph Drake of a fever. When the plate fleet came in to Nombre de Dios, Drake marched inland to try and intercept the mule train. A drunken seaman ruined the ambush but, from a tree on a high ridge, a Cimaroon guide showed Drake the Pacific. He was the first Englishman to gaze upon that ocean, and he prayed to God 'to give him life and leave to sail once in an English ship in that sea'.

With a Huguenot ship, he made another raid on a mule train carrying the Peru treasure, and brought it off after hairbreadth escapes. But his ships by then were so rotten that he first had to capture two Spanish craft to bring him and his treasure home. When these two strange craft reached Plymouth it was Sunday morning, 9 August 1573. As word went round, the congregation ran out of St Andrew's to welcome him, leaving the parson preaching to an empty church. Only 30 men of the 74 who had sailed came home, but they brought with them £20,000 of gold and silver. An equal share had gone to France; Spain, in modern values, was a million pounds the poorer.

But the Queen was looking for peace with Spain, and though privateers followed Drake, he himself had to disappear. Two years later he is recorded as serving the Earl of Essex in Ireland, and he may have been running convoys from Plymouth to Ireland all that time. Bigger projects were under discussion in Devon. Sir Richard Grenville, who was busy turning Auckland Abbey into the mansion that it is today, was proposing to round South America, find the unknown land believed to exist in the South Pacific, colonise it (the first English talk of colonisation), and return round the north of America. William Hawkins, Piers Edgcumbe, Grenville's half-brother Alexander Arundell of Clifton, and several cousins were in the scheme. But the Queen would not approve, fearing that the plan might upset Spain. At the same time, Sir Humphrey Gilbert had a project to open the north-west passage, and as this would not upset Spain, Martin Frobisher was sent off in command in 1576. He brought home lumps of ore from the islands between Greenland and Canada, and as everyone thought they contained gold there was a rush to invest money in his second voyage. For this, in 1578, he had 15 ships, and embarked 41 miners at Plymouth. He got as far as Hudson Strait but found no north-west passage, and though he came home loaded with ore, there was no gold in it. Interest in the north-west passage slumped, and Frobisher's stock with it.

Around the World

Drake had come back from Ireland in 1576 and proposed a voyage very similar to the one that Grenville had not been allowed to make. He formed a syndicate of Court people, unlike Grenville's West Country syndicate, and as Spain was becoming more menacing, the Queen was now less averse to upsetting her.

Drake went down to Plymouth to prepare for his voyage and there found his old lieutenant, John Oxenham, planning a voyage of his own. Later that year, Oxenham sailed for Panama and, after hiding his ship, crossed the isthmus he had explored with Drake, built a pinnace and became the first English sea captain to sail the Pacific. The unarmed Spanish ships were easy prey, and Oxenham began to hide hoards of silver. But he made no hurry to get away. Had he, perhaps, arranged to wait for Drake, and was this a part of the plans they had made in Plymouth?

Life in the town was much as usual. The English had given up the privateering business but the *Castle of Comfort* had brought a Breton prize into Cawsand Bay the year before and the Hawkins family were 'ransoming; Huguenot prizes. London merchants were financing Guinea voyages out of Plymouth. Ships were still sailing to the Caribbean, eight Hawkins vessels and half a dozen others in 1575. In 1576 John Horseley, from Dorset, brought a little ship into Plymouth laden deep with silver and gold from Darien. Apart from Oxenham, a dozen Caribbean voyagers had left Plymouth in 1576.

Drake did not get away until November 1577 and,

Left: Sir Richard Grenville.

officially, he was going to trade with the Turks at Alexandria. He had five ships and 160 men. Thomas Moon, who had been his ship's carpenter in 1572, was in command of a pinnace, and others with him included Drake's brother, Thomas; a young cousin, John Drake from Tavistock; his nephew William Hawkins (son of the second William) and a John Hawkins of uncertain relationship. It was a rough autumn, and within a few days the ships were back in the Cattewater, with the *Pelican*, the flagship, dismasted. They were away again on 12 December. Then there was silence.

Sir Humphrey Gilbert sailed the next November with a bigger squadron but was back in February, having been mauled by a Spanish fleet. Captain Sharpham and Mr Fortescue sailed about the same time with five large ships, planning a settlement on the coast of Brazil, but it came to nothing. Then, in June 1579, one of Drake's captains, William Winter,

Looe Street, running down to the harbour. The houses on the right have been restored and are owned by the Barbican Association.

58

struggled into Ilfracombe. Drake had scrapped two of his smaller ships, lost another in a storm and executed an officer, Thomas Doughty, for mutiny. Winter's own men had mutinied in the Straits of Magellan because they had not signed for such a voyage, and he had been forced to turn back. News began to leak through Seville to Plymouth that Drake was on the Pacific coast of South America, marauding at will. There were fears that, in his fury, Philip might declare war on England, but he was too busy planning to take over Portugal, which he did in 1580.

Then, in October of that year, some fishermen off Rame Head were hailed by a homeward-bound ship: 'Is the Queen alive?' Drake was back.

He anchored under Drake's Island and remained there while messengers rode to London to tell the Queen of his return. Drake had raided the major Pacific ports of Spanish America, from Valparaiso to Callao, without firing a shot, and had stripped treasure ships until his own craft (now renamed the *Golden Hind* in honour of the crest of his patron, Sir Christopher Hatton) could hold no more. He had heard of the capture of John Oxenham and had pleaded for his release in a message to the Viceroy of Peru (it was in vain, for Oxenham and his officers were hanged in Lima a year later). He had followed the coast of North America until cold and fog had forced him to give up hope of the north-west passage and come home through the East Indies. There he had made a treaty with a sultan who had fallen out with the Portuguese, and found room for six tons of spices and a drinking-cup made of a coconut shell which, mounted in silver, is now in the wardroom of HMS *Drake* at Devonport. He had exposed Spain's weak flank, opened a door to the Indies, had sailed round the world. Magellan had also done this but he had died on the voyage, whereas Drake was the first captain, and the first Englishman, to make the circumnavigation.

While he waited under Drake's Island for the Queen's reaction, his wife, Mary, rowed out to him with the mayor. No doubt William Hawkins went out as well, but Plymouth was an unhealthy town that autumn. The plague had killed 600 people and even mayor-choosing was done on the windy heights of Cattedown for health's sake.

The messenger to London returned with instructions that Drake was to put his treasure into Trematon Castle (his own share he put in the care of a good friend, Christopher Harris of Radford, in the old house at the head of Hooe Lake). He was then to go to London to report to Her Majesty in person. Prudently, he loaded six packhorses with gold and jewels, and the Queen talked to him in private audience for six hours. How much treasure he brought home is unknown, estimates vary between returns of £14–£47 for every pound his backers invested, and from a whole year's revenue of the Crown to £2$\frac{1}{2}$

million of modern money. Drake himself was rich beyond dreams, the most famous seaman of England, and henceforth the Queen's chief adviser on maritime matters. He sailed the *Golden Hind* round to Deptford, where Elizabeth knighted him on his own quarter-deck. All London trooped to see his ship and she was kept in dry dock at Woolwich as a show-piece, as we have since kept the *Victory* at Portsmouth, until a fire burnt her to the waterline. Pieces of furniture made from her timbers were afterwards guarded as precious relics.

In Plymouth, as throughout the country, Drake was a national hero. His town house was in Looe Street, just across the road from the guildhall, in the very heart of the town. When in the town he must have been as familiar a figure as anyone. For a time he was the tenant of Thorn Park, the long-vanished manor house whose site is now covered by Hyde Park School. Richard Grenville, conscious of an ancestry dating back to the Conqueror and of having propounded the very plan Drake had carried out, could not bear to live in the shadow of this upstart and slunk off back to Bideford. He sold Buckland Abbey, which he had just finished converting into the great house it still is, to Drake's friend, Harris, and John Hele, a rising young lawyer, for £3,400. He may have known that they were acting for Drake, but it now became his country house.

In 1581 Plymouth elected Sir Francis as mayor. He put the councillors into red cloaks like the aldermen, and a compass on the Hoe. But national affairs largely occupied him, and with Leicester, Burghley, Walsingham and Hatton, he set up a syndicate to develop his trade links with the East Indies. Ships were assembled at Plymouth under the command of Edward Fenton, John Hawkins's brother-in-law. Young William Hawkins was second-in-command and another boy veteran of the circumnavigation, John Drake, commanded a small ship called the *Francis*. Their orders were to reach the Moluccas by way of the Cape of Good Hope, but when they were in the south Atlantic young Hawkins and Drake persuaded Fenton to go the other way, only to find that a strong Spanish force was guarding the Straits of Magellan. Spain was determined not to be caught a second time. The expedition broke up and came home, with Hawkins in irons. John Drake decided to stay in South America, and joined other Englishmen already living beside the River Plate.

Colonisation

Francis Drake, the Hawkinses and the sea captains of Plymouth had all been brought up to seafaring, trading and fighting. But the gentlemen of Devon, with their university educations and their experience of colonisation in Ireland, saw further ahead. To them, it seemed better to stake a claim in America than merely to steal the fruits of Spanish labours.

Grenville's 1576 project had talked of colonising, and in 1578 his cousin, Humphrey Gilbert, obtained letters patent from the Queen to take possession of lands not 'possessed of any Christian prince... and to inhabit or remain there'.

He made his first attempt, in Florida, that same year. It failed, but one of his captains was his half-brother, Walter Ralegh, who had to do some hard fighting before he got back. Gilbert sent another ship across in 1579, but the main attempt did not take place until 1582, when five ships and 260 men sailed from Cawsand Bay, landed at St John, Newfoundland, and claimed it for the Queen. They then turned south, but on the uncharted coast of America the flagship was lost with 100 men and all the stores. There was no alternative but to sail for home, with Gilbert in the smallest ship of all, the ten-ton *Squirrel*. He would not shift to a larger vessel: 'We are as near to heaven by sea as by land,' he shouted across the waters, and was last seen, before the *Squirrel* foundered in an Atlantic gale, calmly sitting on deck reading a book.

His half-brother, Ralegh, inherited his colonising charter and brought in his cousin, Sir Richard

Left: Plaque outside St Budeaux Church.

Grenville. They sent out two survey ships in 1584 under Captain Philip Amadas of Plymouth (a Hawkins cousin) and Arthur Barlow. On their return, Ralegh named the country they had surveyed Virginia, in the Queen's honour (he was her favourite at the time), and was knighted in reward.

The following year Grenville – since the Queen would not be parted from Ralegh – took out from Plymouth the first party of Englishmen to settle in America. They set up a colony at Roanoke, with Philip Amadas as second-in-command. On the way home, Grenville captured a Spanish ship which he told Walsingham contained only sugar and ginger, forgetting to mention the hides, cochineal, gold, silver and 600,000 ducats which were also in her hold. A contemporary letter said the ship was 'worth a million', and Ralegh hastened to Plymouth to help Grenville keep an eye on it.

Drake's wife, Mary, died in January 1582 and was buried in St Budeaux churchyard. Childless, she had had only a year as Lady Drake and mistress of Buckland Abbey; how much of her 12 years of married life, while her husband ranged the world or was busy at Court, did she spend with her mother at the Newman home at St Budeaux?

Drake, that year, was urging a new plan which the Queen approved but would not let him carry out. Like Ralegh, he had to stay close at hand. So, in November 1582, seven ships sailed from Plymouth under William Hawkins with his brother's son, Richard, only 22, as second-in-command. The scheme was to win over the Portuguese islands in the Atlantic to Don Antonio, the exiled claimant to the throne of Portugal, which Philip had seized. Hawkins went to the Cape Verde islands, where Portuguese treachery led to a number of Englishmen being murdered. Hawkins lost heart in the scheme, sailed first to Brazil and then to the Caribbean. He dredged up oysters for their pearls off the island of Margarita, but all the time he was really waiting for the treasure *flota*. No records survive of what happened, but he came home with treasure, hides and sugar, as well as pearls, and that year the flagship of the *flota* was reported at Seville as missing.

The Hawkinses, Ralegh, Drake and most of the Court then put their money into another plan to open the East Indian trade, but it never materialised. The Duke of Parma was sweeping across the Low Countries, leading a Catholic army intent on crushing Protestantism in Europe. Elizabeth had to help, though she still refused to declare war. John Hawkins proposed that the western men should take

St Budeaux Church, built in 1563 by Richard Budockside to replace the original chapel, which was too close to his house.

letters of marque from Don Antonio. In 1584 the Queen gave Drake her own commission to sail to the West Indies, and then held him back. He spent some of the time getting married again, to Elizabeth Sydenham, daughter of a landed gentleman of Somerset.

Descent on the Indies

Philip himself gave Elizabeth the excuse she needed to take action. The Spanish harvest had failed and English merchants were invited to send in grain. Then, when the ports of Spain were filled with English ships, they were seized and their crews flung into prison. The barque *Primrose* escaped from Bilbao and came home with the story. So, in September 1585, Drake took to sea again, the first time for five years. He sailed from Plymouth Sound, flying his flag in the royal ship *Bonaventure*, with Frobisher as his vice-admiral in another royal ship, and accompanied by 19 private ships. There were old shipmates among their captains, Thomas Drake, Thomas Moon and Richard Hawkins, as well as over 3,000 seamen and soldiers. A week before they sailed, Don Antonio came into the port:

The kinge of Portingall arived at Plymouth the 7th Daye of September verye poore & was Driven from his cuntry by the kinge of Spaine ii years before, & was relieved by the Quenes majestie, & was sente for by her majestie to the Corte, where he was Condocted with 50 horses or more.

So the Black Book records, while legend says that he was entertained by both Drake and the Edgcumbes.

Excitement was high as the expedition prepared to set out; even the Queen's new favourite, Philip Sidney, had ridden down to Plymouth to join the fleet. The Queen commanded him to return and told the mayor, John Sparke, to arrest him if he did not instantly comply.

Drake sailed for Vigo in northern Spain, sacked the town, and after freeing English ships and crews, watered his fleet and stocked up with green vegetables. He remained in Vigo for eight days, and then moved on to the Cape Verde islands and took over Santiago. Here a ship's boy was murdered and, remembering the murders of three years before, the town and two others were burnt to the ground. Drake sailed on for the West Indies and captured the two chief Spanish cities there, San Domingo and Cartagena, in brilliant operations. John Sparke sent word from Plymouth to London that Drake 'runneth through the country like a conqueror'.

Among the Plymouth men who died was Tom Moon, Drake's former carpenter and later an officer in the *Golden Hind*. He had led the boarding party over the rail of the first treasure ship in Valparaiso harbour, shouting 'Down, dog!' in Spanish to the first seaman he met on her deck. He had gone up the beach at Cartagena before dawn in the first landing party and had been killed in the first fight. For 14 years he had been at Drake's elbow, reliable, brave and loyal.

Drake took a ransom from Cartagena as he had from San Domingo (though not as much as he wanted) and sailed on. He called at Roanoke, where the colonists had come through their first winter. It had been a hard time, and Grenville was two months overdue. Drake gave them a choice of supplies or a passage home. They decided to leave, and when Grenville arrived a fortnight later he found his first colony deserted. After much searching for them, he left another 15 men in their place, and they were never heard of again. On his way home Grenville sacked the Azores, and reached Plymouth to find Drake's stature greater than ever after his 'descent on the Indies'. King Philip's financial credit was ruined, and Drake was now a European figure – El Draco. 'Truly,' wrote Burghley, 'Sir Francis Drake is a fearful man to the King of Spain.'

Drake spent the summer of 1586 ferrying reinforcements to the army in the Netherlands. Sir Walter Ralegh sent two pinnaces off from Plymouth in June, the *Mary Sparke* and the *Serpent*. They captured the governor of the Straits of Magellan and brought him home prisoner; off the Azores they tackled a treasure fleet of 24 ships, including two 1,000-tonners and, though beaten off, they still had a rich haul of ivory, hides and Brazil wood. Jacob Whiddon, Thomas Drake and Richard Moone of Saltash were in this dashing little expedition. Their three deeply laden prizes reached Plymouth six hours ahead of them, and when they themselves came in:

... wee were received with triumphant joy, nor onely with great Ordinance then shot off, but with the willing hearts of all the people of the Towne, and of the Countrey thereabouts; and we not sparing our Ordinance (with the powder we had left) to requite and answer them again.

On 21 July Thomas Cavendish, a Suffolk gentleman who had been with Grenville when he set up the Roanoke colony, sailed from Plymouth for the South Seas. Three days later, three ships commissioned by the Earl of Cumberland came into the Sound, joined up with some others (including Ralegh's *Dorothy*), and they, too, sailed on 17 August, on Drake's old route, with Robert Withrington in command. They met a lot of trouble in South America, but one odd capture was a Portuguese account of the New World with records of Drake's 1572 raid on Nombre de Dios, Oxenham's forays in the Pacific and a graphic account through enemy eyes of the efforts the Spanish had made to catch Drake on his circumnavigation. It recorded that, in all, Drake had taken from the coast of Peru 1,390,200 ducats of silver and 150,000 ducats of gold, apart from precious stones and plate.

At Buenos Aires Withrington heard that John Drake, the young nephew of Drake who had stayed behind there in 1582, had been captured, but was alive and in good health. He had been shipwrecked, and after having been held prisoner by the Indians for a year, had escaped, only to fall into Spanish hands. At first, he kept secret his relationship to the great Sir Francis, but a Portuguese pilot who had met the circumnavigator recognised him. Withrington reached Plymouth in 1587 to tell Drake that his nephew was being sent to the Inquisition at Lima. It is doubtful if Drake ever heard of him again but, in fact, he was set free in 1595, though forbidden to leave Peru. As escape was almost impossible, he probably married, as did other English released prisoners, and settled there. At the end of the last century there was a noble family called Drake del Castillo in Spain who claimed descent from the great admiral.

But while Withrington failed, as Fenton had failed, to get through the Magellan Straits, Thomas Cavendish succeeded, and made a prosperous voyage, even though it did involve less pluckings and more fighting than Drake's. A Plymouth man, William Stevens, was killed on the Pacific coast. Cavendish made his major capture off California and came home by way of the South Sea Islands, the Philippines, the Java Sea and around the Cape of Good Hope.

Singeing the Beard

While these voyages were starting in the summer of 1586, John Hawkins had been cruising the Channel with the fleet in case the Spanish sought revenge for Drake's descent on the Indies. That winter reports began to reach England that, in every port of Spain, the 'enterprise of England' was going forward. The long struggle, the undeclared war, was coming to a head. Philip had resolved to crush England and a mighty fleet was to be his weapon.

Drake was ordered to form a counter-fleet at Plymouth. The Navy contributed the *Elizabeth Bonaventure* (she had been his flagship in 1585), *Lion*, *Dreadnought* and *Rainbow*. John Hawkins had been in charge of the Navy Board since 1577 and these new ships were the fruits of his experience at sea. They sat lower in the water than those of earlier design, and were better seaboats, being faster to windward and steadier in a sea. Unlike their predecessors, they

Left, top: *Elizabeth Sydenham, Drake's second wife*; left: *Sir Francis Drake.*

were not designed to serve as floating battlefields for soldiers but as artillery platforms from which to sink the enemy by gunfire. Hawkins, in fact, had created the battleship, and Drake was the man to demonstrate how it should be used. London merchant-men, Plymouth ships and Levanters, long used to forcing their way through a hostile Mediterranean, joined him until he had 30 ships.

Drake had clear instructions; he had permission 'to distress the enemy ships within the harbours', to stop the Spanish flotillas from joining up, to halt their supplies and to intercept the *flota*. But he feared that the Queen might still change her mind as she had before, and he was bursting to be off. '... the wind commands me away. Our ship is under sail... Haste. From aboard Her Majesty's good ship, the *Elizabeth Bonaventure* this 2nd April, 1587', he wrote from Plymouth.

Hardly had he cleared the Sound when messengers came clattering into the town with new orders. He was not to enter forcibly into 'any of the King's ports or harbours... or do any act of hostility upon the land'. Hawkins sent a pinnace after Drake with the Queen's new orders but they never caught up with him. The pinnace captured a prize worth £5,000 instead; no doubt Hawkins had privately briefed her captain.

On Wednesday, 19 April, Drake sailed into Cadiz and smashed the galleys defending the harbour. In one day his new ships ended the age-old ascendancy of galleys over sailing ships in confined waters. He burnt or removed some 30 vessels, amounting to 10,000 tons of shipping. He came out on the Friday morning, after having treated a port of Spain like some small West Indian town. Then, anchoring under Cape Sagres, he captured the castle that had been Prince Henry the Navigator's headquarters, and stopped all coastwise shipping, confiscating their stores and burning the staves they were bringing round from the Mediterranean for supply barrels. That did more harm than the Cadiz raid, for when the Armada did sail it had insufficient casks and most of them were of green wood.

Next Drake anchored off the mouth of the Tagus, and when the Marquis of Santa Cruz refused to come out and fight, he ran south to the Azores and captured a carrack homeward bound from the East Indies. She was the *San Felipe*, and her cargo of calico, silk, carpets, taffetas, sarsanets, lawns, indigo, pepper, cinnamon, maize, ebony, saltpetre and a casket of jewels, fetched £114,000, the richest prize yet taken and the first East Indiaman. 'It taught others,' wrote Hakluyt, 'that carracks were no such bugs but that they might be taken...' Her charts and sailing directions opened up to England the secrets of the East Indies.

Drake brought this treasure ship into Plymouth Sound on 26 June 1587 and sent her up to Saltash to be unloaded under the care of Sir John Gilbert and Sir Francis Godolphin. All England buzzed with the stories; Drake had singed the King of Spain's beard and reduced his credit in Europe to its lowest ebb. No wonder that two judges of circuit went out of their way 'of pleasor to see the Town and harborough'.

But Drake also had his troubles; in his domineering, determined way he had refused to hold conferences of his captains while at sea, and when his vice-admiral, William Borough, had protested he had charged him with treason, court-martialled him, sentenced him to death, and brought him into Plymouth a prisoner. Eventually, Borough went back to his job at the Admiralty and the argument died away; he was even given a ship again the following year, but it never left the Thames.

The English Fleet

It was war now, and Spain was still preparing her fleet. That winter, the Lord High Admiral, Lord Howard of Effingham, was at Chatham with John Hawkins and Frobisher, watching the Low Countries. Drake was in Plymouth, building up a fleet of 30 ships and, by January, had over 2,000 men under his command, just about the population of Plymouth itself. His orders, once again, were to ravage the Spanish coast, and he worked night and day to fit out his fleet. Then the Queen changed her

mind and told Drake to pay off half his men. Nevertheless, he continued equipping his ships, and in February heard that the Marquis of Santa Cruz, who had refused his challenge at Lisbon, had died. The Marquis of Medina Sidonia, who had tried to rally the land defences of Cadiz against him, was the reluctant new commander of the Armada.

Grenville was fitting out five ships at Bideford for Virginia, but was now ordered to take them round to join Drake. They arrived in early May, with Grenville's second son, John, in command of one, but Grenville himself went back to Bideford. Drake had been preaching to the Queen the basic naval dictum of seeking out the enemy on his own coast. She was sufficiently impressed to order Lord Howard to leave only a small squadron in the Thames and to sail his fleet round to Plymouth.

At eight o'clock on the morning of 23 May the Lord High Admiral approached Plymouth; 11 great ships of the Navy with eight pinnaces, 16 great ships of London with four pinnaces, seven ships of the Lord Admiral's and 20 ships from the Channel ports. Drake led his 30 ships out to meet them, sailing three abreast. Howard in *Ark Royal* was flying the Royal Standard and a vice-admiral's pennant; Drake in *Revenge* an admiral's pennant. As the ships came abreast both struck their pennants.

Howard sent his vice-admiral's pennant in a pinnace to *Revenge* and the entire fleet came into the Sound with Howard as admiral and Drake flying a vice-admiral's pennant. The office of Lord High Admiral was hereditary; it was only fitting that a great noble should hold the office.

Howard and the biggest Navy ships anchored in the Sound and the rest in the Cattewater. Drake was under St Nicholas's Island. John Hawkins, who for so many years had striven to prepare this fleet, was able to leave his Medway dockyard in June and join the fleet as rear-admiral. His brother William, now

The Cattewater, with a Polish training brig going to sea.

over 70, was appropriately enough mayor of Plymouth that year, and Anthony Goddard, who had been captured after San Juan de Ulloa, was treasurer of the town. Richard Hawkins commanded the Queen's ship *Swallow*, and the mayor's son, William, had the *Griffin*.

Apart from the Admiral, Lord Thomas Howard, the Earl of Cumberland and Lord Sheffield, there were no noblemen afloat. Nor were the country gentry, like Ralegh and Grenville, at sea; their place was with the county militia forces in case the Spanish landed. There were some county names in the fleet, such as that of John Harris and Tristram Gorges in the little *Advice*, John St Leger, Humphrey Sydenham, Ambrose Mannington and Thomas Chichester, but they were either younger sons out for the sport or men like Grenville's son, John, and his cousin, James Erisey (who had married a Carew of Antony), who followed the sea as a profession.

For this was, essentially, a fleet of professional seamen. The Queen's ships were commanded by sea captains of long experience; Sir William Winter; Edward Fenton, John Hawkins's brother-in-law; Luke Ward, Hawkin's vice-admiral of 1585; Thomas Fenner, Drake's flag captain of 1585; the other Fenner brothers, Robert Crosse, Ralegh's captain Jacob Whiddon; John Davis, a Gilbert man from the Dart with several Arctic voyages to his credit. Frobisher's lieutenant was an Eliot, and Drake's lieutenant was his first wife's nephew, Jonas Bodenham.

In the 24 ships listed as 'merchant ships appointed to serve westwards under the charge of Sir Francis Drake' there were many Plymouth names: William Sparke, John Tranton, Thomas Cely, James Founes, John Yonge, John Grisling. Plymouth surnames also crop up in many of the ships' names. There was a general stay upon shipping; no doubt every Plymouth ship and every captain of the port was serving in the fleet; better, if nothing else, to be on the royal payroll than idle.

There were some famous ships in the fleet. The Lord Admiral's flag was in the *Ark*, built the year before by Walter Ralegh and sold by him to the Queen, and variously known as *Ark Ralegh*, *Ark* and *Ark Royal*. Lord Cumberland was in the *Elizabeth Bonaventure*, Drake's flagship in the Indies and at Cadiz. Drake had the *Revenge*, one of John Hawkins's best, launched at Deptford in 1577. John Hawkins himself had the *Victory*, and it was typical of the man that he chose not a new ship but an old one that he had rebuilt, to demonstrate his faith that they were as good as any. He was right enough. *Victory* had been launched in 1561, and had been rebuilt as a low, fast galleon in 1586. She was to be rebuilt again in 1610, to serve as flagship both to Blake and Monck, and was wearing an admiral's flag when she finally went aground fighting the Dutch and was burnt by them in 1666. For a wooden battleship, an active life of 105 years is astonishing.

Frobisher had the biggest ship of all, the unconverted *Triumph* of 1,100 tons, twice the size of Drake's *Revenge*.

Apart from the Queen's ships, there was also a strong force of London merchantmen, including tough vessels like the famous earl's *Galleon Leicester* and the Levanter *Edward Bonadventure*, which in 1591–93 was to be the first English ship to make the voyage to India and lead to the formation of the East India Company. It is noticeable that the London ships were bigger than the western vessels, indicative of where the centre of trading had moved.

All English ports were required to provide some ships, furnished at their own cost. From the west, Bristol sent four, Bridgwater one, Lyme Regis two, Weymouth two, Exeter and Topsham three, Plymouth two (the *Charity* and the *Little John*), Saltash one (the *John Trelawny* under Thomas Meek, who had been round the world with Drake), Fowey and Looe one.

How did Plymouth manage to feed and water so great a fleet? Howard's first letter to Burghley declared: 'there is here the gallantest company of captains, soldiers and mariners that I think were ever seen in England. It were pity that they should lack meat..'. In another letter he wrote: 'I know not which way to deal with the mariners to make them rest content with sour beer.' Victualling ships were constantly coming in from other ports to supplement the local efforts.

In his winter fleet Drake had had 2,900 men in Plymouth, and when the other squadrons joined him in May there were 9,500 men. In July, Lord Howard and John Hawkins sent an estimate of costs to Burghley. Of £6,000 already sent, £5,500 had been spent, and another £19,570 was needed at Plymouth. In September, James Quarles, the chief victualling officer, set out his accounts for 300 days, 1 December 1587 to 20 September 1588. Victualling and ships' stores alone, without pay, came to £21,155. A significant item was 'victualling on shore at Plymouth, at 6d. per diem, £2222.6s.0d.'. This must have paid for the 1,000 soldiers that were in the fleet, and arithmetic suggests that, apart from the 9,500 seamen, the 2,000 inhabitants of Plymouth had these 1,000 soldiers billeted on them for three months.

It was a stormy summer, and it was just as well that it was not fine and hot. The big Navy ship *Elizabeth Jonas* came in with Howard in May, and 200 of her crew of 500 were dead within a month. Lord Howard had the survivors put ashore, the ballast taken out and the whole ship fumigated with fires of wet broom. He brought the crew up to full strength with new men, 'very tall and able as ever I saw', but by 10 August, after the Channel fighting, the infection had broken out again and Lord Howard had to send her into reserve at Chatham. The fighting was not such as to cause heavy casualties but, by the end of the summer, there were few ships that had not lost a third of their crew or more. Lord Sheffield's *Bear* had fallen in strength from 500 to 260, Frobisher's *Triumph* from 500 to 325 and Drake's *Revenge* from 250 to 176. Even John Hawkins, with his great reputation for looking after his crews, lost 150 of his 400 men in *Victory*. 'The companies do fall sick daily,' Hawkins wrote to Burghley.

The Armada Sails

The fleet had assembled in Plymouth just in time. A week after Howard came in, Medina Sidonia led the Armada out of Lisbon on 30 May. Foul winds pushed him as far south as Cape St Vincent, and when he did at last struggle north a gale hit him off the northern corner of Spain. Most of the fleet took shelter in Corunna, but a few ran north to the appointed rendezvous in the Isles of Scilly. Howard had spent two days watering his fleet in Plymouth and then put out to patrol the mouth of the Channel. But the storm that hit the Armada drove him back into Plymouth.

Then, on Saturday 22 June, when ten victualling ships came into Plymouth, word came that on the Thursday a Mousehole boat had sighted large ships off Mount's Bay with red crosses on their sails, and had been chased back into harbour. More reports came in on the Saturday and the Sunday of two Spanish squadrons in the mouth of the Channel.

Howard sailed again on the Sunday, taking with him the victualling ships and the provisions they had not yet trans-shipped to the fighting vessels. But Medina Sidonia had already sent a pinnace to recall his scattered ships to Corunna, and Howard found nothing. Drake slipped round Ushant into the Bay, but still the sea was empty. The English fleet stayed in the chops of the Channel, with Drake pleading all the time for a descent on the Spanish coast where the Armada must be. Finally, Howard agreed, and on 7 July the whole might of England sailed for Spain. Halfway across the Bay another gale hit them, and on 9 July they were forced to turn back.

The fleet was in Plymouth again on 12 July, leaving only fast pinnaces to patrol the Channel approaches. Gale damage had to be repaired, provisions made up and the ships watered again. It was a hectic time, with old Mayor Hawkins taking charge of the shore work, beaching the ships that needed cleaning and caulking, driving his men on the Cattewater beaches by day and working through darkness by the light of flaming torches.

The gale that drove the English back to Plymouth brought the Spanish out of Corunna. Medina Sidonia, his fleet rewatered and revictualled, sailed on 12 July, the very day Lord Howard had regained Plymouth. On Friday, 19 July, he was sighted off the Lizard by Thomas Fleming, a relation of John Hawkins's wife, who was in a pinnace named *Golden*

The famous game of bowls; Drake checking the Lord High Admiral as he prepares to deliver his wood. A beacon flares in the background.
(A NINETEENTH-CENTURY ILLUSTRATION)

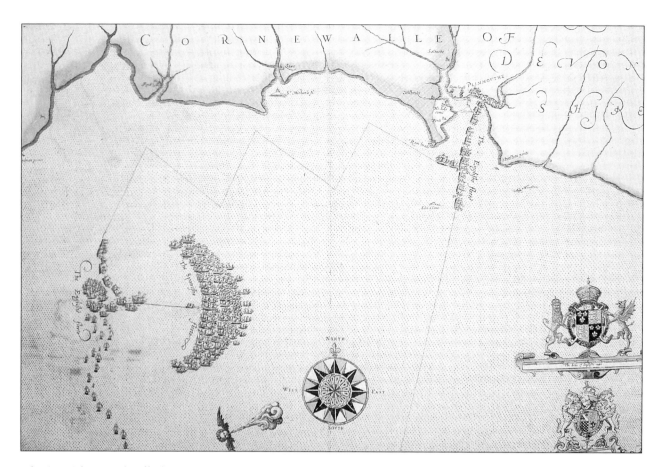

The Spanish Armada off Plymouth, with the English fleet having manoeuvred behind them, one of a series of charts by Robert Adams showing the progress of the fleets up the Channel.

Hind, after Drake's great ship. Fleming reported his sighting to the admiral at Plymouth on the afternoon of that Friday.

Legend says that Howard and Drake, together with all their senior officers, were playing bowls on the Hoe, that Drake stopped, wood in hand, to listen to the news and then bent to play his shot, exclaiming, 'We have time to finish the game, and beat the Spaniards afterwards.' The story is fully in keeping with everything about Drake; the bravado, the refusal to be rushed, the joke in the hour of danger, the need to keep men calm and free from panic. And bowls, after all, was a Plymouth game; a 1584 town record talks of 'playing at booles' and a Spanish jibe set down in 1625 says 'we caught you playing at bowls'.

Moreover, the fleet was ready. Two days before, John Hawkins had written to Burghley: 'the four great ships are in most royal and perfect state... the strength of the ships generally is well tried'. Howard wrote the same day saying he had heard that the Spanish fleet was ready to leave Corunna, that the royal ships were in good shape, Drake and his ships ready; and that all would be in three or four days.

So when, at three o'clock on that Friday afternoon, Drake heard that the Armada was off the Lizard, he knew there was no more to be done for the ships. The light south-west wind blowing the Spanish slowly up the coast was also blowing straight into the Sound, which meant that the English would have to be warped out, towed by their seamen rowing the ships' boats. But that could only be done on the ebb tide, of which there was only an hour or so left, not enough to take the ships far. Only after high water at 11 that night could the fleet move; time enough to finish his throw, indeed the game, to keep everyone calm and for all the officers to be aboard in ample time to make ready for sea.

When the tide is ebbing in Plymouth Sound the tidal current outside is setting up-Channel, but close around Rame Head a back current sets westwards. So, as the English fleet warped out behind their boats, pushed along the tide, they could pick up the back current under Rame to slip them into Whitsand Bay. Six hours of ebb to get them all round Rame, then six hours of west-going Channel current to help them west past Looe. Wrote Howard on the Sunday:

Although the wind was very scant we first warped out of harbour that night, and upon Saturday turned out very hardly, the wind being at south-west: and about three o'clock in the afternoon descried the Spanish Fleet, and did what we could to work for the wind (ward), which by this morning we have recovered.

In fact, it was Drake and the local ships who slipped

inshore of the Armada; Howard and his big ships chose the risky manoeuvre of sailing across the bows of the Spanish fleet and then beating to westward. John Davis in *Black Dog* was Howard's pilot and one of the greatest navigators of the age, but Dartmouth, not Plymouth, was his home port.

That Sunday, Mayor Hawkins and Mr Darrell, the port victualling officer, wrote to London as well:

The Spanish fleet was in view of this town yesternight... Since which time we have certain knowledge, both by certain pinnaces come from his Lordship, also by plain view this present morning, that my Lord, being to the windwards of the enemy, are in fight, which we beheld.

So on Sunday, 21 July, was fought the battle of Plymouth. It raged from nine in the morning till three in the afternoon, with three hours of heavy cannonading. The windward gauge was decisive; with their nimble ships, the English would close the Armada inshore rearguard, hammer away with their guns and fall back out of reach of the towering Spanish ships. Recalde, the rearguard admiral, was hulled several times and his foremast splintered. He sent for help to Don Pedro de Valdes, who was commanding the Biscayan squadron just ahead of him. Don Pedro fouled two ships in turning back, finally losing his bowsprit, foremast and main-topmast. The *San Salvador* partially blew up and was eventually taken as a prize into Weymouth. That night, off Bolt Head, Drake cut out and captured Don Pedro's limping ship, the *Nuestro Senora del Rosario*.

Sailing with Drake as a volunteer was Nicholas Oseling. He had been a merchant in Spain for many years and was also one of Walsingham's chief agents there, moving about from port to port watching the Armada preparations and sending intelligence to London. Captured, he seems to have bribed his way out of prison and got back to England, where Lord Howard wrote of him as 'one adventuring his life in so many ways in Her Majesty's service'. Even in battle, our chief secret service man in Spain could play his part, and he interrogated the prisoners from Don Pedro's ship, as he did other prisoners during the long struggle.

Drake sent his prize into Torbay, with Jacob Whiddon

in Ralegh's *Roebuck* as escort. The Spanish crew were imprisoned in Torre Abbey, the ship taken round to Dartmouth and Drake in due course was the richer by Don Pedro's ransom. He was the third senior officer of the Armada, and this capture was the only rewarding prize. Frobisher, who saw much hard fighting with no such reward, was furious. He was overhead to say that if he did not have his share he would make Drake 'spend the best blood in his belly'. Frobisher also complained that Drake had extinguished his stern lantern, which was intended to guide the fleet, and had left his comrades floundering while he took his prize. But no one else made such a complaint; Frobisher was always unlucky and always jealous of Drake.

So the Spanish fleet was edged away up Channel, always harried by the English but never quite able to get to grips with them. The weather gauge which had been captured by that use of the tides out of Plymouth was decisive. At last, the Spanish ships anchored among the sands off Calais, hoping to join forces with the Duke of Parma. At midnight on Sunday, 28 July, fireships were sent in and scattered them.

Legend credits Drake with the fireship plan, and certainly five of the eight fireships were Plymouth vessels. These were Drake's own *Thomas*, John Hawkins's *Bark Bond*, William Hart's *Angel*, Captain Yonge's *Bear Yonge* and the *Bark Talbot*. Plymouth men sailed them down on the Spanish fleet, lit the fires, touched off the cannons and then took to their boats. At night, with a tangle of sandbanks to leeward, the Spanish fleet had either to stay and burn or else cut their cables and take their chance. At first light on the Monday morning the English ships, with Drake in the lead, stormed in to the attack. This battle of Gravelines was the greatest of the campaign. Of the 124 Spanish ships that had anchored in Calais roads the English could only count 86 on the Tuesday morning, and these were streaming away northwards, broken and defeated.

Howard followed them with the main English fleet until a severe storm that brought no comfort to the scattered Spanish forced the English to sail south again.

King ♣

The English Fleet whereof the L.d Charles Howard was L.d Admirall & S.r Fran. Drake vice Admirall

Left: *A seventeenth-century playing card from an Armada pack.*

Thomas Cavendish.

'We left the enemy so far to the northwards as they could neither recover England nor Scotland,' wrote Drake to the Queen. It had been a long-drawn-out struggle and everyone was exhausted. Drake finished another letter to Walsingham on 8 August, his always bad scrawl getting more and more illegible; '... your Honour's most ready to be commanded but now half-sleeping, Fra. Drake'. Ralegh and Grenville, fresh men, were sent to sea with a small squadron to ensure that the Spanish did no harm on the Irish coast. The main fleet could then pay off, the naval ships returning to winter quarters on the Medway and the merchantmen going back about their business. The men were in even worse shape than their officers. Only one English captain, Lucas Cocke of Plymouth, and some 200 men, died in the actual fighting, but plague had hit the ships' companies hard and, through the Queen's parsimony, the men were put ashore penniless round the Thames as the royal ships paid off. Drake and Hawkins fought hard for the men's rights and argued about their pay; in 1590 they took the lead in founding the 'Chatham Chest', the forerunner of all naval charities.

The Spanish fleet was in even worse straits. Only 50 or 60 ships ever got back to Spain. It estimated that they lost 5,000 men at Gravelines alone. One Spanish supply ship, the *San Pedro Mayor*, quite lost after wandering round Scotland and the west coast of Ireland, came back into the Channel to be wrecked on 28 October in Bigbury Bay. The following January, a Hamburg ship, the *Falcon Blanco Mayor*, which had got back to Lisbon, was sailing home again when she was captured in the Channel and brought into Plymouth.

Finding her way home through the storms that decimated the Armada was the *Desire*, in which Thomas Cavendish was completing his voyage round the world. He had sailed from Plymouth in July two years before with three ships; one had been burnt in the south Pacific for want of crew, the second had disappeared off California. *Desire* was the third ship, and Cavendish the second sea captain, to make the circumnavigation. On 3 September, they heard from a Flemish hulk of the 'overthrowing of the Spanish Fleet, to the singular rejoicing and comfort of us all'; six days later, 'after a terrible tempest which carried away most of our sails... we recovered our long-wished-for port of Plimmouth.'

CHAPTER 6

The Second and Third Armadas

All through the winter of 1588, in spite of the general rejoicings and the thanksgiving in St Paul's Cathedral for the defeat of the Armada, the English commanders were aware that Spain had been hammered but not beaten. In November, John Gilbert, as a Vice-Lieutenant of Devon, wrote that he had heard Medina Sidonia was back in Spain, and that a new expedition against England was to be prepared. He had ordered Dartmouth, Plymouth, and the Cornish ports not to carry any fish to France, as the Spanish were buying up victuals there for their fleet.

Various counter-measures were advanced. Sir John Hawkins (he and Martin Frobisher had been knighted by Lord Howard during a lull in the Armada fighting) wanted to keep six warships blockading the Spanish coast. The bills were now coming in for the Armada and, compared with Cadiz, it was clearly cheaper to fight on the enemy coast. The bill from Plymouth for those five fire-ships alone was £3,650. Drake wanted a direct assault on the Spanish coast, and he was supported by a solider friend of Irish days, Sir John Norris, 'Black Jack', now Marshall-of-the-Field of the Queen's Army in the Netherlands. As joint-commanders, they planned to capture Lisbon and restore Don Antonio to the throne of Portugal. Dutch ships would join them, and cavalry and artillery would be brought from the Netherlands.

Drake, in *Revenge*, started gathering the forces in the Downs, but the Dutch ships, the cavalry and artillery, never turned up, and he sailed down to Plymouth early in 1589. Norris came in with a squadron of royal ships, and the names of the two commanders brought in further support. Soon they had 20 ships, 2,500 seamen and 11,000 soldiers – a rough crowd, mostly veterans from the brutalities of fighting in the Low Countries and Ireland. The stormy summer was followed by a stormy winter, and the sailing date of 1 February was twice put back. Food was running short. Plymouth and the West had been scoured bare, and old William Hawkins was at his wit's end to victual an expedition already eating its campaign stores.

Twice the fleet put to sea, and twice it put back. Norris wrote to Burghley saying that unless the Queen victualled his soldiers, he would have to turn them ashore to forage for themselves. With their numbers swollen to 20,000 this was unthinkable, and the Queen agreed to feed the fleet until it sailed. There were 80 ships now. To add to the Queen's

displeasure, her new favourite, the hot-headed Earl of Essex, emulated Philip Sidney of five years before, and ran away from Court to join the fleet. He did manage to get to sea, one of the ships picking him up in Falmouth.

By mid-April, the whole expedition was launched. Drake and Norris spent a fortnight capturing Corunna, ignored the Armada ships still in the Biscay ports and sailed for Lisbon. The mouth of the Tagus was still too well defended for frontal attack, so the army was landed north of the river. The soldiers marched to the walls of Lisbon but they had no siege artillery, were short of food, and rotten with plague and the results of over-drinking in the sack of Corunna. They fell back on their ships and, when Vigo was stormed on the way north, only 2,000 soldiers were fit to go ashore. By June, the expedition was back in Plymouth.

The Queen was furious that her orders (the usual mass of instructions) had not been carried out. The men from the expedition, on the other hand, thought they had not done so badly. Anthony Wingfield, a soldier, wrote:

In this short time of our adventure we have won a town by escalade, battered and assaulted another, overthrown a mightie prince's power in the field, landed our armie in 3 several places of his kingdom, marched 7 dayes in the hearte of his country, lien three nights in the suburbs of his principall cite, beaten his forces into the gates thereof, and possessed two of his frontier forts...

It was more than the Armada had done in England. What was even more important, the fleet had taken sixty Hanseatic League ships off the Spanish coast, replenished their own supplies and stopped the vital supply of masts, ropes, copper and tallow needed to refit the Spanish fleet.

The Queen was not to employ Drake at sea again for six years, but he was busy in public life as the leading citizen of Plymouth and as a Member of Parliament. The war went on but followed a new pattern on the lines suggested by Sir John Hawkins. The Drake raids had led Spain to spend a lot of money improving the defences of the Indies, so the new plan was to hover about the Azores seeking to intercept the homeward-bound *flotas*. There were still the emulators of Drake seeking to reach the Pacific through the Magellan Straits or the Indies round Good Hope, and new money was coming into the business. Merchants from Barnstaple and Exeter were in it, and more and more of the big London houses. An increasing number of expeditions fitted out in the Thames, but nearly always Plymouth was the final point of departure. London men sent the *Richard of Arundell* off from Plymouth in December 1588 for the south Atlantic, and she was back in Cawsand Bay the following December.

While Drake was on the Spanish coast in 1589, George Clifford, Earl of Cumberland, was in Plymouth with the Queen's ship *Victory*, collecting a squadron. Cumberland had inherited his title in 1569 as a boy of 11 and been made a ward of the second Earl of Bedford, Drake's godfather. He had married his guardian's daughter but she left him when she found him having an affair with a lady of the Court. Cumberland rapidly spent his family fortune and turned to seafaring to recoup. He had financed Withrington's 1586 expedition, and commanded the *Elizabeth Bonaventure* against the Armada. Lord Howard sent him to the Queen at Tilbury with news of the Gravelines victory, and ever afterwards Cumberland wore the Queen's jewelled glove in his hat.

In this 1589 foray, he took three French ships in the Channel, passed Drake homeward-bound from Lisbon and, in the Azores, took a Portuguese ship full of sugar and Brazil wood, and finally a West Indian ship said to be worth £100,000. He sent this last prize home under the command of a friend, Christopher Lister, who had long been a prisoner of the Barbary pirates, but she was wrecked in Mount's Bay and Lister was drowned.

Cumberland was not alone in the Azores that summer; there was a small ship called the *Drake*, some ships of Walter Ralegh's under John Davis, and a Weymouth ship. So alarmed were the Spanish in the Azores that they unloaded the West Indian fleet there until one quay was covered with chests of silver – over five million pieces of eight, apart from gold and pearls uncounted. Frobisher was roaming the islands too, but his bad luck persisted, and the best prize he sent home in that rough winter of 1589 was wrecked on Eddystone. In August of that year, John Chudley (who had been a volunteer in the *Ark Royal* against the Armada) sailed from Plymouth for the Pacific, but after six weeks of struggling against headwinds to get through the Straits of Magellan, he finally turned for home, one of his ships being wrecked off the French coast.

The Hoe Fort

William Hawkins died at Plymouth in the autumn of 1589. He was 70, and worn out by the strain of helping to fit out four major expeditions in five years.

Left: *Sir William Hawkins II.*

He may have been a boy on his father's first trans-Atlantic voyage of 1532, and in his time he had seen the opening up of the New World. His younger brother, John, had taken a year's leave from the Navy after the Armada, but now he came back into service.

Spain was building a big fleet of new ships to escort her *flotas*, ships built on the English model, a tribute to the work of John Hawkins. Through the winter of 1589 John Hawkins prepared to go to sea, for it was feared that this new Spanish shipbuilding presaged another Armada. The alarm in Plymouth was such that:

... the towne uppon this late reporte was strucken with such feare that some of them had convaied their goods out of the towne and others, no doubte, would have followed if they had not been stopped by the cominge of Sir Francis Drake who, the more to assure them, brought his wife and family thither.

This is from a letter which the mayor, John Blythman, and Drake wrote in May 1590 to the Queen asking for financial help in building a fort upon the Hoe. The joint authority is interesting. For centuries, the mayor had been captain of the castle quadrate and commander in time of war, and Drake had held this office as mayor in 1581. But at the end of his term of office, his successor, Thomas Edmonds, petitioned the Crown that Drake should be made captain of the fort and island. No confirmation of the petition exists, but from that time Drake did exercise a vigorous lead in Plymouth's defences, and county lieutenants sent to him their returns of soldiers available for Plymouth.

St Nicholas's Island had been fortified in 1549 and more money spent on it between 1573 and 1583. The barricades under the Hoe had been strengthened, and Sir Arthur Champernowne, Vice-Admiral of Devon, in the 1570 'cold war' with Spain, had set up his headquarters in the island; it was the key to the whole harbour rather than the castle quadrate, which only guarded Sutton Pool. This letter to the Queen reports 13 pieces of ordnance on the Hoe, four on the castle towers ('which is of no strength'), and 23 on the island, but most of them borrowed. The island defences had been built up and armour stored there for 350 men. On May Day ('as their custom in every yeare') the town had paraded at least 1,300 men on the Hoe and, from that day forward, Drake had ordered that there should be kept watch and ward every night as if it were a garrison town:

Of which watch every Master in his tourne as captain is to have the charge and to watch with them himself until midnight, and then to be relieved by his deputie, who shall be a man of like substance and truste. This watch did Sir Francis himself beginne on Friday laste.

Legend has it that Drake mounted his guard on the island itself, and from that day the name of Drake's Island gradually ousted the old term of St Nicholas's Island. That letter was written in May 1590. In June, the Duke of Parma invaded France from the Low Countries and a Spanish force captured Port Louis at the mouth of the river Blavet in southern Brittany. By August, Spain had a squadron of ships there, by October an army of 3,000 men. It was a threat to our shipping routes, and to the West Country. Plymouth did not wait for the Queen's help; the Black Book for that year records:

The northwest tower of the Castell was covered with leade, and 7 brass piecs [guns] were placed yppon the iiiior Castells. This yere likewise were the platteformes [for guns] at Hawe tymbred, the gate a cocksyde wch is to be shutte everye neight was newe made, and the greatte platte forme by the gate att Iland, and the wall neere the same contayninge 257 fote was nowe newly made. Mor bought two demy-colverines and two [w]hole colverines of Iron and mounted them at the barbigan and bulwerkes.

The platform by the gate at Drake's Island is still there. Clearly, the old town walls were patched up and an extension made at the eastern end to enclose Breton Side, advancing the wall from Martyn's Gate to Coxside.

Grenville's Last Fight

Hawkins had been ready for sea in the spring of 1590, but the Queen would not allow him to leave the coast uncovered. He did take a squadron down the Spanish coast later in the year, and Frobisher went to the Azores, but they had missed the first treasure fleet. Spain halted the rest for the year. In April 1591 three ships sailed from Plymouth for the Cape of Good Hope and India. Only James Lancaster in the *Edward Bonadventure* reached Ceylon and the East Indies, where he tried to plunder the Portuguese ships, but his crew were in such low health that they compelled him to turn back, only to be wrecked in the West Indies and the survivors brought home in a French ship. In August of that year, Cavendish left Plymouth with Ralegh's *Roebuck*, the *Desire* under John Davis and a ship of Adrian Gilbert's, intending to repeat the voyage round the world. But they came to grief in the Straits of Magellan, Cavendish died at sea and Davis just managed to limp back to Ireland.

By 1591 Spain had accumulated two years'

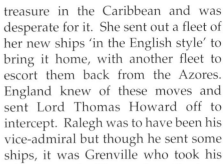

Left: *Sir Walter Ralegh.*

treasure in the Caribbean and was desperate for it. She sent out a fleet of her new ships 'in the English style' to bring it home, with another fleet to escort them back from the Azores. England knew of these moves and sent Lord Thomas Howard off to intercept. Ralegh was to have been his vice-admiral but though he sent some ships, it was Grenville who took his place. Cumberland was in Plymouth with them fitting out a squadron of his own. They were away in the spring, and for three months cruised round the Azores with little profit.

By the time the *flota* sailed, having lost one or two ships to English raiders, the English fleet in the Azores was hard hit by sickness. They tried the old device of putting men ashore on the island of Flores to recover, free from the pestilent air of the ships. They expected the *flota* to appear from the west; instead, they were caught by the escort fleet from Spain, 55 ships strong. Cumberland managed to send a pinnace to warn Howard and he sailed with six fighting ships and six supply ships, just in time to get to windward of the Spanish. Grenville, in Drake's old flagship the *Revenge*, was last away, too late to weather the Spanish fleet. For a day and a night Grenville fought, then, mortally wounded, he ordered the last of the powder to be used to sink the ship. The master refused, and surrendered. Grenville was carried to the Spanish flagship, where he died. The *Revenge* went down in a great storm that sank some 70 Spanish ships as well.

So passed another of the great sea captains, two years after William Hawkins. Richard Grenville had grown up on Tamarside, inherited estates at Efford, made Buckland Abbey into a dwelling-house; if not a Plymouth man, he was a close neighbour.

At home, a government engineer, Robert Adams, was surveying Plymouth and consulting with Drake and Sir Arthur Champernowne on the town's defence needs. John Sparke, the mayor, sent off their report in February 1592 with a map made by Adams. They recommended a fort on the Hoe to cover the bulwarks from land attack. It would cost millions to environ the town with a royal strength ('for nature hath commandment of it'), but it could be protected with a wall and ditch from sudden surprise.

On 30 May 1592 Queen Elizabeth signed letters patent declaring that Plymouth was an ancient port, of frequent resort by her Navy and by merchants, and was to be made defensible by enclosing it with a ditch, wall, bulwark and other defences towards the sea, according to a plan made upon view of the town by skilful persons. She was not willing that the inhabitants should be burdened with the cost, as it would benefit the whole country, so there was to be a tax upon all pilchards exported, a grant of £100 a year out of the customs of Devon and Cornwall, half the forfeitures from carrying prohibited wares, and 'as many as have had relief from Plymouth, special persons are to be appointed to receive benevolence from them'.

Sir John Burrough, Ralegh and Frobisher were in Plymouth preparing for a Panama raid, but they were so long delayed by head winds that they decided to try the Azores again. Cumberland already had a squadron there. No *flota* came their way, but they did fall in with a Portuguese squadron from the East Indies and made the biggest capture of the whole war. The 'Great Carrack', as she is always called, was the *Madre de Dios*, laden with jewels, spices, drugs, silks, calicoes, carpets, ivory, ebony, Chinese porcelain – all the riches of the East. She was said to be worth £150,000. The Hawkins ship *Dainty* first sighted her; Burrough in Ralegh's *Roebuck* played the main part in taking her, helped by a Queen's ship, three of Cumberland's ships and a Caribbean privateer. The seamen plundered her all night, and when the motley fleet returned to Plymouth sailors were laden with pearls and selling porcelain dishes for sixpence. Sir Robert Cecil was sent down from London to supervise her unloading at Dartmouth, and while seven miles from Exeter he could 'smell the loot on sailors making for London'. Sir Walter Ralegh had been recalled by the Queen before the ships set out and imprisoned for his affair with Elizabeth Throckmorten; now he had to be released and sent to help because the sailors would listen to him. Drake, too, was called in, and Richard Hawkins. The western ports had a spree unparalleled in their history. Only Frobisher was unlucky again; he had not been in at the capture.

Small wonder that Spain was angry, and in February 1593 John Sparke was urging the Privy Council to hurry over the Plymouth fortifications, as the inhabitants were much alarmed by reports from Spain threatening to burn it in the next summer. 'Many inhabitants are abandoning the town and cannot be persuaded to stay for the defence thereof.' Robert Adams came down in May and sent off a plan showing that work was in hand on the fort. The work was going slowly because 'the hardness of the rock has been extremely painful', and more money was wanted. 'The town had good will and small means, and there is less hope of the cold charity of their small fellow-feeling neighbours.' Local records show that four gates were also set up round the town in 1593, so it seems that a start had been made on turning the improved medieval defences into the stronger walling of the Adams plan.

That summer, Richard Hawkins put to sea. He had built a ship on the Thames, which his mother named the *Repentance* but the Queen herself rechristened the *Dainty*, for the express purpose of following Drake's route round the world. (She had been in the Azores the year before.) Now, after one false start from Plymouth in which a storm nearly cost him his new ship, he was finally away in June 1593. When he sailed, he saluted the crowds on the Hoe with trumpets and gunfire, to which the town replied. It was to be a long farewell, for though Richard Hawkins became the third Englishman to complete the Magellan passage, he was captured in the Pacific. Spanish naval power was not to be caught a second time: Hawkins had ten long years in Spanish prisons before he saw Plymouth Hoe again. Perhaps in Lima he even saw his distant cousin, John Drake, but while John never left Peru, Hawkins was eventually transferred to Seville and finally won his freedom.

Cumberland was in the Azores in the summers of 1593 and 1594, but the war was moving nearer home.

The Spanish troops broke out of Port Louis and established a strong position threatening Brest. So, in 1594, a military expedition formed up in Plymouth, under the joint command of Frobisher and Norris, to deal with the threat. Drake held himself in reserve in Plymouth (he was back in royal favour and busy at Court again) and the Queen ordered that 500 men should be ready to move into Plymouth for its defence, if needed. The army was landed in Brittany and the Spanish strength broken, but in the fighting Frobisher received a mortal wound. He was brought home to Plymouth to die; on 22 November 1594 his entrails were buried in St Andrew's Church and his body taken to St Giles Cripplegate, in London. This blustering, rough-tongued Yorkshireman who fell out with so many of his comrades, who saw so much of the fighting and so few of the rewards, died alone in his adopted home port.

But it was increasingly clear that Spain's strength lay in the flow of treasure from America, and so long as it came in every year she could rebuild her ships and her armies as fast as they could be broken. Attacks on her coast and blockades in the Azores were winning battles but not the war. Drake's original plan of striking at the source of her wealth seemed to be the best after all.

There was a belief, too, that Spain had found a new source of treasure, as rich as her original conquests in Mexico and Peru. William Parker of Plymouth, who had been with Drake in the 1587 raid on Cadiz and became one of the most successful privateers in the Caribbean, had several years earlier brought back stories of a new city of gold, El Dorado, in Guiana. The ports of Spain were buzzing with similar stories. Ralegh's imagination was fired; he sent Jacob Whiddon to prospect in 1594 and himself sailed from Plymouth in 1595. With him were John Grenville, who was killed in Guiana, John Gilbert, a Gorges from St Budeaux, Jacob Whiddon and a company of West Countrymen. The same year, two other expeditions sailed from Plymouth under Sir

Robert Dudley and Sir Amias Preston. None of them found El Dorado, but they had their successes, in common with the swarms of privateers from half the ports of England who were pin-pricking away at the wealth of Spain.

Drake's Last Voyage

In 1595 a more determined effort was set afoot. Sir Francis Drake and Sir John Hawkins were off to sea again, in joint command of a major raid on the West Indies. They began to assemble their fleet in April; six naval ships, 21 merchantmen, including many Hawkins ships like the *Salomon*, which, a few years before, had been captured by Barbary pirates. They had between 2,500 and 3,000 soldiers under Thomas Baskerville. Spanish intelligence was good, and to upset the English plans galleys from Port Louis raided the Cornish coast. They kept a respectful distance from the forces at Plymouth but they threatened Scilly, appeared on the north Cornish coast, captured a Cornishman off the Manacles and then landed troops at Mousehole. That village, Paul Churchtown, Newlyn and Penzance, were all burnt. The Cornish levies were hastily summoned to march against the invaders, and Drake sent ships round from Plymouth to cut them off. At the first sight of this opposition the Spanish disappeared. This was closer to home even than anything in Armada year, and the Queen (as Spain no doubt intended) was loth to see Drake and Hawkins sail and leave the coast unguarded.

Plymouth, too, was worried about its unfinished fort. The money was slow in coming in, the neighbouring gentlemen were not anxious to make benevolences (however much they profited from Plymouth's prosperity) and the fishermen avoided the pilchard tax as much as they could. There were fears, too, that a professional soldier was to be appointed governor, and two visits of Sir Ferdinando Gorges, a cousin of the St Budeaux family and a

successful young soldier in the Netherlands, had not helped allay this suspicion. Plymouth even offered to pay for the completion of the fort if they could have a royal grant, an annual allowance and Sir Arthur Champernowne as governor.

News that the Spanish *flota* flagship was lying dismasted in Porto Rico finally persuaded the Queen to let Drake and Hawkins sail. Other news had also come in; Hawkins's son, Richard, was a prisoner in the Pacific. It was an added burden for John Hawkins to bear; he was now 63 and his joint-admiral was attracting so many men anxious to follow the magic name that they already had more men than rations. Drake was 50; it was 27 years since they had first sailed together for the Spanish Main. Drake had been the junior then; now he had equal rank, and greater fame.

For the last time, on Thursday, 28 August, the two cousins sailed out of the Cattewater and under the Hoe, no doubt to the sound of guns and trumpets

Drake's drum, now preserved in Buckland Abbey.

Elizabethan pilchard cellars on the foreshore at Kingsand, latterly used as boat stores.

and the town waits. Overnight, they anchored in Cawsand Bay and on the Friday stood out to the south-west. Baskerville in the *Hope* struck upon the Eddystone but came clear; already the voyage had that Friday-sailing smell.

An attempt to land in the Canaries did not come off but enabled Spain to warn the Indies of their approach. Five of Spain's fast new warships were sent in pursuit, and, off Dominica, they captured the Francis, of Hawkins' squadron. Sir John fell ill; 'his sickness began upon newes of the taking of the *Francis*'. He took to his bunk in the *Garland* on 2 November and never left it again; he died as the fleet anchored off Porto Rico on 12 November. The Spanish guns thundering defiance at the English fleet were his death knell, a fitting final tribute for this Plymouth man, the creator of the Elizabethan Navy which established English sea power. In the same cannonade, a round shot went through the quarterdeck of the *Defiance* and took the very stool from under Drake as he sat at supper. Two of his officers were killed, including Brute Brown of Tavistock, an

Left: Drake's coat of arms over a fireplace at Buckland Abbey.

Armada volunteer.

This was a new, well-defended Main. Three million ducats were ashore in the strongest fort and, though Drake could burn the ships in the harbour, he could not take the town. He sailed on to capture Rio de la Hacha, and Santa Marta, and Nombre de Dios, without reward; on an alerted coast the Spaniards had emptied the small towns and would not even ransom them. So Drake burnt them, and sailed on. Off Rio Captain Yorke of the *Hope* died, and Thomas Drake took command. Sickness was rife, and soon Jonas Bodenham had to take over the *Adventure*.

From Nombre de Dios, Baskerville marched the soldiers across the isthmus for Panama, the treasure centre of the Pacific. It was Drake's old dream. But there were forts on the road now, and Baskerville was back, much mauled, within four days. Drake sailed west for a lonely island where he careened and watered his ships; he had not been in these waters for

Cawsand Square in 1918, just a few yards from the beach. At that time it had probably changed very little over the years.

20 years, but it was the stamping-ground of his youth. He was having no great success but he had gone on longer, and lost more men, before his luck had turned in 1574. But the sickness was still in the fleet and it was an unhealthy coast, still called 'Golfo de los Mosquitos'. Captain Plat died at the island and Drake himself 'began to keepe his cabin, and to complaine of a scowring of fluxe'. They sailed back for Porto Bello, the town Spain was building 20 miles west to replace Nombre de Dios, but Drake was dying of dysentery. He signed his will on 27 January, making one alteration; Sampford Spiney went to his nephew Bodenham, who was at his side.

In the early hours of 28 January 1596, Drake asked his servant to put his armour on him, that he might die like a soldier. 'He used some little speeches at or a little before his death, rising and apparelling himselfe, but being brought to bed againe within one hour died.' It was four o'clock in the morning, Drake lying dead in the great cabin of his flagship *Defiance* as she led a mixed squadron of Queen's ships and Plymouth ships along the coasts of Panama. That afternoon they anchored in Porto Bello, from which, in spite of the fine new fort, all the people had fled. With the whole fleet assembled, and to the sonorous cadences of the new prayer-book, the greatest Elizabethan seaman was committed to the deep, in death as in life lying athwart the treasure route of the New World. He was not to lie alone; the following day Captain Josias of the *Delight*, Captain Egerton, Abraham Kendall and the chief surgeon, James Wood, all died and shared Drake's grave. Seamen lie with him too; for at the next muster the fleet had but 2,000 men left, and three ships for which there were no crews had to be scuttled.

With Baskerville now the admiral and Bodenham commanding Drake's *Defiance*, the fleet sailed for home. In the Indies they met 20 ships, part of the 60-strong fleet that Spain had sent to deal with them, and beat them off very creditably. Scattered by storms, they were back in Plymouth just after Easter. Thomas Drake had brought home his great brother's drum and hung it in the hall of Buckland Abbey.

After Drake and Hawkins had sailed, it was clear that Plymouth needed a permanent garrison and commander. Strode of Plympton and Harris of Radford had orders to supervise the completion of the fort, and on 6 September Burghley made a note that Sir Ferdinando Gorges was to take charge of it. Gorges came to Plymouth in October and seems to have been accepted. The mayor was James Bagge, a Weymouth man who had moved to Plymouth the better to operate his financing of Caribbean privateers. He wrote to the Privy Council about Gorges, welcoming 'a gentleman of his worth and experience amongst us in these dangerous times'.

Three days later there were reports of more galleys at Port Louis and, on Gorges's advice, 40 men were put into the island under the command of

Anthony Goddard and Ingrim Barker. But Gorges was not going to relinquish his governorship of Brill until his Plymouth commission was signed, and he went back to the Netherlands. On the night of 14 March a Spanish pinnace sailed into Cawsand Bay and landed 25 men armed with muskets, who fixed barrels of gunpowder to the doors of five houses. They fled at the first shot of the villagers, who then extinguished the burning fuses. This finally convinced the Queen; she appointed Sir Ferdinando 'captain or keeper of the castle or fort lately built and fortified near Plymouth, and captain of St Nicholas's Island'. Gorges was back in London on 3 April for orders, and in Plymouth on 12 April. A fortnight later, Captain Troughton came into the Sound in *Bonaventure*, the first to return of the Indies squadron, bringing the news that both Drake and Hawkins were dead.

Plymouth was jumpy with invasion scares and spy stories. The previous December a suspected spy had been taken out of a London ship and notes in his possession were found to relate to the new fort. These had been sent up to Robert Cecil, but he was one of Cecil's own agents. In June 1596 a suspicious character was reported riding to London, a little man of swart complexion wearing a black doublet of uncut velvet and sea-green velvet hose. He had talked of a plot to seize the new fort at Plymouth and hold it against all England. All London was searched in vain for him.

Gorges was not helping; he brought to Plymouth the arrogance of a garrison commander in a foreign town. Two months after his appointment, he wrote to the Privy Council complaining that the town council had been discussing defence and had sent a sergeant to summon him to them. He 'scorned such a manner of sending for and made answer that if Mr Mayor and his brethren had anything to say he prayed them to come to his lodgings'. This broke up the council in a great fury and the mayor came to tell him that he did them a great wrong 'in so foolish and so braving a manner'. Gorges wanted a commission 'sufficiently ample to exclude all cavil or contradiction of so ignorant and stubborn a people'.

This was Gorge's version. The mayor also wrote to the Privy Council complaining that Gorges refused to let the civil authority arrest his soldiers for felony or debt, and that when the deputy town clerk, John Hele, had been sent with a message, Gorges had impressed him and sent him to the island as a soldier. The town asked for his release, for relief from billeting soldiers and for the old right of mustering the townsman.

In the end, the Privy Council called both parties before them and ruled that justice, the old castle, the townsmen and shipping were all matters outside Gorges's jurisdiction, but that the town and its equipment should be at his command when the enemy threatened.

The arrogance of Gorges is explained by his back-ground. Of ancient lineage, he had started soldiering in the Low Countries in his teens, had served under Norris in Drake's Spanish raid of 1589, had been with Essex helping the Huguenots in the siege of Rouen and had been knighted in the field for bravery. He had gone back with Essex to the heavy Netherlands fighting and had become governor of Brill while still in his twenties. He was just 30 when he came to Plymouth. But after the initial disagreements he learnt that a different standard of behaviour was required in an English town. He bought a house at Kinterbury, just below Saltash Passage, invested in Caribbean privateers and settled down.

His old commander, the Earl of Essex, was in Plymouth when the ships came home without Hawkins and Drake. Spain had captured Calais and a counter-stroke was wanted. A major expedition was forming, 100 ships under the Lord High Admiral, with Ralegh as the leader of one squadron. Essex, no longer the runaway courtier of 1589 but now Earl Marshal of England, had 2,000 trained and disciplined soldiers from the Netherlands. The force was quickly prepared, secretly and swiftly assembled and sailed out of the Sound on 3 June 1596 to strike Cadiz like a bolt from the blue. Ralegh forced the inner harbour; Essex hurled his troops ashore on the western sandspit of the port; the two rival favourites of the Queen fighting like heroes as they raced to be first into Cadiz. They held the town for a fortnight. Medina Sidonia burnt his ships rather than allow them to be captured and 36 vessels went up in flames, together with 12,000,000 ducats' worth of cargo. Philip lost 40 fighting ships as well, including the ship which had crushed Richard Grenville at Flores. The town was systematically looted and then burned; after that the splendour wanes. In the looting it was every man for himself, and when the fleet got back to Plymouth it was the story of the 'Great Carrack' over again. The great men had their hoards, and every seaman was bartering with London hucksters in the inns and on the quaysides around Sutton Pool.

More Armadas

That autumn, Philip gathered together what was left of his fleet and sent a second Armada against England in revenge. The season was too far gone and the Biscay storms spreadeagled his fleet and sank 20 out of the 30 ships he had left. But the alarm had been raised in Plymouth, where Gorges and the new mayor, Humphrey Fownes, checked the town's defences and barricaded the land approaches.

As soon as the weather began to improve in 1597, Lord Thomas Howard, Essex and Ralegh were again in Plymouth preparing the counterstroke. They assembled 42 ships and 6,000 soldiers, but again weather held them up for months, forcing them to eat

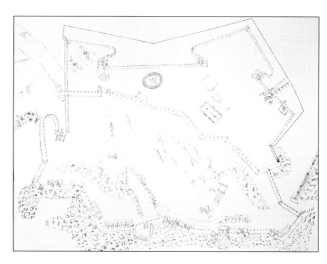

Fernando Gorges's drawing of Drake's fort on the Hoe, which he was sent to command in 1596. The gateway in the front left-hand wall, and the path to it, are still there.

their voyage supplies. Then sickness developed, and after one fruitless attempt to get to sea Essex paid off most of his soldiers. When the fleet did finally get away, it made little more than a gesture off Ferrol before heading south for the Azores and the Spanish treasure ships. Even then they found themselves at the wrong end of the islands when the *flota* did appear, and although William Monson gave chase with a few ships the Spaniards managed to gain safety under the guns of the islands. A prisoner in one of the Spanish ships hit by Monson's gunfire was Richard Hawkins, who was being brought from his captivity in Peru.

Deciding that England was now wide open to him, Philip scraped together every ship he had and sent off his third Armada, 136 ships strong. Their orders were to make for the mouth of the Blavet, pick up the Port Louis galleys and then, after making a feint at Falmouth, to land 8,000 men in longboats west of Plymouth and capture the town from the landward side. There was a report from Spain that Plymouth had been 'bought for 50,000 crowns'. With the English fleet at sea, Gorges drew 500 men into the completed fort on the Hoe and into the island. As it happened, storms scattered the Spanish from Lizard to Blavet and Essex reached Plymouth first. When his ships appeared off Rame Head that October they were taken for Spaniards and people in Plymouth barricaded their houses, ready to fight street by street if need be. The alarm spread throughout the country, and even Parliament was prorogued. Plymouth furi-ously strengthened the Hoe defence and flung up timber gun emplacements on Mount Batten; it cost the town an extra rate the next year.

Essex wanted to be off to sea again in pursuit of the Spanish, but was ordered to stay in Plymouth and take charge of its defences. The Queen's old fears had actually come true; her fleet away and the Spanish on the coast. But there was no need to chase

Above left: *A gateway on the south side of the Citadel, saved from Drake's fort, and* right, *the Hoe Gate, built about 1594 at the same time as Drake's fort. Hoe Gate was demolished in 1863.*

the Spaniards; storms soon broke up their fleet and never again were they to menace the western coast. Philip made peace with France in 1598 and gave back Port Louis and Calais. But his war in the Netherlands went on; English privateers still raided his convoys in the Channel and his ships in the Caribbean.

By now Gorges had a regular garrison at Plymouth, consisting mainly of Low Country veterans, and told Essex in November that, as there were not enough lodgings on the island, he had billeted his soldiers in Plymouth and Stonehouse, and was sending out a guard each night. By the following year the strength of his garrison had increased to 200 men. No doubt his high standing with Essex helped him in Plymouth, while his national reputation was such that he was appointed sergeant-major to the Army which Essex took to Ireland in 1598. He was back in Plymouth that autumn, but in 1601 he was implicated in Essex's plot against the Queen. Plymouth raised money to help his defence, and he not only kept his head but was back as governor by the end of the reign.

Soon after his first appointment to Plymouth, Gorges sent a map of the fort to London. It shows the bulwarks along the cliff-top in great detail, and a path leading up from them to a sallyport. The path is still there, and there is a granite gate of the same shape as the one in Gorges's drawing in the present Citadel wall. The plan of the Citadel follows a regular geometric pattern all round until it reaches the Drake fort; it then takes the shape of the fort and,

clearly, the 1595 walls were incorporated in the Citadel of 1666. Inside are a number of granite gate-ways carved with the same details as the sallyport; obviously pieces of the Elizabethan building used again.

Hoe Gate, the last town gate to be demolished, stood late enough to be photographed, and the same characteristics appear in its granite archway. No doubt it was one of the four new gates of 1593, carved by the same mason as the fort gateways. But how much stone wall was added to the town defences is incalculable; it proved difficult enough to raise the money for the Hoe fort, and the probable answer is that after the Coxside extension had been completed and the key points walled, the rest was left in its 1590 'improved medieval' condition.

After Spain had seized our wheat ships in 1585 the English Government had issued 'letters of reprisal' to private citizens and these licences were used by professional seamen, merchants and the Court gentry to continue their plundering right up to the time King James I made peace with Spain upon his accession. Seeking only private gain, they worked singly or in ever-shifting alliances out of Plymouth and half the ports of England, a constant stinging scourge to Spain. Sir Anthony Sherley left Plymouth in May 1596 with a mixed company that occupied Jamaica's only settlement and, in March of 1598, Cumberland led a fleet of 20 ships out of Plymouth on an expedition which ended in the capture of Porto Rico. Early in 1601 Sir Richard Leveson left Plymouth with a fleet that met the

The line of cobbles along the Barbican marks the division between John Hawkins's 1572 quay, to the left of the line, and the 1892 extension to the quay to the right of the line, when the fish market was built.

Spanish *flota* in the Azores but was not strong enough to attack it. However, he had better luck when he sailed back to Portugal, cut an East Indian carrack out of Cezimbra roads and brought her safely home to Plymouth.

All these were amateur adventurers, and the leading professional in the business at the end of the war was William Parker of Plymouth. After serving with Drake in the 1587 Cadiz raid, he found enough money to buy his own ships, with which he captured Puerto de Caballos in the Honduras in 1594 and a second time in 1595, and Campeche in Mexico. In November 1601, sailing from Plymouth with five little ships and only 208 men, he captured Porto Bello itself in a raid worthy of Drake. The town was the new Atlantic terminal of the treasure route, and though Parker missed the main bulk he managed to collect 10,000 ducats. He refrained from sacking the town and released his prisoners. Then, before departing, he brought his ships up 'somewhat to the eastward of the Castle of Saint Philip under the rocke where Sir Francis Drake his coffin was throwne overboard' – the last salute to Drake from a Plymouth Elizabethan. Today, the ships in and out of the Panama Canal pass only a few miles to the northward and pay no attention at all. Parker was the most distinguished of the last Caribbean privateers; he may or may not have been mayor of Plymouth (there is a conflict of dates), but certainly the captain of one of his ships, Robert Rawlyn, was mayor in 1620.

In 1603 Queen Elizabeth died, James I made peace with Spain and the long war was over. Declared or undeclared, Plymouth had been fighting it for over 30 years, fitting out ships and victualling fleets. Her streets had been filled with sailors and her ware-

houses and merchants regularly enriched with the captured treasures of the Indies. The town was going to feel the pinch of peace, though the economic centre of the business had for some years been passing to London.

The foundation of the East India Company in 1600 was a direct result of Drake's voyage and his treaty, with an Indonesian potentate had provided the legal basis for the early voyages. These had started from Plymouth; now the company was founded by London merchants and their ships sailed from the Thames. A John Hawkins appears in the original list of men granted the East India patent, and William Hawkins III sailed in the company's third expedition of 1608. He lived for four years in the emperor's court at Agra, near Delhi, and took an Indian wife, but died in 1613 on the voyage home. William Parker sailed as vice-admiral for the company in 1617, only to die in the East. Just as Plymouth had launched the American trade, so it was her enterprises which opened up the long association with India.

The leading sea captains, the Hawkinses, Drake, Parker and so many more, were Plymothians by birth or adoption. The leading gentlemen were also linked with the town; Grenville had a Whitleigh grandmother; the mother of both Ralegh and the Gilberts was a Champernowne, descended from the Valletorts, and the Budlocksides and Gorges were Champernowne cousins. Behind them were the Plymouth merchants: Trelawny, Amadas, Fownes, Sparke and Treville. The story of Elizabethan England is very much that of Plymouth; at no other time since has the town contributed so much to England's history, and it left a great mark upon Plymouth itself.

CHAPTER 7

The Elizabethan Expansion

From old Master Hawkins's first trans-Atlantic voyage of 1532 to the end of the Spanish war, Plymouth's prosperity had grown steadily, and the town with it. The greatest growth came (as always) at the end of the good years and, over the period, the town very nearly doubled in size. The main addition came on the South Side, the area now called the Barbican and wrongly regarded as the oldest part of the town. In fact, it is an Elizabethan suburb, and a good two centuries younger than the area north of Notte Street.

The quay at the Barbican was built in 1572 to serve the Protestant privateer fleet; ten years later steps were constructed where the Mayflower Pier now is to enable seamen to reach their boats at low water. In 1584 a new street leading towards the new quay was paved, and this was undoubtedly Southside Street. It had started life as the pathway to the castle, but was probably fully lined with houses before the roadway was paved, even though it was not named Southside Street until 1591. The little streets branching off on either side, to the waterfront and to the Hoe, were all created about this time, as shown by the number of late-sixteenth-century houses they contained until the demolitions of the twentieth century. Only one of these streets is documented; an entry in the town accounts for 1584 shows 4s. paid 'for convaienge of the water over the Southside Kaye thatt rennes from Mr Sperkes newe streate'. New Street is still there, sloping downhill to the quay, the Elizabethan houses that John Sparke built still standing. Sparke's energy, which sent him travelling to the Caribbean, survived into his later days, for here he emerges as the town's first known speculative builder.

The open space between Looe Street and Vauxhall Street was filled up, Looe Street was largely rebuilt (some of the houses again survive) and much rebuilding was done in High Street. Several of the now-demolished houses boasted rich plaster ceilings, as did the 'Ring o' Bells' at the corner of Vauxhall Street. In 1574 the new guildhall had 'sylynges' set up, no doubt, in the same ornamental style. Other contemporary ceilings can still be seen in the great hall of Buckland Abbey and, rescued from Saltash, inside the doors of the City Museum.

A doorway now in the Elizabethan Gardens off New Street once graced the Mayor's House on the corner of Vauxhall Street and Batter Street: it was removed when Brock House was erected. A mural outside the Batter Street entrance to Brock House tells the story of its predecessor. In the Mayor's House the town held formal banquets in the seventeenth century and it later became the mayoral stores. The house is believed to have belonged to William Page, the 'merchant of Plymouth' whose murder was of such national interest that Ben Johnson and Thomas Dekker wrote a play (now lost) called 'Pagge of Plymouth'. In his dotage Page had married Ulalia Glandfield, daughter of a Tavistock tradesman, after her lover, George Strangwidge, had gone off on the Cadiz expedition of 1589 and been reported killed. But George came back, and he and Ulalia hired two villains to murder the old man in his bed. Another accomplice was Ulalia's maid, and all five were hanged at Barnstaple Assize (moved there because of plague at Exeter) in 1591. The episode had all the bloodcurdling qualities of an Elizabethan melodrama; even the judge, Glanville, said to be a relation of Ulalia's, was so horrified that he never sat upon the bench again.

The town was beginning to spread northwards, where Treville Street was named after a family trading with the Mediterranean and North Africa. Further north again, Week Street was first mentioned in 1585, and houses were being built at Friary Green, at the Coxside gate, in 1587. All these new houses had pleasant gardens at first (Thomas Doughty, whom Drake executed on the circumnavigation, is said to have plotted in Drake's own garden in Looe Street), but they were filled by cottages very quickly

Southside Street in the nineteenth century, looking towards the gin distillery. The arch has been removed but the opening remains to Mitre Court.

The doorway of the mayoral house when still in its original position, with a garage built around it.

Eldred's drawing, c.1900, of the Elizabethan customs house on the Parade; it is in rather better shape now.

for apprentices and servants. There was such building in Drake's garden in 1587, and the foundations of the cottages can be seen in the gardens behind New Street.

The harbour that produced all this prosperity was also taking its modern shape and becoming lined with wharves. Many of them were not open quays as now, but had warehouses on the water's edge into which cargoes were directly unloaded. The largest warehouses, built round a central courtyard, were called palaces. Smart had a 'pallais' on Smart's Quay (now the fish market) and a dock was dug alongside it in 1598. The Parade inlet was lined by the New Quay, and Hawkins or Custom House Quay. The Elizabethan custom house, with 1586 carved on a lintel, is now a bookmaker's office on the Parade.

Many of these warehouses and new quays were built out over the harbour bed and limited the water area; the Parade inlet was so reduced at this time. It also led to much litigation with the Crown (which claimed the seabed as royal property) in the seventeenth century. The medieval Sutton Wharf was continued with a dung quay at the bottom of Looe Street (where probably the street sweepings and stables refuse were dumped for removal by barge to fertilise the fields). William Weekes built a quay at Coxside, in the north-east corner of the harbour, where John Sparke had his quay. Sparke also provided a cellar for 'strangers goods' in 1578, and the 'long seller adjoyninge the Crane Quay' served as

a bonded warehouse. There had been a crane quay by 1519; by the end of the century there seem to have been at least two cranes.

Another pointer to the growing population is the provision of a gallery in the north aisle of St Andrew's Church in 1596. Church attendance, after all, was then compulsory.

Maps appear as important sources of information, and three generations of the Spry family served the town as painters, artists, and map-makers. In 1546 John Spry painted a drum and 'made a plott'; next year he made 'a plotte of the haven'. Robert Spry was active by 1570, when he painted both the maypole and 'the ball at Mr Mayor's'. Equally cryptic is an entry for 1580, when Robert painted 'a picture of the Turk on Mayday', but he was not above painting targets, either. In 1584 he made a map which was sent to the Privy Council with a Water Bill. Lord Burghley was the chief man of the Council; his son was the first Lord Salisbury and this map is still (like John Spry's 1547 map of the haven) in Lord Salisbury's library at Hatfield House.

The Countryside

Robert's leaf map is on too small a scale to afford much information about the town itself, but there are some details, such as the fire beacons on the Hoe, at Pennycross (hence Beacon Park) and on Roborough Down. Roborough village is marked by a 'Great crosse', and the Buckland Monachorum turning by 'Broken Crosse', obviously the crosses which still mark the remote Dartmoor roads then marked the road out of Plymouth.

All the great houses of the neighbourhood are shown with the names of their owners beside them. The Harris family had been at Radford since the reign of Henry V; John Harris was a sergeant-at-law (the highest rank of barrister) in Henry VIII's time, and Christopher Harris was MP for Plymouth in 1583 and a friend of Drake. Strodes had been at Newnham since the middle of the fifteenth century. Parker, at Boringdon, was a member of a new family from north Devon which, in the next century, moved to Saltram and took the title of Morley. Drake is shown as residing at Buckland Abbey, his friend Rous at Halton beside the Tamar, and Arundell (Grenville's stepfather) further down.

The Copplestones had been at Warleigh since the Wars of the Roses, and had in them the blood of the Hawleys of Dartmouth. An unhappy legend of Elizabethan times says that the head of the house murdered his godson outside Tamerton Church on a Sunday. Though he bought a pardon by selling much of his land, it was felt that justice was done when he died without sons and his lands passed through daughters to the Elfords and the Bamfields. The Copplestone Oak, still standing outside Tamerton Foliot Church, is said to have been the scene of his crime.

Gorges is shown as living at Budockshead, and Wise at Keyham. The principal Wise residence was at Sydenham, near Lifton, and though they owned Keyham from 1428 they paid little attention to the estate.

These were all old county families, but the map shows a new development, the new country gentlemen. Ham, for example, was an old possession of Plympton Priory; now it was a Trelawny home. A younger branch of this important Cornish family had moved into Plymouth, made a fortune as merchants and, though still active in the town, had moved out again to set up as country gentry as well. Kinterbury, Manadon, and Pennycross were undergoing similar development. The Spry map does not reach south of Plymouth; had it done so it would have shown Wembury House, built in 1592 as the most magnificent mansion in Devon with a gatehouse big enough to house any ordinary family. The builder was John Hele, one of the numerous family which originated at South Hele farm, near Cornwood, and became extensive landowners. John Hele, born in 1540, became a lawyer and did much business for Plymouth; by 1592 he was the town's recorder, and a sergeant-at-law.

Left: *The Copplestone Oak, outside Tamerton Foliot Church.*

The Heles were to become an important family in South Devon in the next century, particularly in Plympton.

It is estimated that Plympton Erle had a population of 615 in 1522 but prospered sufficiently during the rest of the century to become a borough in 1602 (even though it pleaded poverty in its petition). Plympton St Mary, like Plymstock, Tamerton, St Budeaux and Egg Buckland, went quietly on with its rural pursuits. Oreston and Hooe appear as small villages, creations of the busy shipping in the Cattewater.

For information on Plymouth there is the map which Spry helped Adams, the architect of the defences, to make in 1591. The town accounts show it was a careful job; Robert Lampen, a builder of St Budeaux, was called in to help 'take the levell of the ground', and surveyors' tapes and other instruments were bought. The wall which Adam proposed is the main feature; how much of it was built is another matter, but the gates certainly were. In the centre of the harbour entrance is the built-up island which served as a defence against both sea and enemy; on it is the fish house where pilchards were cured.

The streets are accurately mapped and identifiable. At the junction of High Street, Buckwell Street and Whimple Street there is a building with a tower, which must be the guildhall, and beside it there is a drum-shaped edifice that must be the market cross, of the lantern type best represented in the south of England today in Salisbury. The town records of 1564, covering the rebuilding of what is most likely the guildhall, mention the purchase of a dozen moorstone pillars and contain a note that 'the forefront of the market-house was made this year'. The following year's accounts mention the leads of the market cross, and leads can only mean a roof. In 1611, after a new guildhall had been built covering the site of both the old guildhall and the market cross, the 'morestone pillars of the Market Crosse' were sold to James Bagge, the mayor of 1595. Whether Plymouth had a covered market cross before 1564 is uncertain, but it provided not only a roof for trade but also an assembly point for civic occasions.

Stonehouse is shown on the map with its own quay (first mentioned in the time of Henry VII) at the end of Newport Street. The name explains itself, and the quay is probably part of that which now lies just south of Stonehouse Bridge. Houses had spread from High Street up the slope of Chapel Street (now called Durnford Street, the stretch from the barracks to Union Street), which was the road to St Lawrence's

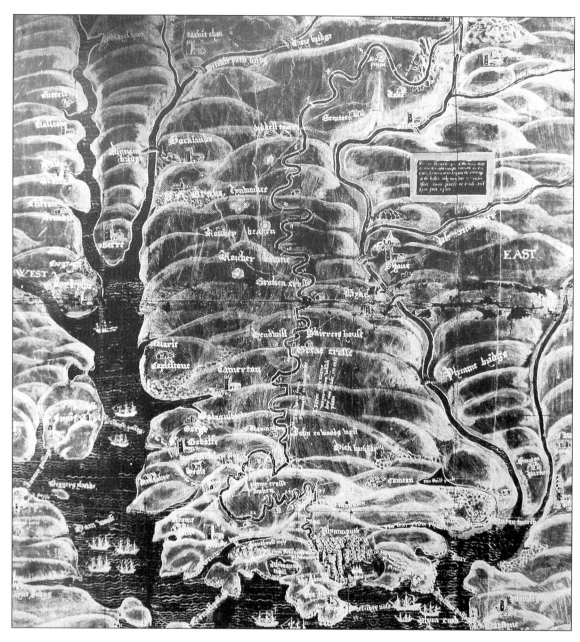

Spry's plot showing the course of Drake's leat to Plymouth.

Chapel as well as to Cremyll Ferry. 'The waye from Stonehouse to Tavistock' is marked along the line of modern North Road. The crenellated manor house wall (part still survives) goes right across the road to the ferry, with an impressive gate, to join a deer park on the shores of Sourpool.

There are more payments to Spry, the painter, in 1594 and 1595, but the only surviving map is a 'plott of the forte and of the hawe' of 1595, which is clearly by a different hand and probably the work of Robert Spry junr, who was still working for the town in 1621. What happened to the other Robert, probably his father, is uncertain, but the St Andrew's registers for August 1591 record the death of three daughters of Robert Spry. Only plague could so decimate a house-hold; the father may well have moved out of town with his remaining family and his death may be

hidden in some neighbouring village registers. Young Spry's 1595 map has a most spirited rendering of the old castle and, beside the plan of the new fort, there is what looks like a circular dining-table. It must be the compass Drake set up in his mayoralty, with the points of the compass marked on the flat top and a revolving spindle which could be used to take the bearing of ships in the Sound. The 'spille', or spindle, was repaired in 1585.

Drake's Leat

The growing population and the large fleets all made heavy demands on the town's water supply. There was, early on, a water course to take supplies from the Sutton farm stream to the quaysides, for the 'cunditt' was mended in 1495. 'Conduit' is used both to describe a gutter for conveying water and for the small buildings from which water gushed from a pipe at bucket height, but these early references must be to simple gutters. A well on Southside, whose pump was mended in 1549, was useful to shipping, and William Hawkins made a new conduit in 1570, probably to serve the privateers' new quay.

The local water sources were soon inadequate, and in 1560 the town paid 26s.10d. to 'Mr forsland of bovy and his company for vewinge of the ground wherebei freshe water myght have byn brought unto the towne'. Mr Forsland was a tin-streamer of importance, accustomed to carrying water long distances over the Moor in leats. A fresh survey was made in 1577, this time costing 52s.5d., but still nothing happened; legislation was needed and Elizabeth did not call many Parliaments. But Plymouth was obviously prepared; the next Parliament met on 23 November 1584 and the Plymouth Water Bill had its first reading on 21 December. The preamble set out the need to water Her Majesty's ships in the port, and the difficulty experienced by mariners who often had to go a mile or more to fetch water. Clearly, large fleets exhausted the local supplies and parties of seamen had to be sent to the brooks flowing down to Pennycomequick and Lipson. The second reason was the danger of fire, the third the need to scour the harbour. There was nothing in the bill about water for the townsmen, and its full title was 'An Acte for the Presvacon of the Haven of Plymowth'.

The bill was sent upstairs to a committee which included Sir Francis Drake (his first Parliament as MP for Bossiney, a village near Tintagel) and Mr Edgcumbe, the member for Liskeard. It completed all stages and received the Royal Assent on 29 March 1585. Plymouth now had authority to tap the headwaters of the Meavy and bring the water to the port by a leat, or open waterway. The town wasted no time. The justices of Devon (sitting in quartersessions, they exercised the functions of the modern county council) came down to view the course and were well entertained. Spry made his map of the route and this was sent to the Privy Council.

But that spring our wheat ships were seized in the Spanish ports; Drake made his descent on the Indies; the cold war turned hot and it was not until after the Armada and the counter-Armada the following year that the water project began to move again. The vast fleets assembled year after year since 1585 must have emphasised the need.

Robert Lampen planned the course of the leat in detail, and his brother, James, seems to have taken charge of the work, with William Stockman and John Stevane as his foremen. The work began in December 1590 and the water began to flow on 24 April 1591. The leat was 17 miles long, a simple ditch about six feet wide and two feet deep. Not until a century or more later did it get its modern hard floor and cut granite sides. The head weir is now covered

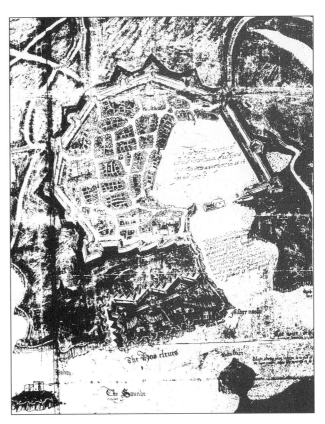

Part of the Adams map of 1591 sent to the Privy Council with proposals for new defences at Plymouth. It is the first map with any great detail: the roofed market cross is shown with the guildhall and its tower beside it. The 'Old Tree' of later centuries is shown at the junction of Bretonside and North Street.

by Burrator Reservoir (for Plymouth still takes its water from the same point). Around Yennadon, the ground was so rocky that a wooden trough carried the water over the ground. Surplus boards were given to Walter Elford, whose house at Langstone was also drowned by the reservoir. Drake, out of favour with the Queen and free to turn to local affairs, was the moving spirit; Plymouth gave him £200 to pay for the actual construction and £100 out of which to compensate the owners of land through which the leat passed. The town had other expenses; messengers to Drake at Buckland; wine and milk at the Church House, Meavy (forerunner of the 'Royal Oak' inn); wine and meals for the justices on their inspections.

Then there was the celebration on 24 April, when the water first flowed to Plymouth. Messengers took invitations to Drake at Buckland and Mr Harris at Radford, the mistresses rode out, wine and provisions were assembled and four trumpeters were sent out on hired horses. It is not hard to translate the bare accounts into a picture of the mayor, Walter Peperell, and the ex-mayor, John Blythman, riding out with the aldermen and councillors and their wives to Head Weir, and there meeting Mr Harris, the MP, and Sir Francis. There were presents to the

Lampen brothers, and to the foremen, and a gift to the rector of Meavy. No doubt he blessed the enterprise, the trumpets were sounded, the sluice was opened and the water began to flow down to Plymouth, where it was greeted with gunfire and the company entertained to dinner.

There is an old legend that Drake rode to Plymouth on a white horse and that the water flowed at his horse's tail. Like many legends, it may well have foundation in fact. Water can only be let into a dry leat slowly, otherwise it scours the bank, and the actual head of water is little more than a trickle moving at walking pace. If Drake and all the local dignitaries had been at Head Weir for the opening and a dinner awaited them in Plymouth, it would have been natural for them all to have ridden back over Yennadon and Roborough Down to Plymouth, keeping pace with the water. The leats that are still earthen ditches make excellent horse trails, and one can well imagine Drake, with his gift for the right gesture, jumping his horse down into the leat and, indeed, letting the water flow behind at his horse's tail. It is a splendid

Left: *Mr Sparke's New Street.*

picture; the men and women in their best clothes, bright with the panache of the Elizabethans, the trumpeters, the jingling harness of the horses, all riding down to Plymouth through the flaming yellow gorse of an April day, with the greatest living Englishman at their head and the water at their heels.

Drake has been accused of making money out of the leat. He may, indeed, have shown a profit on his contract, for he even fought his national wars on a joint stock basis, but it was nevertheless his energy which produced the water supply, and Plymouth gave him credit for it. The Black Book for 1590 records:

This yere on the – daye of December Sr Fraunces Drake Kneight beganne to bringe the Ryur Meve to the towne of Plymmouthe wch, beinge in length about 25 miles, he wth greate Care and diligence effected, and brought the Riur into the towne the xxiiijth day of Aprill the next after psentlie after he sctt in hand to Build six greast

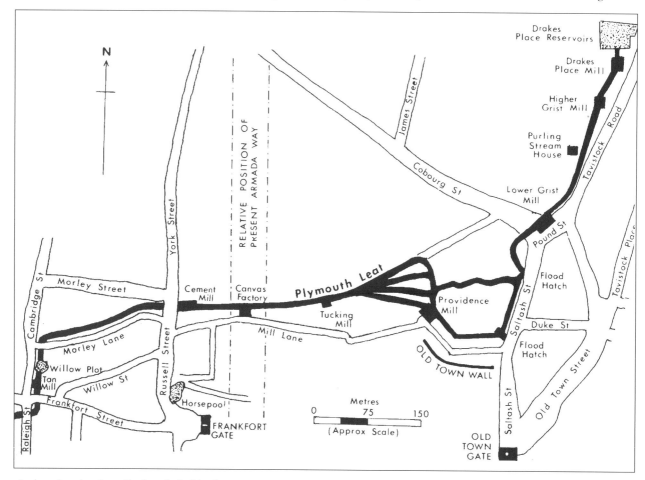

A plan showing how the leat forked in the town to serve a number of mills. The flood hatch is about the site of the Central Hall.
(ILLUSTRATION BASED ON A SEVENTEENTH-CENTURY MAP IN THE WEST DEVON RECORD OFFICE AND TAKEN FROM *WATER FROM THE MOOR* BY DAVID J. HAWKINGS)

milles, the two at wythy in Eckbuckland pish, thother 4 by the towne, the tow at wythy and the two next to the towne he fullie fynished befor michelmas next after, and grounde Corne wth theym.

The mills had been included in the authority of the Act by the Parliamentary committee of which Drake was a member, and he has been charged with lining his pocket in this respect, too. But corn must be ground, fleets need bread as well as water, and the Sourpool, which for so long had driven the manor mills, was drying up. Drake bought them from the Hawkins family and they ceased work in 1592 when the Sourpool was 'made drie for a meadow'.

The Widey mills were at Crownhill. Thence the leat made a great circuit round Pennycross, came across the west side of Mutley Plain and around Houndiscombe Road to drive the first town mill at Drake's Reservoir in Tavistock Road, the second where Cobourg Street leaves the Drake Circus round-about, and the other two in what was called Mill Lane. Thence it flowed into Millbay (it never did scour Sutton Pool), and parts of the leat still carry storm water from the lower parts of Plymouth.

The new mills upset the other mill-owners in the district and a bill was presented to Parliament in 1592–93 seeking to have them closed. The bill was killed by a committee of which Drake was chairman, and though this has been seen as his final villainy in the business, it may simply have been he was aware that his new mills were closer to the ships than those at Weston Mill, Lipson, Mill or Egg Buckland. This same committee passed two other bills, one of which empowered Stonehouse to cut a leat for a water supply. It was a lesser enterprise than Plymouth's and merely involved tapping a small stream at Tor (the Houndiscombe Brook, which flowed down to Pennycomequick). Boundary stones still mark this water supply, and the long-disused reservoirs beside Peverell Park Road are remnants of a later century.

The other bill was for 'the inning of Plympton Marsh', the first work of reclamation at Marsh Mills. This reduced the width of the Laira and made it possible in 1618/19 for Long Bridge to be built over the Plym, so saving travellers the discomfort of the Ebb Ford or the devious route over Plym Bridge.

Once in Plymouth, the water was piped, and the town accounts for 1592 show bills from Moore, and another plumber from Totnes, and for nearly five tons of lead 'for to conveye the water'. A great frost in the winter of 1607/08 burst many of the pipes. For the ordinary townsfolk, there were conduits about the town, little stone buildings with pipes from which the water gushed. The Guildhall and wealthy citizens were directly connected to the supply; Peter Silvester paid 30s. and Mr Kympe 15s. in 1593 as water money; in 1602 the Corporation ordered that no one should pipe water into his house without prior permission; by 1608 38 houses were connected.

Pilchards

During the years that Plymouth was struggling to get enough water there was also trouble over what was really the town's staple diet, fish. Early in her reign, Elizabeth not only enforced meatless days but made them three a week, Wednesdays, Fridays and Saturdays. By encouraging the fishing industry, she built up the nation's reserve of seamen. Increased demand led to greater production, and seine-netting developed, with three or four boats to a net and half-a-dozen men to each boat. The merchants moved in to develop export markets and, by pressing fish in hogshead instead of the old curing, they were able to catch the oil that ran out of the barrels – train oil – and market that, too. These merchants built cellars between Penlee Point and Cawsand, close to the fishing grounds and clear of the congestion of Sutton Pool. Next, they began dealing in 'futures', selling the next season's fish before they were caught, and by 1578 the people of Devon and Cornwall were petitioning against this 'big business'. They complained that the fishermen were getting poor wages and that now nobody could buy fish to eat. Dr Rowse suggests that behind this petition were really the Plymouth merchants, who were feeling the pinch of competition from Cawsand.

While Drake was mayor in 1581, the council forbade the selling of pilchards before they were caught, and in 1584 they ordered fishwives not to sell at prices fixed by the merchants. That year Plymouth went to the Privy Council and complained that the cellars at Cawsand were a great hindrance to the trade of the town. In 1588 the towns of Plymouth, Millbrook, Saltash and Stonehouse joined against the merchants of Cornwall. The Privy Council decreed that no more cellars should be made at Cawsand, that two-thirds of the fish should be taken to Plymouth and that no Londoners or people from outside Devon

Port Wrinkle with its little harbour built by Richard Carew in 1612, and the pilchard cellars on top of the cliff. The harbour has been partly destroyed by storms, but the cellars (right) survive, and served fishermen well into the twentieth century. (AN 1825 ENGRAVING BY WILLIAM DANIELL)

and Cornwall should have cellars at Cawsand. Clearly, bigger men were moving in.

There were more such orders in 1589, and commissioners, Drake among them, were appointed from the two counties to enforce them. But exporting fish had always been good business, and in the end both the Government and Plymouth, failing to halt the trade, turned it to good account. An export duty was levied on all fish exported from Devon and Cornwall to pay for the new defences of Plymouth. The merchants did their best to defeat this duty and in 1595 were taking their catches to Fowey, where the exporters refused to pay taxes to help Plymouth. That year, a letter to Sir Robert Cecil complained that there were two million fish in Plymouth, and every ship was claiming that they had caught them off Newfoundland. Nevertheless, the fish tax did raise £1,327 for the fort, of which £877 came from pilchards. Plymouth men moved into the Cawsand business, too, and certainly Richard Treville was operating from there by 1597.

The tiny harbour of Pier Cellars, built for this business between Cawsand and Penlee Point, is still there, though the cellars have now gone. There were cellars, too, at Polhawn, Sharrow Point (Whitsands) and Port Wrinkle. The little harbour built there in 1605 is half ruined, but the cellars remain on top of the cliff, a high wall about a rectangle lined with sheds open to the central square and surmounted by lofts. It is hard to believe that from Port Wrinkle's little harbour boats made voyages to Ireland, but still of a summer's night one could until recently see the lights of the pilchard fleet strung across the bay from Looe to Rame.

The other little towns which joined Plymouth in this pilchard battle had their foreign trade, too. The *Speedwell* of Millbrook was trading to Ireland in these years, the *Margaret* of Saltash to San Lucar and the *Judith* of Stonehouse was in the Newfoundland fishing-fleet. Millbrook had 80 houses, a mill, 40 ships, and helped, like all the neighbouring towns, to feed Plymouth.

There were 100 English ships in the Newfoundland business, and half of them were Plymouth-owned. On 23 September 1595 there were 50 Newfoundland ships in Plymouth, all waiting to unload their catches, and French and Flemish ships waiting to take them.

Life in the Town

In these strenuous times the Town Council had also to cope with the social work previously done by the churches. There had been an almshouse just west of St Andrew's tower, certainly as early as 1450, when a chapel was dedicated. It may have been rebuilt in the church rebuilding of 1485–1500. As the town's oldest charity it attracted many legacies, which made it the owner of a number of fields and houses. The mayor

The Rose and Crown public house, one of the last Tudor buildings to survive in Old Town Street. It finally made way for street widening in 1896.

and corporation became the trustees and administrators after the Dissolution.

When, in 1561, the Town Council resolved to fill the education gap created by the closure of the chantry school, the Almshouse chapel became the new school and the apartments over it were the lodgings for the first headmaster, Thomas Brooke. For an annual stipend of £10 he was to 'freelye teache all the children native and inhabitaunt... gramer and writinge'. The mayor, John Eliot, the aldermen and councillors all made donations, as did many other citizens and neighbours of the town. A wall was built around the school and furniture made for it. Bell, Gill, Westlake and Mintern succeeded as schoolmasters until 1584, when William Kempe, a Cambridge Master of Arts, was appointed. He wrote a book on education dedicated to William Hawkins, and another, *The Art of Arithmetic in Whole Numbers and Fractions*, which he dedicated to Francis Drake. Written in Latin, it included a poem praising Drake for bringing in the water. Kempe was one of the first people in the town to pay a water rate and, even more important, he was the town's first-known author. His period of office also saw the town's first grants towards university education – '1583, vjs.viijd. given to a scholar to brynge him to Oxenforde.'

Physicians and surgeons appear in the records,

Looking down Looe Street before the houses on the left were demolished in the 1890s. The Pope's Head had been on the right at the top of the street; later the Arts Centre. The Minerva is further down on the same side.

and they must have had a hard time in those insanitary days when the plague was an annual visitor. The town paid for burying the dead poor, and paid compensation for fumigation, burning bedding and the costs of a form of isolation. The burying of a 'neger' on Cattedown and the removal of a 'molato 'which laye about the streete' shows that coloured men were not uncommon. Indeed, the St Andrew's registers show several, men and women, as servants, and a number of births are recorded.

Sturdy beggars who would not work were sent on to the next parish. Thomas Edwards and Vincent, the town criers, regularly had this job. In 1596 Edwards carried a lame man to Compton in a barrow, and a woman distracted of her wits to Plympton; Vincent took a 'lame and impotent man' to Plymstock. Like their predecessor, Ballemay, they removed 'fackebons' and 'hores' to Compton or Stonehouse. Often the women were punished first, tied to the tail of a cart and whipped through the streets, with a boy walking in front beating a basin. In 1589 there was a 'whipping of six hoares'; no doubt the army of Drake and Norris waiting to sail for Spain had its camp followers. In 1589 sixpence was given to a poor woman who had been 'carted' and fourpence paid 'for caryenge her awaye'. Was it compassion or an over-brutal whipping?

John, the drummer, beat the alarm about the streets for sterner occasions; a bagpiper led the beating of the bounds in 1589. A St Andrew's cross was carved on the Stonehouse boundary stone that year, and the castle carved on many of the stones the next year; clearly the present arms of St Andrew's cross and the four castles were generally accepted. Householders were required to put out 'candles and lanterns' to light the streets.

The boys still had a day out on Freedom Day. In 1592 there was sixpence for a women misused by the boys of her apples and basket on St Matthew's Day (21 September); the next year there was 18s.7d. for wine, fruit and cake on St Matthew's Day, and for the boys' spoil in the market. There was a new bell on the Hoe, and in 1594 nearly £300 was spent on other bells, presumably for St Andrew's Church. Drake and Hawkins gave a broken gun towards the cost, and perhaps that metal is still in the St Andrew's bells. It would be appropriate enough, because for centuries a special peal was rung each year on the Saturday before 25 July, and on the Sunday the mayor and corporation marched to church in their scarlet robes to give thanks for 'the great deliverance' from the Armada.

Plymouth was still a country town with roaming animals, and in 1594 a man was fined 10s. for killing

Joseph Gubbe's pig in the street. But one odour had been removed in 1582 when the 'fumynge howses within the Towne putt downe'. One imagines they were the cellars where the fish were smoked, removed away from the houses. That year, too, the ale stakes (good wine needs no bush) were put down and signs set up. So from that time we have inn signs, although the 'Pope's Head' which was at the top of Looe Street, above what is now the Arts Centre, is named in 1573. There was the 'Turk's Head' in St Andrew's Street (where the 'Abbey Hotel' now is), the 'Rose and Crown' and the 'Old Four Castles' in Old Town Street. All were Elizabethan buildings which were pulled down in the nineteenth century, but whether they were always inns is unknown. The only inn now in a building of that age is the 'Minerva' in Looe Street.

Maybe one of them was the base of 'Russell the Post', and 'Peter the Post' (named in 1591). Some idea of the speed of the mail is given by the inscription on the outside of letters at Hatfield House, sent from the town to Lord Burghley. The date, time and town were written down when the letter was handed from one postman, riding as hard as his horse could go, to the next. A typical example left Plymouth at 11.30a.m. on 23 September 1595. It was at Ashburton at 1p.m., Exeter 4.30p.m, Honiton 6.45p.m., Crewkerne 10p.m., Sherborne midnight, Salisbury at 6.30a.m., Andover 9a.m., Basing (stoke) at noon and Staines at 5p.m. Burghley would have it in London within 36 hours.

In 1600 Plymouth was granted a new charter by the Queen which clarified the town's legal rights. It made the ex-mayor a justice in addition to the mayor and recorder, gave the town the right to a prison and excluded the town from the authority of the justices of Devon. By making the mayor clerk of the market it gave him control of trading in the town. A dispute about Saltash's rights in Sutton Harbour was satisfactorily settled and the two mayors twice dined together in Stonehouse in celebration. The Town Council was obstreperous from time to time; James Bagge and Richard Hawkins were fined in 1591 for being late on St Lambert's Day, mayor-choosing day. Joseph Gubbe (the pig owner) made offensive speeches at the 1601 mayor-choosing, and there were more fines when John Harris and the captain of the watch, John Battersbie, came to blows in the Guildhall, in front of the mayor.

The week before Christmas, 1602, the Black Book records that 'Sr Richard Hawkyns knight, who was taken in the south sea by the Spaniardes in the vioadge he beganne in Maye 1593, came home after he had been prisoner'. Here was a ghost from the past, a Hawkins back in Plymouth, a link with the great ones. But the Black Book's next entry was to mark the severance of a far larger link with the past:

Queene Elizabeth departed this mortal life at

Richemonde the xxiijth daie of Marche in the morninge, and that same daie by nyne of the clocke James the Kinge of Scotlande was pclaimed in London to be oure king of England, and the last daie of the same moneth his Majie was proclaymed at the Markett Crosse here in Plymouth to be kinge of Englande, whiche pclamation was reade by Mr Sargent Hele our late Queenes Sargent at lawe, and was pclaymed by John Lupton our Towne Clarke, at whiche tyme here was greate trivmphe with Bondfiers, gunnes, and ringinge of bells with other kinds of musicke.

The old Queen dead; it must have seemed impossible; she had been on the throne for 45 years, and most of her people could remember no other sovereign. It was not just the end of a reign; it was the end of a dynasty. London knew of the Queen's death, and of the new King, on the evening of 24 March. Plymouth heard the proclamation on 31 March.

Perhaps it is fitting that this proclamation was the last great event at the old Market Cross – that granite pillared, open-sided lantern surmounted by a cross which, for so long, had been the heart of the town. Three years after this proclamation it was pulled down to make way for a new guildhall. But this could not be known to those people of Plymouth standing round on that March morning in 1603, listening to old Sergeant Hele reading out the sonorous phrases in his lawyer's voice, their eyes maybe wandering up Whimple Street to the church tower, or down to the blue water and the ships' masts at the bottom of Looe Street, or down High Street to the Parade and the new warehouses. Maybe some of them sucked little clay pipes or wore hats they had obtained by barter from the Indians; they knew that far side of the Atlantic better than London or even Exeter, and Scotland to them was just another foreign country. They, who had known only the Tudors – Welshmen who had become more English than the English – could not know that the Scottish Stuarts would have stiffer necks, that one would have to be broken before they could settle down together, that the old despotic days of the sovereign and his ministers were over; that the rule of Parliament was in sight.

What were they cheering, as the bells or St Andrew's rang out, the guns roared and the bonfires blazed up on the Hoe? They could not know that the war with Spain, which they had waged for 30 years and more, was finally over. They might have realised that they had brought the Spanish Empire to bank- ruptcy. They could not know that they made England a European power, that they had already ensured that North America would be an English-speaking and Protestant country, that they had written a great page in history. They could not know, that morning around the Market Cross, that they were standing at a great dividing point in Plymouth's history.

✦ CHAPTER 8 ✦

The Puritan Town, 1603–42

Plymouth was a Puritan town when James VI of Scotland became James I of England in 1603. Nor was it surprising, for Plymouth had been fighting Catholic Spain for 30 years and too many of her men had fallen into the fires and tortures of the Inquisition for there to be any love of Papistry. The seamen who came home from the sack of Cadiz in 1596 were laden with their loot from churches, rich altar books and prayer books, 'supersticious books' the records call them. On 15 December 1600 'there was burnte in the markett place 22 chests of the pope's Bulls and pdons'.

Drake and Hawkins were touched by the Puritan spirit, says A.L. Rowse, and Puritan sympathies he reports as widespread among the growing bourgeois of the English towns, especially the more prosperous merchants and tradespeople in commercial centres like Plymouth, and the other ports. In late-Elizabethan days the only two records in St Andrew's, the Parish Church of Plymouth, of 'church briefs', a way of taking special collections for charity, were both to relieve the inhabitants of Geneva, that stronghold of Calvinism whose people were under pressure from the Dukes of Savoy. In that period too the town accounts show many payments for special preachers and lecturers, and at that time lecturers, who delivered the sermon after the incumbent had finished morning prayer, were the common mouthpieces of the Puritans.

Queen Elizabeth had given to Plymouth Corporation in 1572 the right to appoint the vicars to St Andrew's, and in 1603 they chose Henry Wallis from St Dominic, on Tamarside. Perhaps they were unsure of him; he had to give a bond that he would resign the living if they so wished, but they never did, and when he died in 1632, still in office, a characteristic Puritan sermon was preached at his funeral. It is from the sermons of the day that were printed and survived that we can be so sure that we are dealing with Puritans. Many survive from the pen of the Revd Samuel Heiron, for long vicar of Modbury, one which explained his 'Refysall of Sybscrpiton to the Books of Common prayer', was printed in 1607 in Holland, as is made clear in a handwritten note on the title page of a surviving copy:

... and sent over packed in the goods of an eminent Merchant of Plymouth, Mr T. Sherwil. No Bookseller daring to sell it, ye whole impression was given away... Some were dropt in the streets, and others left at the door of Scholars.

Yet Thomas Sherwill, this smuggler of dangerous books, was Mayor of Plymouth the following year and twice again afterwards; he was a Plymouth MP from 1614 until his death. His brother Nicholas was also three times mayor. 'Old Mr Sam. Heiron' had many sermons published in London and one, published in 1616, was dedicated to Sir Ferdinando Gorges, commander of His Majesty's forces at Plymouth, Sir William Strode of Newnham, Sir Warwick Hele of Wembury, Sir Christopher Harris of Radford and Mr George Chudleigh of Strachleigh (near Lee Mill, now a farm), who had been led 'to commiserate and to help the spiritual necessity of an vntaught Towne by procuring the establishment of a weekely Lecture in it'. This sermon was one in the series. Heiron was responsible for bringing John Barlow to Plymouth, where he was lecturer at St Andrew's from 1608 to 1619. Barlow had a national reputation and left Plymouth to join a renowned champion of Nonconformists in Bradford. But he still returned to preach in the town, and a 1632 book of his is dedicated to the mayor and magistrates of Plymouth.

Soon after Barlow left Plymouth the Revd Alexander Grosse became vicar of Plympton St Mary. In his 14 years there a number of his Puritan sermons were published, several originally preached in Plymouth. He preached at Thomas Sherwill's funeral in 1631 and again that year at the funeral of Matthias Nichols, lecturer to the town. Grosse later moved to Bridford, near Exeter, but in 1645 he came specially to Plymouth to preach at the funeral of John Cawse, who had just finished his second term as mayor.

The Merchants and Their Trade

We find the names of these Puritans constantly in the mayoral rolls and the lists of merchants in the town; it was a tight community. Thomas Fownes said that there were only 24 true merchant adventurers resident in Plymouth when he was mayor in 1620, but these were the ruling spirits. There were some, like Parker and Rawlyn, who had been active in the Caribbean privateering that brought so much profit to Plymouth in the last Elizabethan decades. Earlier Elizabethan names were fading out; Sir Richard Hawkins, after his ten years in Spanish prisons, largely retired to his new home near Slapton, and the Eliots, old Hawkins partners, were in their great house at St Germans, Port Eliot, built out of the old

Above: *Parker's house in St Andrew Street, probably early in the twentieth century. It is now restored and known as the Merchant's House.* Right: *The Merchant's House restored.*

monastery. Thomas Drake, brother of Francis, and his heirs were country gentlemen at Buckland Abbey. There had been a Fownes with Hawkins and Drake at San Juan de Ulloa in 1568, but the 1620 mayor was a son of a Bristol man; there had always been close family links between the two ports. There was a Gayer mayor of Plymouth in 1592; three Gayer sons stayed in Plymouth and married respectively into the Fownes, Amadas and Sparke families (more Elizabethan Plymouth names), while two others moved to London and became important merchants there. John Gayer indeed became a director of the East India Company (born out of Drake's voyage of circumnavigation), a Lord Mayor of London, a knight and a distinguished traveller in Persia. Some left, some moved in. Abraham Colmer came from Birmingham in 1599, for example, but established himself by marrying the daughter of Nicholas Sheere, a leading merchant.

The basic trade of most of these merchants, and certainly Plymouth's principal business, was in the Newfoundland fisheries. It was essentially a West Country trade dominated by Plymouth and Dartmouth, with Dartmouth holding the major share. Plymouth had 50 ships in the business in 1594, and 60 by 1631; they averaged 100 tons apiece and it has been suggested that they were each crewed by about 40 men. To take 2,400 seamen out of

Plymouth's estimated total population of this period of 7,000 seems a high figure but, even if overstretched, shows how vital the business was in Plymouth's economy. The ships sailed across the Atlantic in spring, set up wooden platforms on the beaches where the fish were split and dried, and returned with their catches in July and August.

Some cargoes came to Plymouth for home use or re-export to France, Spain, the Canary Islands and Italy. But many more ships went direct from Newfoundland to these countries, sold their fish, bought local goods and returned with the profits of a double turnover. Spanish ports had been denied English ships during the long Spanish war, but James had made peace in 1604, opening the ports of Spain and Portugal to English ships. They had been reaching deep into the Mediterranean since 1570 – 'voyages to the Straits', say the Plymouth records – and the Spanish war had not halted this business. The Sherwills were in the Mediterranean trade, and the Trevilles had a factor at Gibraltar.

The true exports from Plymouth's hinterland were tin, lead and woollen goods. Dartmoor tin production was falling in the early-seventeenth century but was not negligible; most of it went out from Plymouth and some was shipped coastwise from Cornish ports for export overseas. Most of the western lead went through Plymouth, partly to

John Hawkins's quay, the Barbican, photographed c.1880, before being widened for the Fish Market. The eighteenth-century Watch House, destroyed in the 1930s, stands at the end.

Newfoundland in the fishery ships and the rest, with some of the tin, coastwise to London. Just as Plymouth was on the edge of the tin-producing areas, so with wool the main production areas were in east Devon and Somerset, better served by Exeter and even Dartmouth. But Dartmoor had large flocks of sheep, east Cornwall was a major spinning area and weaving was another cottage industry along the southern edges of Dartmoor. Tavistock, Buckfastleigh and Ashburton were all woollen towns and while even their output gravitated eastwards, Plymouth did get a share. The six mills which Sir Francis Drake had built beside his 1591 leat were originally planned to grind corn, but by 1608 the two lower mills, roughly situated where Cornwall Street now crosses Armada Way, were fulling mills where cloth was cleaned and shrunk. The slopes above the mills were covered with racks for drying the cloth. The Tavistock and west Devon output was a rough cloth, but the old 'kerseys' were gradually giving way to the new serges as the seventeenth century progressed.

The total volume of trade increased over the years, and Exeter and Barnstaple manufacturers sent some of their produce through Plymouth. The markets ranged from the Atlantic islands to Spain, France and the Low Countries. Through Plymouth too went slates to ports between Copenhagen and Cadiz.

The imports show a richer list: the 300-year-old wine and salt imports from France, with paper, pitch, linen and canvas added; more wine, fruit and sugar from Spain and the Canaries, with iron ore as well from northern Spain; shipping stores from the Baltic (Eastland trade, the Plymouth records call this), rye from Lübeck and hops from Flushing.

Some was for local use, some was trans-shipped into coasting vessels for other English ports, just as the Exeter wool for export came round in coasters. Coal from Newcastle and south Wales, grain from the east coast, all the needs of the town came in by sea from the ports where they were available. The roads of England were still only fit for packhorses, and Plymouth was not helped by a river on either side. Not until 1618/19 was a causeway driven across the mud flats at Marsh Mills and a bridge built over the Plym – the 'Long Bridge' – to cut out the long haul round by Plym Bridge or the Ebb Ford (Efford) available at low tide from Crabtree to Saltram.

The economic life of Plymouth was based on the sea, as it had been for centuries. It is difficult to measure the amount of trade because not all the port books are available, customs returns are an imprecise guide, and in addition all the returns of the Cornish ports (apart from tin, unimportant) are shown in the Plymouth figures. There are also many goods, like the Newfoundland fish, exempt in certain cases. London, of course, dominated all English trade as it had for centuries and, in the west, Bristol and Exeter overshadowed Plymouth as merchant ports. In 1614–20 the London customs returns averaged over £100,000 and the best provincial figures were Hull £7,200, Exeter £4,500, Bristol £3,700, Newcastle £3,300 and Plymouth £2,900. Plymouth, about the twentieth town of the country in size of population, was the sixth port. In her best year of that period, 1617, she outstripped Newcastle.

New England

But Plymouth still held the lead in American developments. The Newfoundland fishermen had very early on reached down from the Newfoundland banks to the American coast, the main ('Maine') land, searching for new fishing grounds. Ralegh had tried settlement in Virginia in 1585 and failed, but the idea persisted. In 1602 Bartholomew Gosnold built a fort on Martha's Vineyard, just south of Cape Cod, but one winter was enough for his men. In 1604 a group of French Huguenots settled in Nova Scotia, the first settlement to persist in North America. But the new start for Plymouth men followed George Weymouth's exploration of the New England coast in 1605. He brought home five Indians to Plymouth, three of whom he gave to Gorges, the Governor of Plymouth. Indian and African servants were already not uncommon in the town.

Gorges joined with Chief Justice Popham, a Somerset man like himself, Ralegh Gilbert, heir to the Ralegh patent for Virginia, and William Parker, the old privateer captain, to form the Plymouth Company of Virginia. They received a charter from the King granting them all America between 41 and 45 degrees north; the London Company of Virginia also had a charter giving them all America between 34 and 38 degrees north. Roughly, Plymouth was given New England and the London Company was given Virginia. Plymouth sent out a ship at once but the Spanish, still claiming all America, captured it. Another ship went out the next year with two of Gorges's Indians as interpreters, Ralegh Gilbert as admiral and Captain George Popham as president. They endured a bitter winter and found nothing but 'extreme extremities', and in 1608 a relief ship brought them all back. Jamestown, which the London Company set up at the same time, survived to become the first unbroken English settlement in North America. Plymouth was to play a great part in keeping Jamestown

going, though it was never very receptive to the pressures Captain John Smith, that great advocate of settlement, constantly put upon the town. Smith was a man of many adventures, chief among them his being captured by Indians and only saved from death through the pleading of the king's daughter, Pocohontas. She was to marry a Puritan settler, John Rolfe, who did much to set up the tobacco industry in Virginia. Rolfe brought her to England in 1616; they landed at Plymouth. Her father also sent home one of his men to spy out the strength of these white men; he landed at Plymouth with a large stick, meaning to carve a notch for every Englishman he saw!

One of the Jamestown support voyages led to the discovery of Bermuda. Sir George Somers sailed from the Sound in 1609 with nine ships and 600 passengers. Eight reached Jamestown but Somers was wrecked on Bermuda, where he wintered. Soon after a permanent settlement was established.

But Plymouth ships were finding trade with the Indians more profitable than settlement. They were setting up trading posts for the summer months to buy fish and above all furs, but bringing these and their men home for the winter. The posts were used year after year, and some were acquiring English names. Gorges and Popham had Plymouth ships in this business, as did Robert Trelawny. His father had moved from St Germans into Plymouth in 1578, apprenticed for eight years 'to be enstructed in the trade of merchandize'. Through marriage the family were linked with the Hawkinses, the Sparkes and the Gayers. The younger Robert had a town house in Looe Street and was mayor three times. The Treville family also moved into the New England trade.

The Plymouth men sent Richard Hawkins out to survey settlement possibilities in 1615 but he found Indian wars ravaging the coast and went on to Virginia. Captain John Smith was sent out from Plymouth as well, but, true to form, he was hammered in a storm, captured by French privateers and escaped from his La Rochelle prison the following year. He constantly upbraided Plymouth for lack of enterprise but knew the port's value; it was, he wrote, 'near as much trouble but much more danger to sail from London to Plymouth than from Plymouth to New England'. The Plymouth Company named him Admiral of New England but stuck to trading. It made money with little sickness

or fighting; in 1619 one Plymouth ship of 200 tons was on the coast for six weeks with 38 men and boys and on its return sold the cargo of furs for £2,000. The next year John

The memorial in St Andrew's Church to John Sparke, who died in 1640, and his wife.

Smith said every seaman in the trade had £20 in his pocket for seven months' work. A stay-at-home craftsman would do well to earn £8 in that time, and he would have to keep himself as well.

With such profits it is not surprising to find a new charter being sought by Gorges and his friends in 1620, giving them all trading, fishing and settlement rights from 40 to 48 degrees north, from Atlantic to Pacific. While the negotiations were still in hand the first trespassers sailed into Plymouth.

They were separatists from the countryside between Doncaster and Gainsborough, Calvinists who, despairing of purifying the Church from within (the Puritan aim), became Nonconformists. They had moved to Holland in 1607 to practise their religion in freedom but found their children growing up as Dutchmen. So they resolved to move to the New World, where they could follow both their religion and their English way of life. They had a licence from the London Company of Virginia and had chartered two ships, the *Mayflower* and the *Speedwell*, for the crossing. The emigrants had assembled in Southampton, where a number of English sympathisers joined them, put into Dartmouth for repairs, and again into Plymouth because the little *Speedwell* seemed unfit for the voyage. There they resolved that *Mayflower* would sail alone, and on 6 September 1620, with 102 passengers aboard, she 'loosed from Plymouth, having been kindly entertained and courteously used by divers friends there dwelling'.

There is no evidence of any separatist body in Plymouth as early as 1620, but from what is known of the religious feelings of the town at that time it can be accepted that the Anglican clergy and the people would have understood them. Beyond their religious sympathies, they would have known that these Pilgrims were setting out across the Atlantic at the wrong time of year, when the Newfoundland and the Maine fishing fleets were homeward bound, and they would have known what hardships any settlers in New England would have to face. In fact this company of men, women and children anchored under Cape Cod on 11 November, found a place to settle across the bay and did establish the first permanent English settlement in New England. As it

Left top: *A modern painting of the* Mayflower *sailing from Plymouth. With all the Pilgrims on deck the ship would have been this crowded.* Left bottom: *The memorial on* Mayflower *pier marking the point of departure of the Pilgrims in 1620.*

happened their choice of settlement was a little harbour long used as a summer fishing and trading point; Captain John Smith's map of 1615 of this coast called it 'Plymouth' and the new settlers kept this name in honour of their last English port of call.

But the Plymouth Company got its new charter, and one of the first things the Pilgrims had to do was to regularise their position with the company. From now on settlement was encouraged and the Pilgrims found neighbours, not always welcome, arriving in small numbers round Massachusetts Bay to the north of them. Abraham Jennings, who had the biggest share of the import-export business in Plymouth in the year the *Mayflower* sailed, bought Monhegan Island off the Maine coast from Gorges soon after to support his summer fishing. David Thompson, who had been married in St Andrew's Church in 1613, settled in 1623 where Boston now stands, his new venture financed by Nicholas Sherwill and other Plymouth merchants. He built a strong house, made friends with the Pilgrims and when he died in 1629 his widow married another Devon man, Samuel Maverick. From this Devon pair the famous Texas family of Mavericks has descended. In 1623 too the *Ann* embarked 60 settlers at Plymouth, mainly local people, who spent their first winter with the Pilgrims. Also in 1623 another Plymouth merchant, Leonard Pomeroy, sent his *Providence* up the Piscataque river to settle the first English in New Hampshire. Gorges and his partner Mason had divided their new charter lands between them, Mason calling his New Hampshire after his native county and Gorges calling his New Somerset.

Pirates in the Channel

When James I ended the Spanish war in 1604 he may have opened new trading areas to Plymouth

Radford House from the south, painted by William Payne, c.1785. The house was demolished in 1935.

merchants but at the same time he began to run down the Navy and ceased issuing letters of marque to English privateers. For Plymouth seamen this had been good business and Plymouth merchants handled their prizes. Now out of work, some privateers turned downright pirates and found Plymouth merchants still willing to deal with them. In the early years of the reign the Dutch were still at war with Spain and their privateers, notably the Dunkirkers, were a constant scourge to our traffic.

As the Dutch retired from the scene the galleys of Algiers, the 'Turks', long a Mediterranean danger, moved into the Channel in 1609 and with them the Sallee Rovers from the Atlantic coast of Morocco. Between 1609 and 1616 the 'Turks' took 466 English ships in the Channel. Some of the English pirates linked up with the Turks, notably John Ward, who had long associations with Plymouth. He is said to have gone over to the Bey of Tunis and taught his men the techniques necessary for Atlantic work. On one occasion Ward sailed into Plymouth after a fight with Frenchmen and recruited replacements for his crew. In 1609 two men were paid 16d. for watching at the Barbican to see that no food was taken aboard a pirate ship; clearly pirates used the harbour and had friends ashore. Even Sir Richard Hawkins, Vice-Admiral of Devon, was constantly accused of favouring the pirates. A true Jacobean mixture here, a Puritan town paying touring theatre companies and entertainers to go away, yet consorting with pirates; men of deep social conscience (as will be seen) working with heartless embezzlers.

Into this world came a breath from the past. Sir Walter Ralegh, languishing in the Tower since his framed trial for treason in 1603, was released to seek out his El Dorado in Guiana. He came into Plymouth with his little fleet in 1617, was entertained by the mayor, Robert Trelawny, and the town paid for a drummer to beat the men to their ships. In June 1618 he was back, his son dead and his expedition a failure. His friends advised him to flee but he went to stay with his friend Harris at Radford. His wife

persuaded Ralegh that the King was intent on his death, and got him to agree to take passage in a ship for France. At dead of night they rowed across Hooe Lake and down the Cattewater to join the ship, but Ralegh would not go on. He went back to Radford, and so to London and death on the scaffold.

One man who watched his execution was John Eliot of Port Eliot. It was a turning point for him; from being a man about court and a protégé of Buckingham, that villainous favourite of the King, he came back to Plymouth to work. He became Vice-Admiral of Devon and set about the corruption and the pirates. A plan to attack Algiers, the main base of the Turks, had been talked about since 1617. In 1619 all ports were required to contribute to its cost. Plymouth's share of £1,000 was matched only by Bristol; even Exeter was only asked for £500. Plymouth said its losses to the pirates had been so great that it could not raise the money, but it tried hard to get the Cornish ports – its official outports – to pay their share.

In 1620 a fleet of 20 ships assembled in the Sound with Sir Robert Mansell as admiral. He was head of the Navy Board and, according to Dr Williamson, 'probably the most eminent master of graft in our history'. Sir Richard Hawkins was called out of retirement to join him; the fleet sailed to Algiers and achieved no more than a useless treaty with the Bey. The fleet came home next year, the men were never paid and Sir Richard died arguing their case in the Privy Council.

Sir John Eliot took on the local pirates. He visited the Torbay headquarters of John Nutt, the most notorious pirate on the Devon coast, captured his ships and imprisoned him. Nutt had friends in high places and Eliot not only saw him released but found himself imprisoned for his vigour, as Richard Hawkins had been before him. But Eliot, out again, kept at his work. He brought untried pirates in gaol in Plymouth to trial and hanged them; another 20 caught red-handed he hanged in a day. As MP for St Germans he was vocal in Parliament and hated both by James I and his son, Charles, who came to the throne in 1625.

Eliot found a local enemy in James Bagge the younger. His father, another James, had moved from Poole to Plymouth some time before 1590 to further his privateering interests. He was mayor in 1595 and again in 1605, an agent of the Crown by 1597 and Collector of Customs for Plymouth and Fowey. He was also cantankerous and (one suspects) anti-Puritan: he called Sherwill 'a seditious fellow', threatened to break the neck of Thomas Fownes and called the 1613 mayor, John Scoble, an insolent knave. In 1614 the town replaced him as MP by Thomas Sherwill, and in 1615 the mayor and magistrates took further action and James Bagge was 'clean removed from the Bench'. Even then he got himself restored by suing in the King's Bench. But the old man moved into retirement, resigning his customs posts in favour of his son, buying a farm at Saltram and beginning to built the great house there before his death in 1624. Young James Bagge moved into prominence, an MP for Cornwall in the 1620s and the Plymouth tool of the King's favourite, Buckingham.

The Spanish War

In 1625 Charles I declared war on Spain and began assembling an army of 10,000 strong at Plymouth. Bagge was victualling officer. There were billeting troubles at once; when the fleet came in it brought the plague and seamen were put ashore in improvised tents. There were 20 Sallee Rovers on the coast, no food ships coming in, the soldiers mutinous and plundering the countryside for food. Charles himself came down for ten days, knighted the young Bagge, reviewed the army on Roborough Down and received a purse of £150 from the town. There were many expenses, and the town was also building plague houses at Lipson and Mount Batten to house the worst cases.

Buckingham stayed on at Saltram till the fleet sailed in October; it was back into the Cattewater in two days in complete disorder. It sailed again a week later, failed miserably to take Cadiz or the Spanish treasure fleet, and all through December the ships were limping back into Plymouth with hardly enough men to stand watches. The army was ordered into billets in Plymouth, the soldiers half-naked, plague-ridden and starving. Conditions were so bad in the town that the commissioners of the army had to meet at Plympton. Nearly 500 seamen deserted for a mutinous meeting at Cawsand. Plymouth people were fleeing the town but, like the soldiers billeted in the villages around, they only spread the plague. It reached Buckland Monachorum and Sir Francis Drake, nephew of the great seaman, moved to his house at Meavy, where the commissioners next met. By June 1627 they were writing to London that the plague was so far spread that all commerce had ceased; by July the mayor was writing that only two magistrates were left in the town. Local government was collapsing.

The fleet began to go in May but the soldiers remained till September; when they went they could not even carry their muskets. How many servicemen died is not known,

but Plymouth lost between 1,600 and 2,000 people, a quarter of the population.

In Parliament Sir John Eliot launched a violent attack on royal mismanagement and sought to impeach Buckingham. The Plymouth scandal was the major ground. John Eliot led the attack; he was MP for Newport, Launceston, a pocket borough of Drake's. A childhood friend of Drake's was John Pym, who had grown up at Halton on the Cornish bank of the Tamar and was now MP for Tavistock (Drake's son married Pym's daughter in 1641). Drake became MP for Plympton and William Strode of Newnham, related by marriage to the family, sat for another Drake seat, Bere Alston. The Plymouth members were Thomas Sherwill, that Puritan smuggler of sermons, and John Glanville, son of the great Elizabethan judge, of Kilworthy, near Tavistock.

When Charles tried to dissolve the 1625 Parliament it was John Glanville who moved the protest. When another Parliament was called in 1626 Eliot demanded the impeachment of Buckingham. It was common gossip in Devon that most of the money to feed the army at Plymouth had gone into Bagge's pocket. Bagge was not in the House when the member for Totnes, Sir Francis Seymour, called him 'the bottomless Bagge'. But both Buckingham and Bagge survived; it was Eliot who found himself imprisoned for 11 days and removed from his vice-admiralty. The office went to Bagge, already Vice-Admiral for Cornwall.

That autumn Plymouth had to build a house in the fields, away from the plague-ridden streets, for the mayor-choosing of Thomas Sherwill. Next spring they found another army assembling, this time to aid the Protestants of La Rochelle. Buckingham was in command, staying at Saltram while the same horror story was repeated: burglary, rape, murder, mutiny, plague. The fleet made two ineffective sallies to La Rochelle, the only result being that the Huguenots lost the town. The soldiers were left to winter in Plymouth, plague-ridden again, left in tents on the Hoe, shoeless and frostbitten in one of those bitter winters of the time. Merchants like Nicholas Blake were ruined; the mayor, Robert Trelawny, died in office. After one mutiny was started outside the Guildhall a scaffold was erected on the Hoe to hang the

Left: Fanny's Bower, Saltram: the granite pillars may be those bought by James Bagge from the Tudor guildhall demolished in 1602.

ringleader, but the mob threw it into the sea.

When Parliament reassembled in 1628 it was Eliot and Pym who presented the Petition of Right which Charles was forced to accept. In the 1629 Parliament, when the House refused to answer the King's summons to the Lords, young William Strode was one of the two members who held the Speaker in his seat while he finished his speech. It was the last Parliament for 11 years. Eliot was back in the Tower, to die there in 1632. Strode rotted in prison for 11 years, Pym applied himself to the New England settlements. James Bagge was even made Governor of Plymouth when Gorges resigned in 1629. But his run was nearly over. In 1634 he was denounced to the Star Chamber, a career of embezzlement over many years disclosed, and he was even said to have 'cozened the King himself' of £20,000 over billeting. No wonder the soldiers in Plymouth had fared so ill, the townsmen groaned so loud and Saltram grown so fine. Now Bagge was ruined, and Saltram forfeit to the state until the debts were repaid. Yet when he died in London in 1638 he was still described as holding all his old offices.

His 20-year-old son, George, asked for all these posts, but was only given the governorship of Plymouth on condition that he accepted a lieutenant named by the King. He turned out his uncle, another George Bagge, who had been deputy, but young George did not keep the post long. In January 1639 King Charles gave the post to one of his most experienced soldiers, Sir Jacob Astley, a 50-year-old veteran of the Low Country wars. Young George was only left with Saltram and its debts.

Postwar Trade

Though Charles's overseas adventures brought much of Plymouth's normal life to a standstill, trade did not entirely cease. Some Newfoundland fishing went on, though Abraham Jennings, who supplied £642 worth of fish to the 1627 expedition, was still unpaid when he died 20 years later. There was also a brief revival of privateering; 80 ships of Plymouth had letters of marque in the war years and many prizes were brought in. After the war, trade made an unsteady recovery, with tin and wool going out, but rather less than before the war, and wine imports rather more. But as with most provincial ports, the 1630s saw a failure to recover the pre-war levels of trade. Pirates were still a menace to commerce: the Turks caught the Plymouth fishing fleet in 1636 and took 30 prisoners.

All through the 1620s bodies of settlers sailed from Plymouth, with many from the town and the neighbourhood. In 1630 the *Mary and John* left Plymouth with about 150 people from the Dorset area who founded the town of Dorchester in Massachusetts. But that year saw the big move into New England when a fleet of ten ships from Southampton took out over 700 people, mainly from eastern England. They had their own charter of self-government, and from their town of Boston the modern state of Massachusetts was created. Gorges surrendered his New Somerset rights in 1635 and in time his land became the state of Maine. He is still honoured as its founder, and a tablet in St Budeaux Church – he lived in the parish, at Kinterbury on Tamarside – commemorates the link. It is still remembered that Robert Trelawny, son of Gorges's old partner, together with Moses Goodyear, son-in-law of Abraham Jennings, financed the founding of Portland, the capital of Maine. But in the 1630s New England became for Plymouth what it had originally been, a place for trade, with the new settlers replacing the Indian. By 1637 the colonists had taken over all the fishing on their coast.

The Newfoundland fishing prospered, however, growing stronger than before the war. Plymouth played a leading part in gaining the 'Western Charter' of 1634, which gave the West Country ports control and considerable privileges in the fisheries, and by 1641 declared itself 'chiefly dependent on the fish trade'.

Wealth and Building

In spite of all the problems besetting Plymouth in this first part of the seventeenth century it was not a poor town, at least it had rich and generous merchants. Early in the reign the old Tudor guildhall and the market cross beside it were removed and a new guildhall built. There were two storeys on the old guildhall site and the council chamber was on the first floor, supported by pillars over the old market cross area which was now a covered space where the market could be held, processions to church start and great events be announced as they had through Plymouth's history. The total cost was £794.8s.1d., and detailed accounts down to the last nail survive.

In 1612 William Lawrence, a merchant of Foxhole (Vauxhall Street), left £100 in his will to Thomas and Nicholas Sherwill to build an orphanage, the money to be paid when his good ship *Jonathan* came home from the Straits. The Sherwills and other merchants gave money and endowments of property in and around the town and the Orphan's Aid was built in Catherine Street with the date 1615 over the doorway. Then, in 1630, more money was raised to build the Hospital of Poor's Portion just below the Orphan's Aid. It was the first true workhouse; the need for it may be a comment on the distress left by Charles's wars with Spain and France. The corporation had control of it, and the doorway surmounted by the town arms is preserved in the gardens behind New Street. Thomas Fownes also built almshouses in Basket Street in 1628, yet when he died in 1637 he still left £9,000 in cash with which his son could set up as a country gentleman at

An artist's impression of the 1603 guildhall, made from an older drawing by H.J. Snell. It stood at the end of Whimple Street; High Street can be seen through the pillars on the right.

Whitleigh. Young Trelawny was able to rebuild Ham in 1639. The building still survives as flats. The Trevilles were able to buy Budshead at St Budeaux. The Sherwills acquired the Houndiscombe estate, stretching west of Mutley Plain from North Road East to Ford Park.

The New Church

But these Puritan merchants had not finished their troubles with King Charles when his foolish wars ended. In 1631 Plymouth appointed Thomas Forde, vicar of Brixton, to be the lecturer at St Andrew's. But with the King's support the high church party was gaining strength nationally, and Forde was a notable Puritan. The King ordered that he should not be admitted. Next year the vicar, old Henry Wallis, died after 29 years in office. Plymouth nominated Alexander Grosse of Plympton, another great Puritan. The Bishop of Exeter refused to institute him, so Plymouth put up the already banned Forde. Not only was he banned again by King and Church but the King took back the advowson from the corpo-

ration and in 1634 his nominee was instituted, Dr Aaron Wilson, rector of St Stephen's, Walbrook, and a staunch Royalist. So Plymouth made Grosse lecturer. The King forced him to retire, and appointed Thomas Bedford. The new vicar was soon at loggerheads with his parish. He said the street market was overflowing on to church property, that the councillors had no right to pews in the church, or to appoint a churchwarden.

Within months Plymouth resolved to petition the King, on the grounds of the increased population of the town, that Plymouth be divided into two parishes and to permit 'some worthy and devoted Gentlemen, our neighbours' to build a new church. John Hele of Wembury offered a site, Sir John Gayer of London was among the prospective benefactors, Robert Trelawny was mayor and the not yet discredited Sir James Bagge chosen to present the petition. This was as diplomatic as the 'increased population' reason: Plymouth no doubt hoped for a church as Puritan as St Andrew's had been before Wilson. There were endless arguments over the matter until 1640, when Charles, under all-round pressure, was persuaded to

The entrance to the Orphan's Aid, with the Grammar School doorway beyond.

give back to the corporation the advowson of St Andrew's and permit the new church. The King said it was to be called Charles Church! The necessary Act of Parliament received royal assent in 1641 and building began at once, at the town's expense, on a site on the north-eastern edge of the then built-up area. (The dividing line between the two parishes zigzagged from the Parade to Old Town Street, and thence by way of Cobourg Street, North Road East and Tavistock Road to the town boundary with Compton Giffard outside the boundary added to Charles parish.)

So with interrupted trade, pirates, futile wars, starved mutinous armies, plague and religious strife, Plymouth had no cause to love King Charles. In the 1630s the town resisted the imposition of ship money less strongly than the rest of Devon; it could see the benefits of the resultant stronger Navy with convoys for merchantmen and the qualified success of the 1637 expedition against Sallee. But Plymouth's neighbours, the dowager Lady Drake of Buckland Abbey and Richard Strode of Plympton, brother of the imprisoned William, were the Devon Hampdens in the ship-money disputes.

And when Charles eventually recalled Parliament in 1640 it was dominated by the Plymouth neighbours. John Pym led the House, John Glanville was Speaker. When this Short Parliament was replaced by the Long Parliament, Strode was back from prison. When the King came to arrest the five members chiefly opposed to him, two of them were Pym and Strode. Their chief defender was John Maynard, MP for Totnes and Recorder of Plymouth. The five escaped, but from that moment Civil War was certain. There was no doubt where the sympathies of Plymouth lay.

CHAPTER 9

Civil War, 1642–46

When the Civil War did come in 1642 there was a great searching of men's minds; many who had opposed the King in Parliament drew the line at fighting against him. In Cornwall Lord Robartes, whose father had bought the title out of the fortunes the family had made as merchants of Truro, and built the great mansion that still stands at Lanhydrock, near Bodmin, stayed with Parliament. So did Francis Rous of Halton, John Pym's half-brother, and Sir Alexander Carew of Antony House, just across the Tamar from Plymouth. Otherwise the Cornish MPs and gentlemen were almost solidly for the King, led by Edward Hyde, the MP for Saltash who became the great Earl of Clarendon. Among them was Sir Nicholas Slanning of Maristow, son-in-law of James Bagge and one of Plymouth's MPs.

Of the country members and gentlemen on the Devon side of Plymouth the notable declarations for the King were the Champernownes of Modbury, John Glanville of Tavistock, John Harris of Radford and Robert Trelawny of Ham. Trelawny, Mayor of Plymouth in 1640, was still trading in the town. He had declared for the King when still a Plymouth member and had been removed from office and twice imprisoned for his views, but once free he began moving his ships quietly down to Falmouth. Plymouth, like most ports – in Devon, Exeter, Dartmouth and Barnstaple – declared for Parliament when the war began; Devon was in Parliament hands and Cornwall held by the King's men.

When Charles raised his standard at Nottingham in August 1642 he had already sent for the Governor of Plymouth, Sir Jacob Astley, to be his major-general of foot. The Plymouth fort and Drake's Island were without a commander and the mayor, Thomas Ceely, took both over without any protest from the garrison. Had the King left Astley as his commander in the west, who knows what different lines the war might have followed. But Parliament sent a distinguished soldier, Colonel Ruthven, later Lord Grey de Ruthven, to command at Plymouth, and young Sir Francis Drake (he succeeded his father in 1641) raised a regiment called the Plymouth Horse.

Sir Ralph Hopton commanded Cornwall for the King. In November he advanced on Exeter but, finding it too strong, fell back on Tavistock and moved against Plymouth, cutting off the town's water supply from Burrator. He drove in Ruthven's outposts and then, with 2,500 men, attacked from Plympton. But Ruthven held the narrow passage of Long Bridge for three hours and Hopton fell back.

Alarmed for Plymouth, Parliament sent Lord Robartes to command the west and raised three regiments of foot soldiers and 1,000 dragoons to defend the town. In December Ruthven successfully broke up a Royalist assembly at Modbury; then in January 1643 he advanced with the Plymouth force into Cornwall only to be badly mauled at Braddock Down, between Liskeard and Lostwithiel. The survivors fell back on Saltash but Hopton flung them back over the Tamar and Plymouth for the first time was closely besieged.

Under the Earl of Stamford, who with his Devon army had joined Ruthven in Cornwall, and the new mayor, Philip Francis, a hasty line of earthworks was built across the vital ridge north of the town, looking down on the mile-wide gap between the head of Stonehouse Creek at Pennycomequick and the head of Lipson Creek, where St Augustine's Church now stands. Five regiments sat round the town, but the Cornish would not cross the Tamar; without them the Royalists felt too weak to attack, and on 29 January 1643 unsuccessful attempts were made to arrange a local truce in a meeting at Ham House.

Parliament built up the Plymouth garrison by sea till it was estimated that there were 9,000 men in the town. The Royalists sat tight around, but their foraging upset the Devon countrymen who rose and attacked a concentration at Modbury again. As the defeated Royalists streamed into Plympton they found the main army on the move back to Tavistock; the Plymouth garrison had attacked to support the Devon men. Now a local truce was arranged that lasted from 28 February until 22 April.

But Parliament disapproved of these local arrangements, sent commissioners and reinforcements into Plymouth to stiffen the Committee of Devon, in the town since the debacle at Braddock

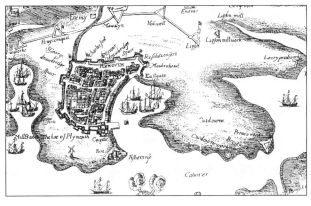

Detail from the contemporary siege map of 1643.

99

Down, and the day after the truce ended there were Plymouth regiments fighting between Lifton and Launceston, and in the advance into Cornwall which was broken in the Battle of Stratton on 16 May. Leaving light forces to watch Plymouth, the Cornishmen advanced across Devon to besiege Bristol, but they had overrun their strength.

Plymouth, left in peace through the summer of 1643, built up its defences. The Elizabethan walls, such as they were, had been allowed to deteriorate; even the gates had been removed in 1620. Now the walls were repaired and the gates rebuilt, but the true defence of the town had to be further out. The key was the line of earth-works already built and it was now strengthened with five triangular forts. Ditches were dug and the earth flung inside to make ram- parts, in turn topped with wooden stockades. Lipson Fort, roughly at the corner of Lipson Road and Queen's Road, covered the London road. Holywell Fort, at the crossroads by Greenbank Fire Station, dominated the second road; Maudlyn, on the site of the Blind Institution, controlled North Hill; Pennycomequick Fort, at the present North Cross roundabout, watched the Saltash road, and Eldad Fort, at the bottom of North Road, covered Millbridge. The only other ways into Plymouth then meant water crossings. There were two smaller forts in Stonehouse watching that waterfront, and two more at Prince Rock and Cattedown covering the Cattewater. An outlier, Fort Stamford, above Turnchapel, was meant to control the Mount Batten peninsula and the entrance to Sutton Harbour.

The siege was resumed in August 1643. There were 900 Royalist troops based on Plymstock and Prince Maurice advancing; Barnstaple, Bideford and Exeter were all captured. Sir Alexander Carew was in command of Drake's Island. He was suspected of communicating with the Royalists at Mount Edgcumbe and when the mayor went to arrest him on 19 August he found the garrison already holding its commander prisoner on the beach. Carew was sent to London by sea and executed for high treason. New Parliamentary soldiers took command of Plymouth, Colonel James Wardlaw and Colonel William Gould. They launched raids on the besiegers at Hooe and Roborough, but Prince Maurice had taken Dartmouth and was advancing on Plymouth, the only place still held by Parliament in Devon or Cornwall. Of Maurice's regiments 14 supported the 900 men already investing the town, billeted at Plymstock, Plympton, Buckland Monachorum, Tamerton and Cawsand. Royalist ships from Falmouth closed the sea approaches. For 17 days

Left: *Sir Alexander Carew.*

Royalists battered the isolated Fort Stamford and, after a heroic struggle, the men there had to yield; they were allowed to march out with colours flying, bag and baggage. A Royalist battery was set up which could bombard the Hoe. An Oreston battery had already closed the Cattewater, and with Stonehouse Creek closed by Mount Edgcumbe guns, Millbay had become for the first time in history the harbour of Plymouth.

It was a desperate situation. The bickering between townsmen and the imported military ceased, Colonel Gould took full command and all the beleaguered took a solemn vow and covenant 'to the utmost of my power faithfully to maintain and defend the towns of Plymouth and Stonehouse...'. Work parties brought in timber from close at hand to strengthen the defences; a covering force at Thorn Hill chased a Royalist patrol back to Crownhill on 11 November, but it was the last raid for a long time. The whole western army was tight round the town, with Prince Maurice setting up his headquarters at Widey Court, recently built by 'Yeoman Hele', of the newly rich legal family.

Then treason was found again. Ellis Carkeet, 'a malignant mariner', was arrested after trying to persuade the gunner at the Maudlyn to blow up his fort. Two of his accomplices. Henry Pitts, a wine merchant, and Moses Collins, a lawyer, fled to the enemy. They nearly brought the town down.

Three hours before daylight on Sunday, 3 December, they guided 400 Royalist musketeers across Lipson Creek to take by surprise a little fort at Laira Point, at the far end of Mount Gould Road. From Plymouth 150 horsemen and 300 musketeers streamed out to the rescue; they failed to dislodge the enemy and found Prince Maurice with his main force had advanced from Compton village around the head of Lipson Creek and, filing left, were moving up the northern slopes of Mount Gould. The rescue party charged the new threat without avail, and some Royalist cavalry broke through the disorganised defenders to reach the very walls of Plymouth. There they were all killed or captured and the main force of the garrison stood with their left flank resting on Lipson Fort. The Royalists held the Mount Gould peninsula; any retreat by the defenders would mean that the attack would be behind the fortified line.

For four hours the defence held. A small gun at what is now the top of Mount Gould Road worked havoc among the Royalist cavalry, and 60 musketeers moved along the southern slopes of Tothill to take the

Cavaliers in the rear. Then, at the sound of a drum, Gould led the advance. Maurice, fading forces behind him, began to pull back.

Retreat became a rout. The incoming tide was filling Lipson Creek and the Royalists barely extricated themselves. One body of 100 horsemen was trapped and nearly all captured or drowned in the tide; the total losses of the attackers are unknown, but the defenders had few casualties. Colonel Gould had one horse killed under him and another wounded; from that day the whole area has been called Mount Gould and a monument in Freedom Park marks the command post.

The Royalist cavalry who reached the inner defences of Plymouth were defeated under the walls of Fort Resolution. Archaeological excavations at Friary Park in 1991 revealed this fort, and it has been preserved amidst the new housing. It is the only point of the inner defences to have seen actual fighting.

Maurice tried, 17 days later, to break the defence line by night infiltration between the Maudlyn and Pennycomequick, and three bloody assaults were needed to dislodge this force. But by Christmas Day he had had enough, and moved his men back to winter quarters at Plympton and Tavistock. They drove all the cattle in the countryside before them and hoped to starve Plymouth out. But 'there came an infinite multitude of pilchards into the harbour, within the Barbican, which the people took up with great ease in baskets... such a circumstance never happened before'.

For the first six months of 1644 Plymouth built up its defences and sent foraging raids as far out as Roborough. Maurice moved his main force to attack Lyme Regis and a new commander, Sir Richard Grenville, took over. A grandson of the Grenville of the *Revenge*, he was a cruel and vicious soldier of fortune, known as 'Skellum' Grenville after a treacherous desertion of the Parliamentary cause. He despoiled the country houses of the Parliamentary gentry, from Lanhydrock to Buckland Abbey, stole their revenues and hanged their villagers. By April he had his main forces in the meadows between Plympton and Marsh Mills, with another force at St Budeaux.

But Plymouth was in good fettle. Morale and discipline had been raised to new heights under Colonel Gould, and after his death in spring 1644 his successor, Colonel Martin, kept up a vigorous offensive. On 11 May 1,500 men drove the Cavaliers out of Roborough and came back with 100 prisoners. Four days later an amphibious assault force landed at Cremyll, captured the peninsula from

The Sabbath Day Fight memorial in Freedom Park.

Millbrook to Maker, and set fire to Mount Edgcumbe House before pulling back.

Then in July the Earl of Essex, with half the Parliamentary main army, marched into Cornwall. The forces besieging Plymouth fell back before him, and Essex even called 2,500 men out of the Plymouth garrison into his army. But the King and Prince Maurice were on the heels of Essex; he was trapped and defeated between Fowey and Par, and the remnants of a shattered army took refuge in Plymouth.

Robartes, escaped from the Cornish chaos, resumed the Plymouth command, and eight ships of the Parliamentary navy under Vice-Admiral Batten were in the port. Fort Stamford had been retaken earlier and Admiral Batten had fortified the tip of the peninsula; it has been called Mount Batten ever since. Colonel Martin was buried in St Andrew's that October, like Gould before him; Plymouth took a heavy toll of its defenders.

The King reached Widey

Left: *Excavations at Friary Park, 1991, reveal the walls of Fort Resolution.*

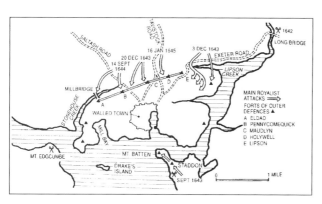

The Siege of Plymouth, showing the line of the main Royalist attacks on the town.

Widey Court before it was demolished in 1954. King Charles made this his headquarters during the siege.

Court on Tuesday, 9 September; his main army of 15,000 men and 28 'great guns' menaced the town. Each morning he rode down Tavistock Road with his staff and generals to be received on the southern slopes of Hartley Hill with much ceremony and saluting. 'Vapourings', the veterans of Plymouth called it, looking across from their defence line; Vapouring Hill stuck as a name and there is still a Vapron Road there. Did Charles remember that nearly 20 years before he had led an army up that hill from Plymouth for manoeuvres on Roborough Down?

He launched his attack the following Saturday. Lipson had been tried, and the Maudlyn; now it was a frontal attack on Pennycomequick, with a side thrust across Mill Bridge. The battle raged from dawn till nightfall; sailors from the fleet played a heroic part in the defence of the line, and it was never broken. Next morning Charles and Maurice rode away. Widey Court was pulled down between the wars, and all that remains of 'Our Court at Widey' are the lodge gates, now positioned at the northern end of the pedestrian way under the Manadon flyover.

Robartes was left facing Grenville. In October the garrison captured Millbrook and Saltash only for Grenville to retake them. Grenville kept up the pressure all that winter, even though plague and cold were filling Plympton St Mary churchyard with his men. In January 1645 he flung 6,000 men against the whole line of Plymouth's defences, concentrating on the main forts. He did capture the Maudlyn but it was retaken and the Royalists were cast back down the hill to Mutley Plain; they lost 300 men there alone. In February Grenville captured the ruins of Fort Stamford only to be turned out again. In March he

went off to the siege of Taunton, leaving 2,000 men facing Plymouth. Robartes too was recalled, a Committee of Defence taking control in Plymouth. By December, as the Royalist cause collapsed, so the garrison moved out, capturing St Budeaux and even Buckland Abbey. Col Sir Francis Drake with the Plymouth Horse was with the army that Fairfax and Cromwell were leading westward.

There was one last piece of cloak and dagger; Fairfax did not want to advance into Cornwall with the Royalist concentration at Mount Edgcumbe on his flank. He sent his chaplain, Hugh Peters (whose mother was a Treffry of Fowey), into Plymouth where Phillipa Coryton (the family is still at Pentillie) came in disguise to meet him. The two, fanatic Roundhead preacher and Royalist maiden, both disguised, made their way by boat and horse through the armies to Mount Edgcumbe and back to Fairfax, with the assurance that the Mount Edgcumbe men would not move.

Parliament recaptured Dartmouth on 18 January, and that day the last Royalist marched away from the Plymouth siege. Fairfax advanced to Bodmin, on 12 March the Cornish army surrendered and on 25 March Fairfax and Cromwell were welcomed into Plymouth; '300 pieces of ordnance were discharged to welcome them thither'.

Left: The title page of a tract published in 1645 describing an attack on Fort Stamford on 18 February the previous year.

A TRVE
RELATION
OF A
BRAVE DEFEAT
Given by the Forces in *Plimouth*, to
SKELLUM GREENVILE,

On Tuesday, the eighteenth of
February, 1644.

Written thence by a sure Hand to a speciall friend
in *London*, and confirmed by many that were
eye-witnesses of the same.

With the taking of one Lieutenant Colonell,
one Major, foure Captaines, foure Lieutenants,
two Ensignes, 92 Common Souldiers.

There were also taken about 300 Armes, good store of
Mattocks, Shovels and Faggots.

Published according to Order.

LONDON,
Printed by E. P. for *Francis Coles*, dwelling
in the Old Bayly. 1645.

CHAPTER 10

Commonwealth and Restoration, 1646–48

The resolution of Plymouth during its three years of siege may have been a vital factor in the final victory of Parliament, but it cost the town dear. St Andrew's parish registers show 3,000 deaths for the period, when a normal figure for the 46 months of war would have been 300. The town had suffered little physical damage but all its energies had gone into the struggle. For the last two years the Committee of Defence kept the town going by borrowing money, totalling from £2,000 to £5,000 a month, from the merchants, even the service leaders, against the next ship bringing in cash from Parliament. Even the funds of the town's charities were used. At the end of the war food was short and the soldiers' wages unpaid; it took two grants totalling £16,000 to clear the debts.

The countryside round had been stripped by the besieging forces. Plympton St Mary church registers show the death rate for the last three years of war up threefold; Leigham and Boringdon had been ransacked, Saltram damaged and all its gardens, orchards and woods cut down. George Bagge, already saddled with his father's debts, was a broken man, and disappears from view after 1654. Francis Drake retired from the command of the Plymouth Horse and set about putting Buckland Abbey and its ravaged estate in order; in 1650 he had to sell Werrington Park to Pay his debts.

Trade and the Navy

Plymouth, with this ravaged countryside around it, could take little comfort from the sea. The Newfoundland fisheries had kept alive during the war, at a much reduced scale. In 1652 there were only five Plymouth ships on the banks, and this the trade on which the port, ten years before, had been 'chiefly dependent'. The New England fishing had been

What was left of the Lambhay Victualling Yard before the 1930s demolition. It is now called Commercial Wharf.

taken over by the colonists before the war; thrown on their own resources during the war they had built their own ships and were carrying on their own trade, reaching down to Virginia, Maryland and the West Indies, taking what had been the growth area for Plymouth shipowners in the pre-war years. On top of that the remnants of the Royalist navy were at sea as privateers, with bases in Scilly and the Channel Islands until 1651. But Cromwell was building up the navy, which introduced a convoy system for merchantmen in 1649, crushed the Royalist privateers and within a few years cleared the Barbary pirates from the Channel.

Left: Robert Blake.

More seriously for our shipping trade, the Dutch had taken over much of our foreign carrying-trade during the Civil War. The Navigation Act of 1651, forbidding foreigners to trade with our colonies, provoked the first Dutch war in 1652. Plymouth became a naval base again under Captain Henry Hatsell, who had commanded Drake's Island in the latter years of the Siege. He eventually lived at Saltram, close to the repair yards at Turnchapel and Teat's Hill. A hulk was also anchored in the Cattewater to house shipwrights, and stores were set up. The old castle became a hospital after de Ruyter mauled Sir George Ayscue's fleet in mid-Channel and chased him back into Plymouth. Later a house was taken over as a hospital and in 1654 a victualling establishment was established at Lambhay.

Once peace was signed with the Dutch, Cromwell launched a Spanish war which made Jamaica an English colony, kept Plymouth busy and frequently brought Robert Blake (who had commanded Lyme Regis as a soldier during the war) into the port as an admiral. In 1657, after crushing a Spanish fleet off Santa Cruz and dealing with the Sallee Rovers in their home port, he anchored in Cawsand Bay to die before he could come ashore. His heart was buried in St Andrew's Church beside that of Frobisher.

Industry

Industry also was helped by the navy. In 1665 their agent paid Thomas Teate the ropelayer £880 for 20 tons of cordage and Daniel Barker £962 for cable yarn – large sums for those days. A little earlier Teate had been buying land beside Sutton Pool which is still called Teat's Hill, and the town's largest ropewalk survived there until nearly the end of the nineteenth century. Barker was to be twice mayor.

Apart from the work engendered by the navy, there are signs of growing local industry. A yarn market had long been held weekly in St Andrew's churchyard, where the spinners sold their yarn to the weavers. In 1653 the town built a proper Yarn

Market in Old Town Street to serve them, though subsequent rents suggest that it did not do as much business as was hoped. The term 'clothier' begins to crop up in local records; these were the capitalists of the trade who bought the finished products and often financed the spinners and weavers, who were small men working in their homes. Among those described as clothiers were new men of substance and members of old families, a Trelawny, and Harris of Manadon.

A new meat market, the Shambles, was also built down the middle of Old Town Street in 1657–58 with a Leather Hall above part of it. Here the tanners did business with the butchers and farmers; the manufacture of leather was the most important English industry after textiles and Plymouth had its share. The town seems to have had more than its share of brewers: indeed Captain Hatsell wished they could all be shipped to the West Indies, because their beer produced so much drunkenness.

Religion

The town was sufficiently recovered from the war to complete the building of Charles Church in 1657 (though the tower was only 20ft high) and to build a new grammar school within the Orphan's Aid in 1658. At the outbreak of the war the walls of Charles Church had reached roof height and it is thought that a canvas roof was improvised and the first services held there in 1643 by a Presbyterian chaplain to the garrison, Francis Porter. His communion table was in the nave and, to make it clear that this was a Puritan church with no altar, a door was built in the east wall. At the outbreak of war the town imprisoned the hated Dr Wilson of St Andrew's and sent him off to Portsmouth; on Wilson's death in 1643 the King named the lecturer Bedford as vicar. Plymouth then sent him packing by sea and appointed their own vicar, the saintly George Hughes. During the war all kinds of dissenters practised their religions freely but only the Baptists survived as a congregation. A Plymouth fuller, Abraham Cheare, whose father was tenant of one of the lower mills, became their pastor. In 1651 a meeting-house was built in the Pig Market, the later Bedford Street, now roughly the frontage of Dingle's store on Royal Parade.

When two Quaker missionaries arrived in 1654 they marched into both St Andrew's and the Baptist meeting-house to protest at the services being held. They caused an uproar, and two more Quakers who arrived the following year were arrested and sent for trial at Exeter. But a Society of Friends was estab-

The ruins of Charles Church during a service in 1991 to celebrate the fortieth anniversay of the wartime destruction of the church.

lished; they continued to protest in the older churches and neither fines nor imprisonment could check them. Arthur Cotton, a shopkeeper, and his wife Priscilla, and Nicholas Cole, a merchant, and his wife Mary, were early adherents, and the women made their protests and stood their imprisonment as much as the men. George Fox himself was in Plymouth in 1655 and there are prominent names among the Society's members: John Harris of Pennycross, John Light the clothier, and Elizabeth Trelawny, who became a regular correspondent with George Fox. For all their pacifism the Quakers brought a stormy atmosphere into Plymouth's religious life and in turn met much hostility from the other churches and the town leaders.

The Quaker unrest was paralleled by discontent in the countryside. The Royalist gentry, once they had settled the fines they had to pay for backing the losing side in the war, became restless. When the 'Sealed Knot' was formed in 1654 to coordinate the Cavalier efforts, they gave Sir John Grenville, son of the admirable Bevil and nephew of 'Skellum', the task of securing Plymouth as the first act in any rebellion. He actually found himself in gaol in Plymouth the following winter when the plans leaked out. They fizzled out in the abortive Penruddock uprising in the west in March 1655, when Plymouth hastily 'made up' the lines on North Hill, but the

leaders were executed and 70 of the rank and file transported from Plymouth to Barbados. The rule of the major-generals was extended to the west and General Desborough took over the western counties. He had served Cromwell in the west before and visited Plymouth. St Andrew's Church was lining pews for him and his wife, Cromwell's sister, in 1652. I n May 1659 Desborough was made Governor of Plymouth.

The Restoration

Cromwell was forced into the near-despotism of the rule of the major-generals not only by the old Royalist-Episcopalians on the Right, but by the new forces of the Left, the Levellers, Fifth Monarchy men, Quakers, Anabaptists and Ranters. The old Parliamentary-Puritan men of the Civil War were the middle party now, and alarmed as much by the new Left as by the old Right. Fears for the future grew when Cromwell died in 1658 and his unpromising son Richard became Protector. Many old Parliament men like Robartes in Cornwall and Sir Francis Drake and John Maynard in Devon preferred the idea of a king to that of a left-wing republic. Of similar mind was William Morice who had bought Werrington Park from Drake and early in 1660 became Governor of Plymouth. (Seven years later he bought the Keyham, or Stoke Damerel, estate from the Wise family.) Morice arranged the vital meeting between his north Devon neighbour, General Monck, and the emissary of the king-in-exile, John Grenville. As a result Monck played the vital part in bringing King Charles II back to the throne in 1660. Monck became Duke of Albemarle, Grenville the Earl of Bath, Morice the king's Secretary of State and a knight. Maynard, the king's serjeant-at-law, was also knighted and sat as MP for Plymouth almost constantly for the next 30 years. Morice was Plymouth's other MP, but in spite of his important part in the Restoration of Charles he retired into private life in 1668, saying that the king was debauching the nation.

Plymouth clearly had divided feelings about the Restoration, but the majority view preferred a king to the new Left. Charles was proclaimed in Plymouth 'with great tryumph, the Cunditts Runing two dayes with wyne'. Apart from political concern, Plymouth had not prospered in the latter days of the Commonwealth. The wars had hit normal trade, and though the needs of the fleet brought business, the bills were not paid. By January 1660 the agent-victualler in the port reported six ships in the Sound with starving crews, and six more expected. His credit was exhausted and no one could go into the streets without being pestered for money. Wages for the Navy were four years in arrears.

So Plymouth welcomed Charles II, but was aware of its past record in royal eyes. The £400 spent on a silver wine fountain for the king (it still has a proud place among the Crown Jewels in the Tower of London) was probably placatory, but its effect did not last long. In 1662 the Puritan mayor, William Allen, was removed from office along with six magistrates, 13 councillors and the town clerk. The new mayor, William Jennens, was a 'church and king' zealot and applied the 1662 Act of Uniformity with vigour. Francis Porter of Charles Church conformed and kept his place but George Hughes of St Andrew's and his lecturer, Thomas Martyn, were ejected and imprisoned on Drake's Island, to be released after a few months and forbidden to come within 20 miles of the town. Abraham Cheare was in and out of Plymouth and Exeter gaols for three years before he too finished up on the island, where he died in 1668. Drake's Island became a notorious state prison; among its sufferers were Colonel Lilburn, one of the judges of Charles I, and later General Lambert, who had tried to set up a republic in place of the king's restoration. Both died on the island.

But the Puritans' spirit was not easily quenched. Driven from the parish churches, they formed their own, meeting in secret in private houses. The Revd Nicholas Sherwill of the old Plymouth family was one leader, Obadiah Hughes, son of the ejected vicar of St Andrew's, another. There had been ejections from both Plympton churches, from Tamerton, Brixton, Ugborough and many other villages; some

Left: *The Hospital of Poor's Portion in Catherine Street, the Elizabethan workhouse demolished to make way for the 1870 guildhall.*

or these pastors now came into Plymouth regularly to minister to the Nonconformists. With the Declaration of Indulgence of 1672 five Nonconformist ministers emerged to be granted licences, and a number of meeting-houses were permitted. Sherwill led a congregation at the old town debtors' prison, now the gin distillery in Southside Street. Thomas Martyn, the ejected lecturer of St Andrew's, ministered in Green Street, near Charles Church. There was another congregation in Stonehouse, and the Baptists had survived, though their numbers were declining. The Quakers continued, though more quietly, mourning the death of some early leaders and the defection of others. They suffered most because they refused to hide, and met in the street if denied their meeting-house.

The pattern of persecution seems to vary with the government of the town. Jennens was mayor until November 1663 and he regularly had Presbyterians, Baptists and Quakers in court before him. The persecution kept up until 1665, when even Sherwill had two months in gaol. After 1666 nonconformity 'seems to be winked at', to quote R.N. Worth, apart from a bad spell in 1669 when Jennens had some influence with the mayor. The Act of Indulgence brought real relief in 1672, and though it was soon repealed, Plymouth paid no apparent attention and the Nonconformists were left with far more liberty than the law permitted. When Jennens stood for Parliament in 1676 the first vote, that of the freemen, was so strong against him that he retired.

With the Toleration Act of 1689 came final freedom, and by 1704 the Southside Street congregation built a chapel in Batter Street. The later chapel buildings on this site are now part of the Virginia House Settlement. In 1689 the Baptists were still in the Pig Market. They had no pastor from the death of Cheare until 1689, when 66 members signed an invitation to a new minister. The Quakers, who had leased a house in Bilbury Street since 1675, bought the property in 1703 and were there with various rebuildings until 1918. The last building ended its days as a labour exchange and was demolished to make way for Bretonside bus station.

One group who had enjoyed this freedom before the Toleration Act were the Huguenots, French Protestants fleeing from Catholic persecution. Some

Batter Street Chapel, built for the Presbyterians in 1705 and now part of Virginia House.

40 or 50 reached Plymouth in 1681 and settled in both Plymouth and Stonehouse. The majority could accept the Anglican services of the day and at first both communities shared St George's Church, Stonehouse, a chapel of ease of St Andrew's. But the French communities grew and the Plymouth group were meeting in the old Marshalsea in Southside Street by 1706, and in 1710 built their own chapel in How Street. About 1690 the Edgcumbes found the Stonehouse community a chapel in Edgcumbe Street, and there was a third, Calvinistic, meeting-house for them in Plymouth. The total community seems to have grown to about 700. Some were landowners, some very poor, but they found ways of earning a living. A French crew from Stonehouse took a Plymouth ship to Barbados in 1691. Two started the first paper mill in Plymouth as early as 1710. But they were gradually assimilated into local life, and their anglicised names are still common in the city.

Charles Church was finally consecrated by the Bishop of Exeter in 1665, and Porter inducted. But that door in the east wall was walled up and the altar moved to the east end of the sanctuary. The walling-up is quite clear in the ruins that survived the Second World War, and in spite of this lapse the church Plymouth built for its Puritan conscience stayed a bastion of low churchmanship into living memory.

Post-Restoration Trade

Plymouth's maritime trade, which in common with that of the whole country picked up slowly during the Commonwealth, enjoyed 30 years of rapid expansion after the Restoration. It also changed direction. London, and to a lesser degree Exeter, merchants had moved into the Newfoundland fisheries with new methods, planting colonies of fishermen and sending out 'sac' boats with supplies and bringing back the fish. The Plymouth fishing fleet built up to 20 ships by 1677 and 12 were working on the sac principle, but the method took much capital which they had to borrow, and the interest swallowed what profit they made. Plymouth had nearly abandoned Newfoundland by 1699, and though there was a revival in the eighteenth century it was short-lived. Plymouth vessels bought Newfoundland cod for south European markets until the end of the sailing ship era, but from the early-eighteenth century this fishing was never a major Plymouth concern.

The new business was with the West Indies and the southern mainland colonies. The Virginia tobacco trade was at first shared by Barnstaple, Bideford, Exeter and Plymouth. The West Indian islands,

of which Barbados was the first to develop, started with tobacco but switched to sugar, with coffee, cocoa, cotton and spices also in the smaller islands. They were fed by New England but the planters, in boom conditions, were getting luxuries, manufactures and cloth from England: such cargoes were in small parcels so as not to swamp the small markets.

During the war years convoys escorted by warships sailed from Plymouth to the Americas and the Mediterranean, and up-Channel to the Downs. There were 56 ships in a 1666 convoy to Virginia and Barbados: a 1672 letter mentions 'the Straits fleet' waiting in the Cattewater for the weather. Customs returns for 1672 and 1676 show Plymouth in sixth place among English ports, with London roughly double all the outports put together, and then Bristol Hull, Dover, Exeter and Plymouth following in order; by 1679 and again in 1681 Plymouth was in fifth place. In the colonial trade alone she was outstripping Exeter and all the western ports by 1692, with 21 ships in the trade. Even Bristol only had 55. Exeter was sending serges by sea to Plymouth for export to the colonies, Spain, Portugal and Italy. Plymouth was the fourth English port for the Spanish and Portuguese ports in 1686, with 32 inbound ships and 42 out.

The West Indian links went beyond trading. In 1651 Francis Drake's brother-in-law, Charles Pym, went to look after the family estates in Nevis and Antigua; he was in Barbados in 1652 when the English fleet arrived, was one of the commissioners who surrendered the island to Parliament (it had been a Royalist stronghold), and in the reign of Charles II became a member of the Council for Foreign Plantations. George Bagge, brother of the Bottomless Bagge, turns up in 1667 looking for admission as a Poor Knight of Windsor (a military charity); he had been in Barbados. In his 1669 will Justinian Peard, Mayor of Plymouth in the last year of the Siege, mentions his interest in a plantation in Barbados. Peard was a North Devon man but he made enough money to rent what is now called the Merchant's House in St Andrew's Street, then his own town house in Notte Street, and eventually to buy Cann House, Tamerton Foliot, as well. He was one of the magistrates removed from office after the Restoration; excluded with him was John Paige, because he had settled in Barbados. A Quaker meeting in 1677 was addressed by 'Katharine Norton, widow, late of Barbadoes'.

Count Magalotti, who arrived in Plymouth in 1669 in the court of that

Left: *the 1586 Custom House on the Parade.*

The Parade; the top end of this creek of Sutton Harbour was reclaimed in 1692 and originally called the New Quay. Before that the buildings either side stood close to the sea; the Elizabethan Custom House still survives.

late Medici prince of Florence, Cosimo III, Grand Duke of Tuscany, wrote:

The life of the city is navigation. The inhabitants export lead and tin in greater quantities than any other article, and with these they go to the Canaries and to the Western Islands. To Barbadoes, in the New World, and in every part of Europe, they act as carriers conveying merchandize from place to place at great profit to themselves. Hence it is that, in Plymouth, only women and boys are to be seen; the greater part of the men living at sea.

He described how well supplied the town was, with all the necessaries and 'articles that administer to luxury and pleasure'. The town accounts tell the story: nearly £300 in 1666 to rebuild the Guildhall; nearly £100 in 1692 to build 'New Quay' – the Parade – and repair all the other quays; streets improved; exchanges for the comfort of merchants built on the Parade and the Barbican. John Lanyon left £2,000 in 1674 for the poor, which, with the Hele bequest of £500 some 30 years before, founded Hele and Lanyon's School.

The Royal Citadel

Lanyon, a Cornish Royalist, had been appointed naval agent in Plymouth when Hatsell – a Commonwealth officer – was dismissed at the Restoration. In 1662 the Naval Board ordered the building of 'yards

and buildings' at Plymouth when a fresh Dutch war was imminent, but in the event the war was concentrated in the North Sea and eastern Channel, and Sheerness Dockyard was built instead. In this 1664–68 conflict Plymouth had care of wounded seamen and prisoners of war, probably at Coxside, but Charles's mind was turning to coast defences rather than ships at sea; he wanted a standing army. So in 1665 the commission was issued which led to the building of the Royal Citadel on Plymouth Hoe. Originally, a self-contained conventional fort of the period was planned west of Drake's fort, with five bastions in the best Vauban style. Later the two eastern bastions were scrapped and the walls extended to take in Drake's fort, the old walls being built up to the new standard. A number of granite doorways from the old fort were used in the new building, and these, with the irregular outline of the eastern end, alone remain of the Drake fort. Sir Bernard de Gomme was the engineer and met some criticism over his unorthodoxy. Samuel Pepys, in 1683, looking over the Citadel with a rival military engineer, wrote that 'De Gomme hath built very sillily'. But the new structure mounted 152 guns as against the old fort's 67. It is still one of the greatest fortresses of the period remaining in Britain, and the gateway, attributed to Thomas Fitz, one of the nation's finest examples of baroque architecture.

The foundation stone, inscribed 'Jo Earle of Bathe 1666', still faces the Hoe, and the walls were at an average height of 20ft in 1667. Twice that summer de

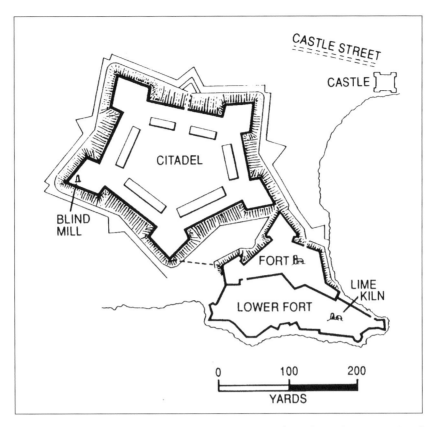

Sketch plan of the Citadel. Sir Bernard de Gomme first planned a conventional five-pointed star-shaped Citadel for Plymouth Hoe; later he amended it to embrace Drake's fort. Note the medieval castle with its four towers.

The Citadel Gate.

(A DRAWING BY C.E. ELDRED, PUBLISHED IN 1901)

mayor and Sir Jonathan Trelawny went aboard the flagship amid much exchange of salutes. De Ruyter was back again in the Sound just after peace was declared. This was the year after the Dutch had towed the cream of our fleet out of the Medway; that they made no attempt to tamper with Plymouth shows their respect even for the half-built Citadel.

Since its completion no enemy fleet has come into Plymouth Sound. The idea that it was built to cow a rebellious town was no doubt current in Plymouth, and the Magalotti account of 1669 quotes it, but both the previous forts on Plymouth Hoe had all-round defence, and they had not been built by suspicious monarchs.

The king himself was in Plymouth in 1671 with the Dukes of York and Monmouth to inspect progress. The king and his brother came again in 1676, this time with Samuel Pepys, the Secretary of the Navy, and on both visits inspections were made of the Cattewater and the Hamoaze, to see potential sites for the projected dockyard. But still no more was done.

The Last of the Stuarts

Ruyter anchored in the Sound with a fleet of 30 Dutch ships, but each time kept well out from the Hoe. On the second visit the Earl of Bath sent out a flag of truce to say that the war was nearly over; the

Though Charles might make flattering speeches in Plymouth, kiss merchant Alien's pretty young wife and touch for the king's evil, and though the corporation might make him costly presents, he did not have the town's love. His first act had been to pack the town council with his supporters. Within a couple of years there was a new town clerk, Edward Pollexfen of Kitley, near Yealmpton, who had been a stout Parliament man in the wars, a man who by the 1680s (when the terms Whig and Tory came into use) could be called a moderate Whig. He retired to Kitley in 1699 (his daughter Ann married William Bastard and the family is still there); his successor, Robert Berry, was another Whig. There were also devoted Tories like James Yonge. He learnt to be a surgeon in the Navy, retired to his native Plymouth in 1670 to start in private practice and be surgeon to the little naval hospital, became a member of the council and eventually mayor. His diary gives a lively picture of the time, full of loyal sentiments with the Commonwealth years marked by a black mourning band which ends opposite the entry 'Cromwell yᵉ great Rebell, went to yᵉ devill in a tempest'. His family is still at Puslinch, looking across the Yealm to the Pollexfen descendants at Kitley.

For much of the rest of this century the parties seem to be about equally balanced in the council. When there was a dispute over a new vicar for St Andrew's in 1679 the two parties reached deadlock and the bishop put his man in, which 'caused great Animositeys'. There were things which upset both sides, like an early lawsuit. The Duchy of Cornwall owned the bed of Sutton Harbour, heart of the town's activity and wealth. It had always been leased to the town; early in the reign of Charles II it was leased to a Cornish cavalier and the ensuing lawsuit was not only lost by Plymouth but cost them some £2,500. It affected the ownership of all the quays, warehouses and private houses which the Plymouth merchants had been building out into the harbour for centuries, an activity which had speeded up with the new shipping boom. The Royal Citadel too spread over 41 acres of the Hoe, which the town regarded as its own property. When the outworks reached into private property in 1679 payments was made, but the town land was just stolen. The royal visits were another drain on the town's purses.

The parish churches also had been forced to use services of a style forgotten for 20 years; it was an offence not to attend, and early in the reign the Puritan conventicles were harrassed and oppressed. But the underground churches were never suppressed, though in a small town they cannot have been so very secret. Indeed, in many mercantile towns the laws were increasingly ignored as Charles's reign wore on, and public opinion increasingly turned against him. There is a gauge of Plymouth's attitude after the Rye House Plot of 1683; Monmouth, who was to have been put on the throne, fled to Holland, other leaders were executed or killed themselves, but two, Lord and Lady Landsdowne, took refuge in Plymouth.

King Charles, having successfully replaced the London Whigs by his own men, turned his attention to the provincial towns in 1683, and Plymouth was among the first. Only five aldermen voted against surrendering their charter; old Serjeant Maynard, still MP for the town and recorder, tried to stiffen resistance, but Lord Chief Justice Jefferys, on assize in the west, advised them otherwise. When a new charter was obtained the following year (two members of the deputation died in London) it was met at Ridgeway, Plympton, with much celebration and ceremony. The king appointed in his charter all the officers, aldermen and councillors. But there had been two Whigs in the deputation; there were Whigs even among the men named by the king, and they were soon back in their old power-sharing position.

Maynard was replaced as recorder by the Earl of Bath, but in practice Pollexfen served for him.

The accession of King James II was sharply followed by the Monmouth Rebellion. Plymouth was not directly affected, but the method of its suppression did not go unnoticed. Within six months a group of Quakers from Plymouth and Stonehouse emigrated in the *Desire* to William Penn's new Quaker colony of Pennsylvania, where they planned to set up a woollen manufactory. James Fox, one of the leaders, was a member of the family prominent among West Country Friends ever since. They were soon to move into Philadelphia, but their original settlement keeps the name of Plymouth Meeting to the present day.

James also looked at the Plymouth charter, and the aid of the Earl of Bath was enlisted by the town. The earl swore that the town 'is now become as loyall as the garrison, which is no small reformation', and the 1684 charter survived. But the new king was rapidly alienating the Tories, and the Whigs had never wanted this Catholic king. When William of Orange landed at Brixham in 1688 his fleet came round to Plymouth. The Earl of Bath, in spite of his long allegiance to the Stuart cause, surrendered the Citadel and arrested the loyalist Earl of Huntingdon, commander of the regiment in garrison. The troops declared for William of Orange. Plymouth was the first town in England to proclaim William and Mary, and the Black Book, the official civic record, has the entry, 'God wrought a wonderfull deliverance in these Kingdomes in rescuing us from Popery and Slavery'.

✦ CHAPTER 11 ✦

Plymouth Dock, 1688–1750

The accession of William and Mary meant the completion of the English Revolution that had begun with the Civil War. They were constitutional monarchs, invited to the throne by Parliament through whom they were to rule. They also inherited from Cromwell and the later Stuarts a professional Army and Navy. No longer would England fight her wars at sea by hiring or commandeering private ships; now there was a state-owned fleet manned by regular officers and seamen, paid by Parliamentary vote.

Since Commonwealth days the naval wars had been with the Dutch, over trade, and mainly fought in the eastern Channel where the existing dockyards, from Deptford to Portsmouth, could serve the Navy. The main need for a western port had been as a convoy base for the growing Atlantic and Mediterranean trades, for repairing warships and refitting prizes.

Cromwell had established the hulk in the Cattewater; ten years later the Navy Board ordered the construction of yards and buildings at Plymouth, and the sale of the hulk. In December 1663 it was 'cried by the bellman according to custom, and put to the candle at £100, but no one would bid a penny'. No dock was built either, so the hulk was repaired, and in 1665 converted at least two Dutch prizes into English men-of-war. A map of that year shows the area between the entrance to Hooe Lake and Turnchapel marked 'the King's land fitting for a dock' and by 1667 the beaches there, and in front of the ropewalk on Teat's Hill, were being used to careen and repair naval ships.

But there was still no dock by the time William came to the throne. The Dutch wars were over, and while the Dutch had gone on fighting the French, we had taken back their maritime trade. William was the arch-enemy of the French and they now turned on us, aiming to restore the Stuarts. The naval harbour which Richelieu had built at Cherbourg 50 years before and Colbert had improved was fortified by Vauban in 1680–88. In 1688 too Louis XIV began building a great dockyard at Brest: England more than ever had need of a western base to cover these French arsenals.

After some debate in which Exmouth, Torbay, Dartmouth, Bideford, the Cattewater (based on Turnchapel) and the Hamoaze were all considered, the Admiralty decided on the Cattewater. It wanted a stone dock (all earlier English docks were of wood) but no one could be found at Plymouth to under-

take such a task. Ideas changed again, and when, in December 1690, a contract was given to Robert Waters of Portsmouth to build a stone dock, the site was fixed at Point Froward, on the eastern side of the Hamoaze. The final decision was urged by Edward Drummer, Surveyor to the Navy, who planned and supervised the work and eventually increased the size of the dock to be able to take first-rate ships and not just cruisers, as originally planned.

A naval dockyard on the Hamoaze had originally been suggested by Walter Ralegh. Charles I had considered Saltash and his naval agent, Bagge, inspected a site with two Plymouth elders. In 1671 Charles II, with his brother James and Samuel Pepys, inspected all possible sites by boat – Sutton Harbour (where naval ships had been repaired alongside Smart's Quay, where the Fish Market now is), the Cattewater and the Hamoaze. The latter site had its disadvantages, as a 1694 progress reports makes clear:

The passage into the River is very crowded, the Current false by many Ecldyes, the tides on Springs rapid, the Soundings fowle, the Shores Dreadful, and the ready bringing in and carrying out of Shipps, too much commanded by the Course of the Westerne Winds.

But, goes on the same report, these disadvantages made it equally difficult for the enemy to attack the yard, which it finally called 'this supereminent treasure of the nation'. Buoys were already being laid to mark the Cremyll narrows, and pilots organised; a report four years later showed Plymouth in

Turnchapel, once thought of as the site for Plymouth Dock. Turnchapel Wharf, in the foreground, is now occupied by the Ministry of Defence. There is now a yacht marina in front of the village and houses fill the clifftop field.

money terms as second only in value to Portsmouth among the English dockyards.

A good naval base required not only a sheltered dockyard but an anchorage whence ships could proceed to sea swiftly; Portsmouth had the advantage in the Solent over Plymouth Sound, disliked by every admiral from Blake onwards, until the Breakwater was built, as being too exposed. Still, Plymouth was the best choice in the west. Apart from a long record of supporting fleets with water, victualling and ship repairs, it now had the Citadel for its better defence, and was still the safest harbour. A breakwater had already been talked of in Torbay but there was no population to support a dockyard. Dartmouth was too dangerous an entrance in bad weather, and the Cornish ports seem not to have been thought of; Fowey was no healthier than Dartmouth and the Fal estuary too remote from London.

The First Yard

Sir Nicholas Morice, son of the Restoration Secretary of State, owned the chosen site, but he was only 13 and his trustees would not sell. With difficulty they were persuaded to move from a one-year to a seven-year lease, but Nicholas, when he came of age, remained difficult, 'the greatest Jew in these parts'. It was said that he would not sell land for less than six times its normal price, so the leases continued. The land passed to the St Aubyn family through marriage in 1749, and though some later extensions were bought by the Admiralty, the Crown did not finally become freeholders instead of leaseholders of all the dockyard until 1857.

Waters began work in 1691. Point Froward, the site of the original yard, can still be identified from a boat, the way most people see the modern dockyard. One cruises past Mutton Cove, the statue of King William IV and the covered building slip and then the waterfront turns sharply from north-east to north. That knuckle was Point Froward, and just north of it a small cove was enlarged to make a wet dock and from the top of the dock a dry dock was cut out of the rocky ground. The rocky headland was levelled and the stone from the excavations and the levelling of the point used to build a flat area out into the stream north of the dock, with a sea-wall giving deep-water berthing and two building slips. In 1693 Richard Annet contracted to erect the buildings. A row of 13 officers' houses were set on a terrace looking over the dock, a large storehouse built on the flattened Point Froward and a roofed ropehouse 1,056ft long ran back from the storehouse, at right-angles to the waterfront. Various other storehouses and workshops were erected and when complete the Navy had its most modern yard. A first-rater could be taken into the dry dock and two into the wet dock, while the great storehouse held all stores and equipment for 40 ships of the line.

A wall enclosed the whole on the landward side by 1696. Then in 1727 a marshy area south of Point Froward was leased, bringing the total yard area to 54 acres. A mud dock which dried at low tide and a mast pond were made in the new area, and the recovered ground used for storing timber. A new dry dock was built in 1727 north of No. 1 Dock, the new No. 2 being a peculiar double dock, with one basin opening out of the other, but capable of taking two ships at once. No. 1 Dock took its first ship, the *Weymouth*, in June 1695. The yard had launched its first ships the year before, the little 'advice boats' *Postboy* and *Messenger*. The first, *Postboy*, launched in April, was

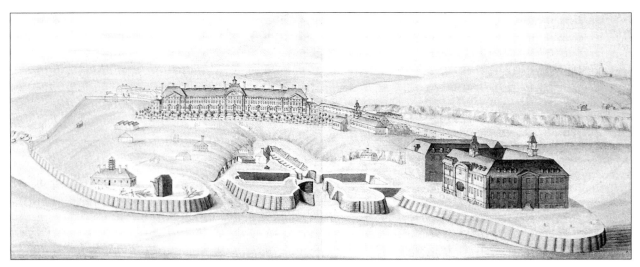

'A view of His Majesty's Dock at Plymouth' from a survey of the Harbours and Dockyards of England. In the centre is the square wet dock with the single dry dock behind it. To the left is a double-wheeled crane and the smiths' shop, to the right is the 'Great Square Store House' with the hemp house behind and the ropewalk running along the southern boundary. Behind the Docks is the terrace of officers' houses. The artist has shown private houses behind the dockyard gate at the top, although it is generally believed that the first houses were built in 1700, running outside the left-hand wall down to North Corner.

unlucky, captured by the French before 1694 was out. Both were probably built from the spare timber from the fourth-rate *Anglesea*, built (probably in the Cattewater) at the same time.

Supporting Services

The Ordnance Board rented the northern area of the yard in 1696 as a gunwharf, from which to supply ships with guns, powder and shot. By 1708, when the Navy presumably wanted more room, the gun wharf moved to Mount Wise, but in 1719 yet another site was leased and a gunwharf built to the designs of the celebrated John Vanbrugh, then in Crown service. The Gun Wharf and many of the buildings survive as the Morice Yard. Vanburgh's buildings are justly renowned, but the earlier dockyard buildings made an impressive pile, as the original drawings show. Most have been replaced over the years in the natural course of development, and the Terrace built for the officers was destroyed in the Second World War bombing, except for the northern end. One side-effect of the importation into the area of national architects and new techniques was the introduction of brick, hitherto almost unknown, into Plymouth building, and much more sophisticated architecture, particularly in the country houses built by the Plymouth wealthy after this time. Plympton House (1720) and Puslinch, built near Yealmpton in about 1726, illustrate the use of brick and the new elegance.

The Victualling Commissioners, since they were appointed in 1654, had rented storehouses first at Lambhay and then at Coxside, in Sutton Pool. In 1705 they built a Victualling Office at Lambhay, in the shelter and protection of the Citadel, though the King's Bakehouse remained at Coxside until replaced by a new bakehouse at Lambhay in 1750. Not that any of their establishments had a good reputation. The first warship built in the dockyard, the 50-rater *Looe*, joined the Navy in 1696 and was sent to cruise

to the westward. Her provisions turned bad; she made for an Irish port to revictual and on leaving struck a rock and was lost.

The 'Commissioners for Sick and Wounded Seamen, and the Exchange of Prisoners of War' also needed premises; by 1695 they had converted the old tidal mills at Millbay into a prison for 300 men. The sick who had been accommodated in Plymouth boarding houses (whose owners were also crimps, supplying seamen to merchantmen and press gangs), or at one time in the old castle, were by 1690 in 'Plymouth Hospital', a building just south of the present Derry's Cross roundabout but then in open country. Even there they were complaining of ill-treatment and they continued to be billeted on the crimps or houses in converted storehouses, including some at Coxside, for another half-century and more.

In 1693 the first English chart of Plymouth Sound was published in *Great Britain's Coasting Pilot*, the work of Captain Greenvile Collins, who had been appointed Hydrographer to the Navy by Charles II in 1682. Apart from the main harbour plan, there is a

This 1854 scene of cleaning cannon balls in the Gun Wharf could have been matched at any time in its history.

Above left: The first Eddystone lighthouse, started by Winstanley in 1696, nearly 120ft high; *above centre:* Rudyerd's 1706 lighthouse, 92ft high; *above right:* Smeaton's 1756 lighthouse, 72ft, with Douglas's 1878 tower, 132ft.

second of the Sound inset in the general Channel chart; the only other inset is of Portsmouth. In 1696 Henry Winstanley began building the first Eddystone Lighthouse, the first rock lighthouse in the world. Because of the French war a guardship constantly protected the men but, while she was away for a spell in 1697, Winstanley and his workmen were taken prisoner by a French privateer. They were all back within a month, Louis XIV sending them home with the comment that he was at war with England, not mankind. But in the great storm of 1703 Winstanley and his lighthouse were swept away. John Rudyerd built the second lighthouse in 1706–09 and this survived until destroyed by fire in 1755. Both these lighthouses were privately owned, the proprietors receiving the light dues collected by the customs officers.

The Officers and Men

In command of the yard was a Commissioner of the Admiralty, who in theory ranked with his brother commissioners in London. He had the central house in the Terrace, which looked down on the new dock, and the pecking order of his subordinate officers is shown by the ranging of their houses in the Terrace. On his right, in order, he had the Master Shipwright the Master Attendant (secretary), the Clerk of the Survey (civil engineer), the Shipwright Attendant the Master Caulker and the Chirugeon (medical officer). On his left were the Clerk of the Cheque (accountant), Clerk of the Stores, Clerk of the Ropery, Master Ropemaker, Master Mastmaker and the Boatswain of the Yard.

The commissioners were serving naval officers posted to Plymouth. The first master shipwright, Elias Waff, was transferred from Portsmouth and it would be reasonable to expect a nucleus of dockyard officers and trained men to be appointed from other dockyards, were it not that the hulk had been at work in the Cattewater on and off for nearly 40 years, and must have built up its own labour force. It is other-

wise hard to explain why Plymouth Dock should have had 69 shipwrights and caulkers and 40 workmen and boys on its books in 1690 when not a stone had been laid in Hamoaze. It seems more likely that these were the men of the hulk, living with their families either in Turnchapel or Plymouth. Certainly a hulk was moved into the Hamoaze in 1689 and two other hulks, old French prizes, were brought down-Channel to serve as living quarters. But the transfer from the Cattewater was not completed until 1696.

A study of Stoke Damerel marriage registers for 1690–1715 shows that well over half the extra-parochial people getting married were from Plymouth and the neighbouring parts of Devon and Cornwall, a few from Chatham and Portsmouth, the other naval yards, and the rest from ports between Northumberland and Falmouth, with London most numerous. Many of these would be sailors in port, rather than settlers, but the evidence suggests that the new town which grew up around the dockyard drew mainly on Plymouth for its people, with the local immigration which had always fed Plymouth plus some skilled men from other dockyard and mercantile ports.

The New Town

Men are not going to live aboard hulks if they can avoid it, and there are petitions in 1692 and again in 1697 asking for houses nearer the work. The January 1697 letter writes of:

...the difficulties which our workmen undergo, by living too far from their business... of very great prejudice to his Majesty's service and a fatigue to them almost intolerable ... this winter seems to have made all our avenues and passes thereto much more rotten and troublesome...

In 1695 Celia Fiennes went from Plymouth to Dock by boat, 'the nearest way'. It was a two-mile walk from Plymouth, either by way of the ferry at Stonehouse or across Mill Bridge, for a day's work

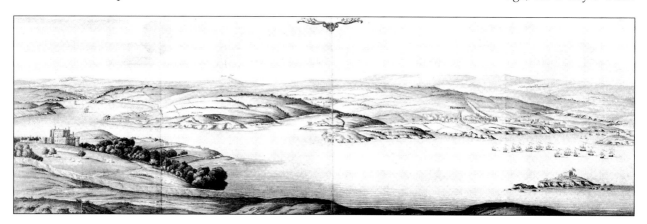

'A view of Plymouth Sound and ye River Hamouze and Catwater taken from ye rising ground above Mount Edgcomb... delineated 1697' by Edward Dummer, at the time supervising the building of the Dockyard, visible right of Mount Edgcumbe House.

which in winter was 6a.m. to 6p.m., in summer sunrise to sunset, with half an hour for breakfast and one and a half hours for lunch.

But not until 1700 would the Morice trustees part with any land for housing, and again it was on lease-hold. The first house was at North Corner and then Cornwall Street stretched up, parallel with the north wall of the yard. By 1712 there were 318 men employed and by 1733 Plymouth Dock, as the new town was called, had 3,000 people. Because of the Cornwall Street development the Gun Wharf was separate from the yard. So the new town occupied a narrow strip running up from the waterfront between the two walls – a corridor which survives – and then gradually filled a gridiron pattern of streets of which Fore Street, leading from the yard gates, was the main axis and the furthest south. By the 1750s the workforce had risen to 1,000 and the town had spread north to Morice Square, east to the top of Fore Street and south by another couple of parallel streets. Daniel Defoe in 1724 wrote of the handsome houses of the yard officers and called the town streets spacious, as did another traveller, the Revd S. Shaw, in 1788. But, he writes:

... as the inhabitants here are chiefly mechanics, &c, belonging to the docks, the houses are slightly built either of plaster or slate stone [he meant slate-hung]... *and will not bear a minute inspection, but have a good effect at a distance.*

Plymouth Dock, in fact, was a working-class town. Within 50 years it grew from nothing to having nearly half as many people as its older neighbour.

The Parish Church, Stoke Damerel, was three-quarters of a mile from the town, a lonely country church in the fields. Apart from the distance it could not cope with its suddenly swelling parish, though a north aisle was added about 1730 through the efforts of Robert Young, a clerk of the dockyard. In the 1740s both Whitfield and John Wesley preached at Dock in the open air a number of times. Though they attracted followers they were given rough receptions and there were no dissenting chapels until the second half of the century. There were no schools, no charities and the market was in temporary wooden shambles outside the yard gates. According to Defoe there was a good cheap market at Saltash and people went there to shop 'by the town boat' rather than walk to Plymouth.

Plymouth Dock was outside the boundaries of Plymouth and was ruled by the county magistrates sitting in quarter session at Exeter. Magistrates living near the town would have conducted petty sessions for minor crime. The lord of the manor had his court. Other local government was in the hands of the parish vestry of Stoke Damerel, which seems first to have levied a poor rate in 1727.

Wages were small, ranging from 2s.1d. a day for shipwrights and caulkers down to 1s.1d. a day for labourers, but there was overtime, $7\frac{1}{2}$d. a 'tide' ($1\frac{1}{2}$ hours) or 2s.1d. for a 'night' (five hours). In 1693 a churchwarden put the master shipwright and several of his men into the spiritual court for working on fast days; a report to the Admiralty said that the men were so frightened that they would not work Sundays or holidays, a common dockyard practice, apparently, and such a refusal had never been known before.

Men paid such wages could not afford to build their own houses and the developers of the new town seem at first to have been the yard officers, whose pay ranged from £100 a year for the master ship-wright down to £36 for the boatswain. The clerk of the cheque in 1706 owned 42 houses, and of these 13 were beer shops. Seeing that the porter's lodge inside the yard gates also had a beer shop, part of the porter's 'perks', it is clear that there was one facility the new town did not lack.

What made the men even more poor was the system of paying; for fear of highwaymen, a frigate brought the money from London once a quarter for the wages to be made up. So every three months Dock had a spree, but in the intervening months the families ran up debts with shops and taverns whose keepers would be as alert to the frigate's arrival as their customers.

Corruption

The one 'perk' that all yardees shared was the right to chips, in theory the waste ends of woods. In practice these chips grew so large that a size limit of 3ft was placed on them; it is said that most of the woodwork in the old houses of Devonport, stairs and all, is based on 2ft 11in. timbers. Apart from these chips – and it was estimated at one time that enough wood went out of the yard in a month to build a sloop – there was straight pilfering of every kind of store. For the men it was a case of what they could smuggle out; for the officers it was a more complicated busi-ness of good stores being condemned or receipts signed with suppliers for goods that went other ways. It would not be surprising if the houses of early Dock were largely built out of yard stores. So much money could be made that large sums were paid to secure quite minor posts in the yard that offered opportunities for swindling. Another abuse was the overtime claimed: a 1710 clerk was paid for a quarter in which he apparently had only two hours off in every 240.

The Government was partly to blame for the frauds, through its tardy payment to the officers. Lanyon, for instance, Charles II's agent in Plymouth, complained at one time to Pepys that he was in great straits, for the government owed him nearly £8,000 which he had laid out on its behalf. Waters, the contractor who built the yard, did some £60,000 worth of work, was always kept waiting for payment and then received credit notes which he could only cash on the excise at heavy discounts.

Yet the agents seem not to have fared too badly. Bagge built Saltram House out of his years of office, though he lost it when found out. Captain Hatsell, Cromwell's agent in 1652, was quite soon able to afford to live at Saltram and was Mayor of Plympton in 1658. After the Restoration he was in custody in Exeter on rather vague charges, but in 1662 he was back and doing naval business, still living at Saltram and a trustee of the new Plympton Grammar School.

John Lanyon, a Royalist Army engineer, had petitioned the king in 1661 for a job, pleading sadly reduced circumstances because of his loyalty. He was made naval agent at Plymouth and in 1664, with two other merchants of the town, offered Pepys £300 a year if he got them the contract to victual the garrison at Tangier. Pepys obliged, and got his money. In 1665 Lanyon was accused of dishonesty in his naval work and the clerk of the cheque in the port was refusing to sign Lanyon's bills. But the deputy governor of the Citadel assured the commissioners that this clerk was a worthless fellow, not fit for employment, who if he had an office at all kept it in

Left: Tablet on the wall of Lanyon's almshouses.

a tavern. Lanyon, already a freeman of Plymouth, is described in local records as a merchant, was mayor in 1672–73, and when he died the next year (oddly enough in Paris) left large sums to charities in and around Plymouth. The almshouses he endowed (rebuilt in Victorian times) still face Charles roundabout. It was remarkable progress in 14 years, but it may have been honest enough in the fashion of the times.

But certainly there was dishonesty in the new yard on a large scale. The storekeeper was dismissed in 1699. It was discovered in 1708 that the canvas contractor was supplying rotten ropes to the sailmaker for bolt ropes, the cause of several mishaps at sea. Then in 1711 the commissioner was replaced and the master shipwright, the clerk of the cheque and the storekeeper all dismissed; 20 years later a number of yardees were on trial at Exeter for stealing. None of this was peculiar to Plymouth Dock. The chips and the scandals were common to all yards. And in its first 60 years Plymouth Dock did build or rebuild 48 ships, as well as coping with all the refit and fitting out of three strenuous naval wars.

The Admiralty Takes Over, 1688–1750

In his *Memoirs* James Yonge recorded: '1690. In° Paige. In this Gentlemans Mayoralty happened nothing memorable, but the dock In Ham hoas was began...'. Over the next 20 years he wrote 'nothing memorable' several times, and a century later Henry Woollcombe, in his history of the town, still unpublished, suggests that Plymouth was asleep up to the beginning of the reign of George III. Indeed the town changed little outwardly; some avenues of elm trees were planted on the Hoe and about the town, a few houses rebuilt, the water supply was improved a little, a pond filled in. But the town was prosperous; trade kept up and people were busy. Underneath it was a vital period for Plymouth, the half-century in which the town was taken over by the Admiralty, that new branch of the civil service which Samuel Pepys had just created when Yonge made that 1690 entry.

Trade

The commercial port of Plymouth was busy enough in this time. The town quay dues, which had doubled between 1670 and 1700, more than doubled again by 1720. In number of ships and tonnage engaged in trade in 1715–17 Plymouth ranked fourth among English ports, and took third place in the trade with northern Spain, fifth place in the trade with southern Spain and the Atlantic islands, and sixth place in the Portuguese trade. In 1733 the port was trading with Virginia, the West Indies and the Mediterranean. There was at least one Plymouth ship in the slave trade.

But the gaps were great. In those 1715 figures London has 244 ships, Bristol 48, Exeter 30, Liverpool 23 and Plymouth 19. Defoe, in his 1724 *Tour through*

Great Britain called Bristol, the second largest town in England, 'the greatest, richest and best port in the country', and it was building new docks and wharves for her expanding trade. Even so, Liverpool, which had been in the Atlantic trades since the mid-seventeenth century, had in 1715 opened the first wet dock in all Britain and by mid-century had outstripped even Bristol as a port. In the trade explosion of the eighteenth century Liverpool and Bristol, with industrial areas behind them to supply export cargoes and away from the war-torn Channel, took the lion's share. Plymouth marked time. Its little commercial harbour, Sutton Pool, was the subject of endless lawsuits over its ownership. Greenvile Collins's chart of 1693 shows its quay drying out at low tide, and in 1744 the fish house which stood where the lock gates now are, and which gave some shelter to the harbour, was washed away in a storm.

Exports from the hinterland were limited; woollens overseas, some lead, tin and copper from Dartmoor to south Wales, paving stones and slates, some of which went to the American colonies. As the century 17 wore on the coal imports from Newcastle fell, to be replaced by supplies from south Wales and increasingly from Whitehaven. The coasting imports consisted largely of corn, groceries and other foodstuffs, together with household goods from London and other sources which supplied Plymouth and were reshipped in smaller craft to West Country ports between Exeter and St Ives; road transport was negligible. In the same way a high proportion of the overseas goods on which duty was paid – tobacco, wine, sugar, fruit, ginger and Newfoundland train oil – was exported again coastwise. In the ten years 1722–31 Plymouth imported direct nearly three

'The East Prospect of Plymouth' from A Survey of the Fortifications of the Plymouth Division, 1716, by Col Christian Lilly. The drawing was made from Cattedown. Note the Victualling Yard under the Citadel.

million pounds of tobacco, the bulk of which was re-exported, and it was still getting some tobacco by the 1750s. As the duties mounted on tobacco so the direct imports increasingly moved to Bristol and Liverpool, where the richer merchants could find the capital required. The sugar crop too was drawn off to these ports. In 1750 Plymouth built its first sugar house for grinding cane (it was near the western end of the modern Mount Gould Road, its ruins long thought to have been an old fort), when Bristol already had 16.

Yet foreign trade was growing in Plymouth in these years; in 1750 there were 16 ships in the West Indies and another 12 sailing to the mainland American colonies, an improvement on the 1715 figures.

If the merchants of Plymouth sometimes contrasted the modest growth of their shipping trade with the meteoric rise at Bristol and even more at Liverpool, they still had a solid and important mercantile business, and alongside it a growing business which these other ports could not take away. War – and there were 32 years of war between 1688 and 1750 – might interrupt trade, and the press gangs were far more active than in the rival ports, but it brought compensations. There were captured enemy ships whose cargoes were auctioned before the vessels were converted to English use, and convoys of merchantmen which, whether inward or outward bound, wanted victuals, liquor and repairs. Ship: could be weather-bound, or awaiting escorts, for weeks at a time, a useful extra market. Defoe in 1724 wrote: 'there are several considerable merchants and a abundance of wealthy shopkeepers whose trade depends on supplying the seafaring people that upon so many occasions put into the port'. It was, he said, 'the general port for receiving all the fleets of merchant ships from the southward, as from Spain, Italy, the West Indies, etc'.

Though the Navy itself might be run down between the wars, as in the 24 years of peace after the Treaty of Utrecht, there was still the growing town of Dock that needed all manner of household goods, clothing and foodstuffs that Saltash market could not provide, and which had not developed its own mercantile community.

In the peace years too the yard and its ancillary establishments were extended and built up; Plymouth merchants were shipping bricks from Southampton, bringing in timber, supplying the workmen to some extent and feeding them. The capital expenditure of the Crown in Plymouth in the century after 1660, from the building of the Citadel to the construction of the dockyard and its steady expansion, injected much cash into the Plymouth economy. The work of the yard and the Victualling Office at Lambhay, building and repairing ships, feeding crews, all brought contracts for Plymouth merchants and ship owners.

Industry

The Plymouth woollen manufactory reached its zenith in this time, largely through the enterprise of three generations of the Shepherd family, who came from Northampton about the beginning of the century. From their home at Coxside, looking down to the creek where they built a quay still called Shepherd's Wharf, they had storehouses and factories close by the waterside, and more near the present Drake Circus roundabout, and in addition at Coxside they made glove leather from the sheepskins, converted the offal into glue and produced thick 'foot oil' from various residues. They had half a dozen looms in private houses in the town, mills at Ashburton, Buckfastleigh, Totnes, Tavistock, and spinners in east Cornwall. Altogether the family had 4,000 people on their payroll, and in Plymouth alone their weekly wage bill was between £500 and £600, plus the wages for the crews of their half-dozen coasters carrying the finished goods to London for the East India Company. The balance was shipped direct from Plymouth to the Americas.

Commercial dynasties were established which have come down to modern times. Collier's the wine merchants were established in Southside Street in 1676 and survived until recent years. William Moore the shipwright died in 1742 and the family business, which continued until a century ago, certainly had a shipbuilding slip alongside Friary Quay, in the north-east corner of Sutton Harbour, soon after the death of this first William.

Smuggling

The country financed its long wars with increasing taxes, and the principal source of revenue was the customs and excise duties. These seemed as iniquitous to the victims as income tax today, and there was little more shame in evading them than in our employing income tax advisers. From the dawn of trade there had been in Plymouth some evasion of duty on woollen goods, and uncoigned tin exported. But smuggling in the modern sense really began with William's French wars, which denied English customers their brandy, wine, silks and fine lace. Very soon the Channel Islands, and notably Guernsey, became the entrepot where these things could be bought, and Cawsand the main centre of the western smugglers of these goods. In Plymouth and growing Plymouth Dock they had the largest population and therefore the best market for their 'free trade'. It is hard to measure how fast this trade grew because the only records are of captured goods and smugglers, and in the eighteenth century the preventive service was little developed. But in 1732 the Plymouth tide-surveyor, who supervised the landguard, was murdered, and two men were executed for the crime. It was 'about the running of brandy', and their bodies were hung in chains at Crabtree, on the Laira estuary. This was usually done at the scene of the crime; one imagines that this was the landing point and perhaps the lonely Crabtree Inn, which disappeared when the dual carriage road was built in 1974 from Laira to Marsh Mills, was a smuggling base.

Apart from the goods brought over from France, there was also the tea, tobacco and rum smuggled out of the incoming ships into the longshoremen's boats, and again Cawsand was admirably placed. As the duties mounted on these goods there was an even bigger business in deceiving the customs officers in the actual port landings, a practice made easier by the corruption of the age.

The New Families

Customs service brought to Plymouth the founder of the town's dominant eighteenth-century family. John Rogers was the son of a Fifth Monarchy man who had been imprisoned for his libellous sermons against Cromwell, whom he had ardently supported until Cromwell made himself Protector, and grandson of the first Protestant martyr of Mary Tudor's reign. John Rogers, born in prison, married the daughter of a London alderman who probably used his influence to get Rogers 'a handsome place' in the Custom House at Plymouth, about 1670. It was in the last days when customs officers were not salaried but took their rewards from the fees they charged the owners of ships with which they dealt. It was possible to make fortunes. At any rate, when Rogers was offered promotion which meant moving to Bristol, he 'quit that employ and continued as a merchant, to which he had been bred, and by his success therein arrived at a considerable fortune', to quote family records. 'He got his estate mostly by tobacco', they continue, although other reports attribute the fortune to pilchard curing. At any rate, Rogers bought Wisdome near Cornwood in 1690, Ivybridge in 1692 and Blachford and other property in 1694. The family estates eventually stretched from the Harford slopes of Dartmoor down to Ermington.

No doubt his links with the Custom House helped him in the tobacco trade, but there was one disaster. His ship *Winchelsea*, laden with tobacco, struck the Eddystone Rock a few days after the storm of 1703 had destroyed the first lighthouse and she was lost with all hands. Rogers, already an important man in Plymouth, was elected MP for the town in 1698 and then made a baronet by King William. In 1702 he was High Sheriff of Devon, this boy born in prison at Windsor, and in 1710 died of an apoplexy while smoking his pipe in a Plymouth coffee house. His family was at Blachford, beside the stripling Yealm, until the 1980s.

This one-generation move from Plymouth business to country estate is remarkable only in its swift-

Mr Parker is saluting the return of King George III and his Queen, in the boat just passing Crabtree across the Laira. Their Majesties stayed at Saltram in 1789. The amphitheatre is still there with the folly (right), but the saluting guns have gone and the lead statue was stolen a long time ago by boatmen and melted down.

ness, but a new development of this time was of country families moving towards the merchant town. A native of Plympton, George Treby was a successful lawyer, became MP for Plympton and its recorder, and then Recorder of London until he was removed by Charles II (who had earlier knighted him) for defending the City's rights. After 1688 he rose rapidly again, Recorder and Lord Lieutenant of London, Lord Chief Justice when he died in 1700. He had four wives as well, the last of whom was an heiress, and acquired much land at Plympton, including much of the old priory land. He had just started Plympton House, splendid in red brick made locally and Portland stone, when he died in 1700. His son George, MP for Plympton by the time he was 24, had finished the house by 1720 and the Trebys dominated Plympton for another century.

Plympton had changed little since medieval days. There were the hamlets of Underwood and Colebrook, St Mary's Church, just a few cottages beside Ridgeway at the Dark Street Lane junction, and the old town of Plympton St Maurice clustered under the Castle. Its rather obscure claim to borough status and a mayor had been clarified by a new charter in 1602, and a later 1692 charter gave the town a recorder and quarter sessions. It was reasonably prosperous, a little market town with some retired Plymouth merchants, and some of its citizens were merchants and ship-owners in Plymouth. Plympton Grammar School had been built in 1663–71 after various law suits over the bequests in which Plymouth gained some authority over the trust. Built in similar style with an arcaded front is the Guildhall of 1696, given to Plympton by Treby and the Strode family.

Close to the eastern side of Plymouth, the Friary estate, which had been in the hands of the Sparke family since Elizabethan days, was breaking up. Through the seventeenth century the Sparkes had

Plympton House, built 1700–20 with a façade of Portland stone but sides of brick, then new to the area. Seen here from Plympton Castle.

Tothill House. The modest villa of the Culme and later Culme-Seymour family which stood just north-east of St Jude's Church until the late-nineteenth century.

lived at the old Whitefriars, rather like father-figures in retirement. Jonathan Rashleigh of Menabilly had inherited part of the estate through a Sparke marriage, and on the death of the last Sparke in 1714 his son-in-law, another Cornish landowner, Sir John Molesworth Bart of Pencarrow, acquired the main part. From Rashleigh, a Plympton farmer, Anthony Culme, leased 28 acres at Tothill in 1680 and ten years later his son bought it outright. By 1730 the Culme estate included Mannamead and Little Efford, and when the last Culme died in 1804 they also owned Freedom Fields, most of Lipson, Compton and Laira. Their house at Tothill was one of the most pleasant in the area, standing just north-east of the present St Jude's Church and looking down the Tothill Creek to the Laira and the woods of Saltram.

Even more important for Plymouth was the Parker move into Saltram. The family came from north Devon and by a series of marriages to rich wives had leased Boringdon, just north of Plympton, by 1564, and finally inherited the manor and Woodford. George Parker bought Saltram as well in 1712 and could afford to lay out the grounds, and his son John created the great house largely as we know it today. John's son was created Lord Boringdon in 1784.

Politics

The landowners of the neighbouring countryside had real influence in Plymouth, even though the controlling element was the central group of merchants and traders, joined as the eighteenth century advanced by professional men, doctors and lawyers. Both Tories and Whigs kept their rich men's fingers in the Plymouth pie. The 1684 charter which Charles II forced upon the town gave them the Earl of Bath, Governor of Plymouth, as recorder. In the first list of freemen there were five peers, two baronets and a range of Tory landowners like Edgcumbe and Slanning (of Maristow). That charter also reduced the number of common councillors from 24 to 12. The 1695 charter of William III restored the common councillors to 24 in number but brought in the Whigs, Sir Francis Drake as recorder, George Treby and three other baronets, and landowners like George Parker as freemen. Pollexfen, town clerk from 1665 to 1669, was basically a country landowner.

The importance of these appointments is shown by the method of local government, almost unique for a borough. The council as such rarely met, and administration was in the hands of the Court of Quarter Session. Here the recorder or his deputy, normally the town clerk, presided. The justices sitting with them were the mayor, the ex-mayor and two senior aldermen. The grand jury of 12 was chosen by the aldermen, the councillors and the freemen.

It was a self-perpetuating organisation. Freemen, who alone could trade in Plymouth, had either to have served an apprenticeship in the town, be eldest sons of dead freemen or be elected by quarter sessions. From the freemen the aldermen elected the councillors. In turn the mayor was elected annually by the councillors and 12 freemen, but the 12 freemen were chosen by two aldermen appointed by the retiring mayor, and two councillors elected by the freemen. Of the estimated 8,000 inhabitants of Plymouth in 1700 there were about 250 freemen.

Yet even in this closed shop the politics were as fierce as the comments in the contemporary records. Of William Cock, mayor 1702–03, Yonge says: 'A good church-man & a Tory, but of no parts, nor temper; he was R. Berryes Bro. Law, who had now screwed himselfe in yᵉ Townclarks chair, and proved as Imperious, & Arbitrary as his Master Polexfen had befor him. He Governed this Mayor...'; of Thomas Darracot (1704–05): 'One whom we all thought honest, but he proved a Shuffler. Abetted the whiggs... '. Yonge makes it clear that the Tories were churchmen, probably high churchmen; the Whigs were dissenters or had Presbyterian leanings. Captain Hambly's Book in the city archives is equally blunt: William Phillips, mayor 1746-7, 'when drunk was carried home in his cook's apron'.

The advantage swayed every year or two from

one side to the other, and many men changed sides; over the years, as in national politics, there were breakaway parties in both Tories and Whigs, and rival factions. Several times in Plymouth there were evenly divided elections, as over the election of a new vicar for Charles Church in 1711, which had (as in the election for a vicar for St Andrew's in 1679) to go to the Bishop of Exeter for a decision. It was almost the same story in 1732 over a new vicar for St Andrew's, when the great Zachariah Mudge only secured the election after the Black Book had been consulted for precedents.

The election of Members of Parliament was further confused not only by party divisions but by the question of who had the right to vote. According to Yonge the two Members of Parliament for Plymouth were elected by the freeholders, but by the time of Queen Elizabeth the freeholders left the election to the corporation and the freemen, to avoid the cost of having to pay the members. In the general election after the Restoration the freemen and the freeholders enthusiastically claimed their old right and elected two members strong for the king's return. The corporation, old Parliament men, in turn elected more restrained supporters of the Restoration, but the Committee of Privileges of the Commons gave the right to vote to 'the Mayor and Commonalty' and accepted the freeholders' men. So the freeholders were considered as electors.

Though this was the age in which party politics took shape, they were still not clear cut or well defined. Not only were both Whigs and Tories split nationally into opposing groups, but locally men were likely to weigh personal interests against these new ideas. It was a corrupt age too, and practices change; the old custom of presents from the corporation to a helpful member – a silver-gilt cup to John Sparke in 1679, for example – gave way to payments to the corporation. In 1710 the two men elected each gave 100 guineas to the corporation. In 1721 there were 20 houses open to supply wine and strong liquor free to the voters, and two hogsheads of beer for 'the rabble'.

The first manager for the Whigs in south Devon was Sir Francis Drake, the third baronet, great-great-nephew of the Elizabethan hero, nephew of the Parliamentary colonel of horse. He was related to all the West Country Whigs, and by the end of his life had in his own control two seats at Bere Alston and

Left: *Charles Church steeple, postwar but before the roundabout was built.*

one each at Tavistock, Dartmouth, Totnes, Plympton and Plymouth. His correspondence shows how the control was exercised: buying up property which carried freeholders' votes, using his influence to get a voter a place in the excise or the Custom House, filling a vacancy for an armourer in the Citadel. The Whigs and the Navy were always close, and a Drake, of course, would gravitate to the Navy. A brother and a cousin were captains in the Navy, and a niece married Sir Charles Trevanion, Commissioner at Plymouth Dock. Even so, Plymouth was difficult to manage. In Lady Elliot-Drake's family history she says of this time that Drake never quite controlled Plymouth, and that the Whigs were always in the minority there.

Yet in spite of this view, and even though Charles II tried to pack the Plymouth Council with his friends when he came to the throne, the town was returning Whigs to Parliament within seven years. William of Orange's accession naturally gave the Whigs further strength, but ten years later his policies were upsetting the merchant class nationally and in 1698 John Rogers and Charles Trelawny defeated the Whigs Parker and Calmady and set the Plymouth Tories rejoicing. The king made Rogers a baronet and so perhaps bought back his support; at any rate, at the 1700 general election the Plymouth Tories secured the nominations for Charles Trelawny again and his brother.

Francis Drake retired from Parliament the next year and entered his management career in earnest. In 1705 Charles Trelawny kept his seat but Drake secured the other for Admiral Sir George Byng, a serving officer and a staunch Whig. Byng promptly gave the command of a ship in his squadron to a Drake cousin! The admiral was to hold a series of senior posts in the Navy for the rest of his life; when he was made Viscount Torrington two of his sons in succession took his seat (the third was the Admiral Byng executed for losing Minorca). The family held this Plymouth seat for 34 years.

Drake got rid of the Tory Trelawny in 1713 by securing the nomination for Sir John Rogers, the second baronet, as a Whig. 'A sensible man', said Sir Francis of him. Indeed, when Drake died in 1717, Rogers became Recorder of Plymouth. The family held this office for 80 years, handing it down with the baronetcy as if it too were hereditary. But the second baronet was an unreliable supporter of the government and on a number of occasions voted the wrong way, so that in 1721, in addition to Byng, the government managers put up William Chetwynd, a junior Lord of the Admiralty. Rogers was going to stand and it looked as if Plymouth was to see its first contested election since 1698, but at the last minute he dropped out. The way the Rogers family could change their tune is shown by two pamphlets which survive. Neither is dated, but one proclaims: 'The Admiralty for Plymouth for ever' and urges a vote for Rogers or 'you'll disoblige the Admiralty your only friend'. The other opens: 'Rise up sinking Plymouth', and in verse attacks the Navy as no friend to the town, principally for having built a brewhouse at Millbrook instead of beside the Victualling Office at Lambhay.

George Treby of Plympton succeeded Drake as the government and Whig manager in Devon, controlling not only Plymouth and one of the Plympton seats but five other Devon boroughs. He was a candidate for the mayoralty of Plymouth in 1727, but Sir John Rogers had shortly before persuaded the previous mayor to add 17 freemen, improperly, to the list. His son John (who never bothered with trade after he had made the grand tour) also stood for the mayoralty, and both polled an equal number of votes. At one point the two candidates drew their swords on each other and a fight was only averted by the alarm of a fire in Gasking Street. The town had no mayor from 17 September until the following 12 March, when the council chose Rogers by order of the King's Bench.

It is not easy to follow the Rogers's politics; the second son, William, was 'bred a merchant', and became Collector of Customs in Plymouth, while the third son, Frederic, joined the Navy a few years later. Yet when Robert Byng resigned his seat in 1739 and the government candidate was Charles Vanbrugh, one of Byng's captains and brother of the Gun Wharf architect, John Rogers stood against him and Plymouth had its first election since 1698. Rogers raked in every freeholder he could find, 'faggot votes', and won; probably the 'Rise up sinking Plymouth' pamphlet is of this date. But Vanbrugh went to petition, and the House of Commons decided that the 'Commonalty' of the 1661 decision meant the freemen only, not the freeholders, and Rogers was unseated in favour of Vanbrugh. Not for another 40 years were the freeholders of Plymouth to try to claim their rights, and the Admiralty and the government went on nominating the men they decided Plymouth should send to Parliament. When Captain Charles Saunders RN was returned in 1750 a contemporary wrote that:

... though neither a man of figure or character [he] *was readily accepted by the vile scoundrel Aldermen in places, and their lacquays the Common Council – one half of both benches having made themselves* slaves and dependants *on the board of Admiralty by getting into places.*

It was unjust about Saunders; he commanded the fleet at Quebec when Wolfe captured the city and was later Pitt's First Lord of the Admiralty for a short spell. Yet one of the Plymouth seats was held by one naval officer or another from 1705 to 1754, and the other had been at the government's disposal since 1713. For 26 years it was held by Arthur Stert of Membland, who steadily served one government after another, had a secret service pension and helped manage the West Country elections. In Plymouth he was said 'to have a precarious interest of his own with the Corporation', and he paid the rent for the Shepherd factories and stores for all the time he was in the House.

The dockyard, the customs service and the Citadel always had enough jobs, contracts, fat commissions and other inducements to keep a majority of the 200-odd freemen happy. Politically Plymouth was a rotten borough, in the pocket of the Admiralty and the government. In business it was finding it easier to make money out of the dockyards than by the old-style trade.

The Great Awakening, 1750–1815

Plymouth was dead by 1750, and only began to wake up with the accession of George III, wrote Woollcoombe in 1819. The three major factors in the revival seem to have been the extensive Crown building programme in Plymouth which grew out of the long French wars, the coming of the turnpike road link with London and the discovery by the county gentry with Plymouth interests that they could make money out of the developing town.

With brief intervals Britain was at war with France and various of her allies from 1738 until 1815. Increasingly the theatre of war was not the Narrow Seas but the Atlantic, the Mediterranean and the West Indies, with Plymouth the most strategically placed naval base. So Plymouth prospered. When the Seven Years War broke out in 1756 Captain George Rodney was senior officer at Plymouth and all that spring he was driving the dockyard and the ships' companies. Invasion was feared and defence lines around Dock, from the high ground just south of the road from Torpoint Ferry to Stonehouse Creek, were started at once. Behind the lines half a dozen squares of small barracks were built, and in 1757 'the best Wages in the county' were being advertised as far away as Sherborne for 50 masons and bricklayers to build barracks at Dock. By 1759 over £25,000 had been spent on local defences.

Land had been bought at Stonehouse at the outbreak of war for a naval hospital, but more land was later bought from Lord Edgcumbe, and building began in 1758 on the shores of Stonehouse Creek.

The Royal Naval Hospital at Stonehouse, built in 1758–62 in the new hygienic style with small separated blocks linked by colonnades.

Left: The 1857 gateway to the Royal Marine Barracks.

The first patients were transferred from the old hospital near Derry's Clock in 1760, and when the hospital was completed in 1762 it was the first in England built in small blocks, so that groups of patients were isolated from one another. With land-ing steps down to the water's edge, sick and wounded seamen could be landed directly from boats: the steps were in use until about 1919 and still survive, along with the graceful grouping of the wards and the officers' quarters.

During the same time the dockyard itself was being expanded across the 'New Ground' to the south. The original ropehouse which had formed the southern boundary of the yard was demolished to open up the New Ground, and another ropehouse built on a north-south line. In the New Ground a mast pond, new store, mast and boat houses were established, and two building slips on the site of the present slips. A new road was made down to Mutton Cove, the little basin still at the southern boundary of the dockyard. On the other side of the yard a third dry dock, the North Dock, was added in 1762, and more building slips. Improvements to the yard went on for another ten years, and in that time over £153,000 was spent.

Much of this work went on in the uneasy peace period of 1763–76, when the Navy was much run down by political neglect. The War of American Independence (1776–82) stirred things up very sharply. A Franco-Spanish fleet off the port with an invasion army threw Plymouth into a panic in 1779. New gun batteries were hurriedly built all around the Sound, and a blockhouse at Higher Stoke. New barracks for the Royal Marines were built in Stonehouse in 1782–83. When the force had been raised in 1755 the Plymouth Division was billeted round Sutton Harbour with an orderly room in Southside Street, a limestone-faced building between Southside Ope and Parade Ope. The New Quay became the rallying point and parade ground, and has been called the Parade ever since. As the force grew so companies were billeted out, in Dock and as far afield as Modbury, Plympton and Tavistock (on the main routes into Plymouth). In 1781 the new

Admiralty House, built 1789–93, was originally Government House and home to the Governor of Plymouth and then to the garrison commander. It only became the home and office of the naval Commander-in-Chief in 1934.

The Breakwater today.

barracks were started, again on land bought from Lord Edgcumbe, a long block for the men running along the western water's edge of Millbay with the officers' quarters at right-angles at the two ends. The block survives, with the officers' mess still in the south wing and senior officers' dwellings next door. It was first occupied in 1783. The familiar block on Durnford Street and the wings which completed the barracks square were not added until 1857. Railings separated the original parade ground from Barrack Street, which disappeared with the Victorian extension, but not before it had acquired nine public houses and a brewery.

In 1789 work on the fourth dry dock, the New North Dock, was started. It was planned as the biggest in the country, and George III came down to see it under construction. A classical summer house on 'Bunker Hill' still marks the spot from which he admired the view. The king, it is said, asked why the new dock was being built even larger than designed and was told that the French were building a new ship, the *Commerce de Marseilles*, which was even longer than the design length of the dock. So it was being made big enough to take her; she was indeed captured at Toulon soon after the outbreak of war in 1793, and was the first ship to enter the new dock.

Preparations for war had long been in hand. Under the authority of the Duke of Richmond, Master-General of the Ordnance, a second wall was built around Dock, behind the main line with its barracks and the civilian houses. He also moved the seat of the Governor of Plymouth from the Citadel to

a new house at Mount Wise, built as Government House but since 1934 known as Admiralty House and the seat of the Commander-in-Chief (since called the Flag Officer). The first governor to occupy this house was General Lord George Lennox, Richmond's brother. It was a rewarding post, 'the first military appointment in Great Britain', so not only was there a smack of nepotism about the appointment but Richmond was accused of building a comfortable house for his brother 'economically with the public money'. Richmond upset a lot of local people, particularly because his new wall cut them off from the little foreshore left, and to placate them he built Richmond Walk, which still runs along the waterfront from Mutton Cove under Mount Wise. Not until 1820 was another residence, now called Hamoaze House, built for the Commander-in-Chief at Mount Wise. In 1810 a start was made in turning the landward defences of Dock into a moat and masonry wall, but this was abandoned at the end of the war in 1815.

With the outbreak of war in 1793 Plymouth was full of troops, some accommodated during the summer in camps at Roborough and Maker. In 1794 Shepherd's woollen manufactory 'behind Frankfort Place' – roughly where Dingle's now stands – was made into a barracks, and another built beside the Millbay prisoner-of-war establishment. After extensive campaigns in the West Indies, Plymouth was flooded with sick and wounded soldiers in 1795. Many died, a temporary, inadequate hospital at Friary could not cope, and the Naval Hospital would not take soldiers. A direct result was the building in 1797 of the Military Hospital, on the northern shores of Stonehouse Creek facing the Naval Hospital, following a similar pattern of small blocks, four in this case, linked by a massive colonnade. The building is now used as two schools.

As the war progressed, so did the number of French prisoners mount. Apart from Millbay and converted establishments at Coxside, there were prison hulks in the Hamoaze. Conditions worsened until in 1805 Thomas Tyrwhitt, close friend and servant of the Prince of Wales and an enthusiastic 'improver' of Dartmoor who had already built himself a house at Tor Royal and founded the new settlement of Princetown, proposed building a prison there. It reputedly cost £200,000, and in 1809 it received its first 5,000 prisoners from Plymouth.

The last, most elaborate and expensive scheme of all began in 1812 when the Breakwater was started. It had been suggested by Admiral Lord St Vincent as early as 1779, when captain of the *Foudroyant*. He, Hawke, Hood and all the great admirals of the time found Cawsand Bay dangerous as an anchorage and preferred Torbay. When St Vincent became Commander-in-Chief Channel Fleet in 1806 he forced the Admiralty to consider various remedies, of which the present Breakwater was eventually chosen. When St Vincent resigned in 1807 things were forgotten again, but work eventually began in 1812. It was not completed until 1848 and cost £1,000,000.

After a century's inflation sums of money mean little in modern terms, but the Crown did invest a great deal of cash in Plymouth between the middle of the seventeenth century and 1815. Local labour and local stone were employed, and each finished project meant local employment or wages spent locally. At the head of the Office of Works were distinguished architects – Sir William Chambers, for instance, who built Somerset House – and they not only provided Plymouth with an impressive and often overlooked collection of great Georgian buildings, but again set new standards for local builders and developers.

The New Roads

For centuries overland communication and transport in England had been so bad that wherever possible coastal shipping was used. The King's Post, in which relays of horsemen rode post-haste with messages of government, was opened to public letters on payment in 1635. John Codd started a packhorse system between Plymouth and London in 1722. But the old system whereby each parish had to maintain its roads was never going to satisfy a developing nation, and in 1663 the first Turnpike Act was passed. In this a private trust could improve a length of road and recover its costs by charging a toll. At the toll houses there were gates, or pikes (long poles) which were turned aside to permit passage after the toll had been paid. So the new roads became known as turnpikes. As the increasing number of French wars after this date made coastal shipping a prey to enemy ships, so the pressure for new roads mounted. Much of the Great North Road, and the roads from London to Bristol, Harwich and Portsmouth, were completely turnpiked by 1750, with many other main roads nearly complete.

By 1753 there was much lobbying for the Great West Road to Plymouth and Falmouth. There was much traffic in wartime, it was argued, and in peace new roads would attract 'such persons of fashion and fortune as make various tours in England for pleasure, health and curiosity'. Many would settle in Devon and Cornwall if they could get to London

comfortably. There was opposition, some from farmers, but by May the Acts had been passed which would permit turnpikes all the way to Exeter. It had been agreed that the improvements would be left to the major towns on the route, each town trust concerning itself with its approach roads. The Exeter Act, for instance, allowed them to improve the road west as far as Chudleigh Bridge. In 1755 the Ashburton Trust was permitted to turnpike the road from Chudleigh to (South) Brent Bridge, and in 1757 came an Act for improving the high road from Brent Bridge to Gasking Gate, Plymouth – the Plymouth East Trust. The Great West Road followed the line of the old post road to London, more or less the present A38 to Exeter and A30 on to London.

The new road was constructed in 1758. Before that time the usual route from Plymouth to London was through Tavistock and Okehampton. The old south road was only ten to twelve feet wide, 'more like a river bed than a road', wrote Woollcoombe, and if a horseman met a packhorse he had to go back to a gate to let the packhorse pass. Invalids could join a coach at Exerer! The new road, wrote Marshall in 1796, was well formed but too narrow, and the lofty hedges were an intolerable nuisance to travellers. In spite of this John Bignell, the landlord of the Prince George Inn on the corner of Stillman Street and Vauxhall Street, had a diligence running to Exeter weekly in the first year the road was open. The journey took 12 hours. Two years later a 'machine' was plying between the White Hart, Old Town Street, and Exeter, and by 1785 there were mail coaches on the road.

Once the main road to Exeter was turnpiked, others were improved. The Modbury turnpike through Yealmpton and Brixton to the main road at Plympton was authorised in 1759. In 1760 the Cremyll-Liskeard road, through Crafthole, Polbathic and Trerule Foot, continued the Great West Road into Cornwall, and subsequent Acts that year took the road on through St Austell, Lostwithiel, Truro and Falmouth to Penzance. This Cremyll route had been the post road into Cornwall at least since 1600, but it was challenged by a new 1761 road from Trerule Foot to Saltash which continued, on the Devon side, to Weston Mill. In 1761 too there was an Act to improve the roads out of Tavistock which authorised roads to Callington, Launceston and Lydford, and above all through Horrabridge and Rock (Yelverton) to Plymouth. A branch road from Manadon Gate took a spur to Plymouth Dock, and this became the new town's main road to London.

With communications so improved from Plymouth and Dock to the outside world, it was time to look internally. A map in Devon County Record Office, from the Bedford Papers, refers to a Turnpike Bill for improving the roads out of Plymouth in 1756, but this seems to have been replaced by the Plymouth East Act of a year later. Apart from improving the Plympton road, it also showed improvements planned to the road across Cattedown to the Oreston passage, to Stonehouse Lane (through King Street and Stonehouse High Street to the Cremyll Ferry), and to the old Dock road by way of Cobourg Street, Pennycomequick and Wilton Street, as well as the road from Pennycomequick through Milehouse to Saltash. At best this was patching, but a major change came in 1768–73 with the building of Stonehouse Bridge, which linked Dock and Stonehouse. Like the new roads it was subject to toll. Pedestrians paid ¹/₂d return, and so for the rest of its days it was the ha'penny gate. By 1775 the first diligences were running from Plymouth to Dock by way of Stonehouse Lane and the Bridge, but the road cannot have received the proposed 1756 improvements. In 1784 a Bill seeking a turnpike from the western edge of built-up Plymouth to Stonehouse Bridge was presented to Parliament. A Dock petition extended the road up the hill to reach the Dock town gate, but a petition from the Mayor and Corporation of Plymouth asked for the road to be extended right through the middle of Plymouth to meet the Exeter road at Gasking Gate, from the bridge through Stonehouse to the Cremyll Ferry, and from the Dock Gate right through Dock to Mutton Cove (which by now also had a ferry to Cremyll). It was impertinent, for the turnpike trust would be responsible for maintaining these roads, and the House of Commons rejected the petition – the appellants were themselves responsible at least for the road through Plymouth.

In 1791 Torpoint Ferry started operating, with passenger boats operating from North Corner (between the dockyard and the Ordnance Wharf) and horse boats running from Pottery Quay, the present

Devonport landing stage. The horse boats had a plat-form between two hulls and a ramp enabled horses, carts and carriages to be taken aboard. The 1760 Cremyll-Liskeard Act had permitted a spur from Crafthole to Torpoint and this road with the ferry made a much shorter route into Cornwall than the old Cremyll crossing. In 1800 this became the post route, with the mail brought across the ferry and loaded into the waiting Truro coach.

Improvements were also going on to the east of Plymouth. In 1784 Lord Boringdon had built an embanked carriage drive from the Longbridge at Marsh Mills to his fine house at Saltram. This kept the tides out of Plympton marshes, which had stretched right up to St Mary's Church. On the other side of the estuary he promoted the Plymouth Embankment Company, which enclosed the Laira marshes, and these two embankments made it possible for the Plymouth Eastern Trust in 1802–09 to avoid the old steep route over Lipson Hill with a new embankment road from Plymouth to Crabtree, and thence from Longbridge straight to the foot of Ridgeway, cutting out the previous route winding along the northern edge of the marshes. Plymouth celebrated the 1810 jubilee of George III by making a new road from Bretonside to Embankment Road and so the present line of the main road was established.

Thus by the end of the Napoleonic wars Plymouth had good communications in all directions. The London mail coaches were making the journey in two days even before the last improvements, and by 1797 a man called Rosedew, who provided the post horses on the road, was building Beechwood House near Cornwood out of the fortune he had made. It was subsequently bought by Lord Seaton, one of Wellington's generals at Waterloo, and his descendants are still there.

The Country Gentlemen

The last male Morice – the family which had owned all the manor of Stoke Damerel since 1667 – died in 1749. He left the manor to his elder sister's son, the 23-year-old Sir John St Aubyn, fourth baronet, in 1749. Like his father, this St Aubyn sat for various Cornish constituencies all his life but, though a Tory, was never as far to the right as his Jacobite father. On his death in 1772 his 14-year-old son succeeded him, a colourful character, in trouble over his extravagances even before he left school, the father eventually of 15 bastards by two different women, a lover of

The Ha'penny Gate; Stonehouse Bridge in the days when tolls were still charged and pedestrians paid a halfpenny. Tolls were finally bought out in 1924. Top: *a ticket.*

the arts and sciences and a patron of John Opie, the Cornish painter. After the St Aubyns inherited Stoke, Dock began to blossom; there was clearly more freedom in granting leases. A market was built in 1762 and talks started with Plymouth to improve the town's water supply (though this was not done till the building of the Devonport Leat in 1795–96). Dock Theatre opened in Cumberland Street in 1762 (the site is now Cumberland Garden, overlooked by Theatre Ope and the Shakespeare Hotel), and decent hotels like the Fountain and the King's Arms developed in Fore Street just outside the dockyard gates. The town began to spread south to George Street, Pembroke Street and Prospect Row, where villas with views across to Mount Edgcumbe were built. The fourth baronet did offer £200 a year to Plymouth in 1766 for a water supply, and he did build Stonehouse Bridge with Lord Edgcumbe in 1767, but the destruction by fire in the last century of the estate office and its papers makes it difficult to trace the extent of the family influence in the development of Dock. The rateable value of the town increased from £4,000 in 1750 to over £20,000 in 1800, and apart from the expansion of the town proper the two village suburbs of Stoke and Higher Stoke began. Though they kept the leasehold system of the Morices, the St Aubyns vastly increased their revenues from the development of their manor, and it is hard to doubt that they actively encouraged it.

Their neighbours in Stonehouse, the Edgcumbes, in the eighteenth century collected three titles. Richard Edgcumbe, a close friend of Walpole's and a minister in his governments, was the Whig political manager for Cornwall and was made a baron in 1742 to prevent his being examined by the House of Commons over his political machinations in Cornwall. He was succeeded in 1758 by his eldest son, Dick, who sat in Parliament to keep the influence warm but had no interest in politics. As a young man he lost his daily 20 guineas at White's Club, made a reputation as a wit, remained a bachelor and had four children by Ann Franks, a beauty of the day. One of the Plympton seats was Edgcumbe-owned, and Dick, himself an artist, became the first patron and encourager of Joshua Reynolds, son of the Plympton Grammar School headmaster. His younger brother George went off into the Navy and was a

Left: *Richard Edgcumbe, the second baron, painted by his friend Reynolds.*

midshipman in HMS *Romney* with Byron and Rodney. All three became admirals and lifelong friends. George had reached captain's rank with a distinguished naval record when he succeeded his brother in 1761.

Like the St Aubyns, the Edgcumbes also made the most of the building boom. Father had sold the government the land for the Naval Hospital, son George was a partner with St Aubyn in building Stonehouse Bridge (which by the end of the century was making them £2,000 a year profit). In 1773, the year the bridge was completed, he leased out the land on which Durnford Street and Emma Place were built, with imposing houses for the new elite of Dock. Durnford Street was named after the fifteenth-century heiress who had brought Stonehouse and Maker to the family, Emma Place after Lady Edgcumbe (who was the Archbishop of York's heiress). He had already removed the barrier gates at the top of High Street, by the new hospital, and at the top of the hill in Durnford Street. The High Street arch became a decorative feature in Mount Edgcumbe Park, on the carriage drive above Redding Point.

In 1780 Lord Edgcumbe, now a full admiral, sold the land for the Royal Marines' Barracks to the government and the year after, in compensation for the damage the new defences of Plymouth Sound had done to his woods, was made Viscount Mount Edgcumbe and Valletort. In 1789 he became the first Earl of Mount Edgcumbe and the following year, with Reginald Pole Carew of Antony, launched the Torpoint Ferry. When the first earl died in 1795 Stonehouse had grown from a village to a town of nearly 4,000 people, almost a quarter the size of Plymouth itself. The second earl, a dilettante amateur actor and musician, saw Stonehouse still growing and one of his daughters is remembered in the name of Caroline Place.

The Sir William Carew who built Antony House in 1710–21 was another Jacobite, who in 1715 was in preventive detention in the Citadel

Left: *The Hamoaze-facing backs of Durnford Street houses, which Betjeman described as 'once a sort of place for retired sea captains'.*

Saltram House, the only National Trust property within the City of Plymouth.

at Plymouth. He and his successors lived very quietly after this, but the estate passed in 1771 to 18-year-old Reginald Pole, of the political and wealthy east Devon family and also closely related to the politically powerful Rashleighs of Fowey, the Morices and half the great families of Cornwall. He added Carew to his surname, became an MP for Fowey and a privy councillor, much improved Antony House and park in best eighteenth-century style, and regained family land lost after the Civil War.

On his estate was the land opposite the growing dockyard, and at Torpoint grew a little community of maritime tradesmen: blacksmiths, carpenters, shipwrights and boatmen. They came mainly from Plymouth. Two ropewalks were built. The Carews had kept Torpoint field clear with an eye to housing development, and helped obtain the 1760 Cremyll-Liskeard Turnpike Act with its spur to Torpoint. There had been an unofficial ferry to Devonport since 1730, and by 1748 the Passage House had been built. But not until 1774, after young Reginald Pole-Carew took over, was Torpoint field formally laid out for development as a housing estate with a regular grid pattern of streets like Dock. As at Dock, even the type of house built was controlled – a very early form of planning. By 1784 there was 'scarcely any ground left untaken', and in 1785 two more fields were laid out and provision made for a church and a market. As it turned out there was no Anglican church in Torpoint until 1819, but a visit by John Wesley in 1787 led to a Methodist chapel by 1792.

But the major development was the start of a Torpoint Ferry proper. Pole-Carew had to bring in Lord

Mount Edgcumbe, who had the right of passage over the river between Cremyll and Saltash. St Aubyn would have been a more likely partner, but though he was a cousin of Pole-Carew's and this branch of the Poles had their home in Stoke Damerel, St Aubyn was not happy with the rival town of Torpoint. Once the ferry was in business he tried to injure Torpoint by manipulating the times and charges. But St Aubyn did become a partner in the ferry within a few years, by 1794 the Liskeard mail was being carried on the ferry and by 1796 there were two rival coaches running from Torpoint to Truro and Falmouth. There were about 1,500 people living in Torpoint by 1811.

Even more important to Plymouth was the second Lord Boringdon at Saltram, who succeeded his father in 1788 when he was only 16. He embanked Chelston Meadows to make a carriage drive to the ferry he created where the Laira Bridge is now, built two slips at Turnchapel in 1793, where many ships were built for the Navy, and laid mooring chains in the Cattewater in 1809 which added much to the commercial facilities of the port. He was active in the House of Lords from an early age but played a full part in rebuilding the trade of Plymouth at the end of the French wars, becoming first president of the Plymouth Chamber of Commerce in 1813 and a leading light in establishing the Exchange in Woolster Street the same year. He was created Earl of Morley in 1815, and Plymouth named a street in his honour.

Naval Influence

The landed families also developed an interest in Plymouth through their naval members. Admiral Lord Edgcumbe was Commander-in-Chief Plymouth in 1766–70 and again in 1773. For 55 years the Commissioners of Plymouth Dock had strong local connections. Frederic Rogers was another younger son sent into the Navy. A captain at 24, Frederic became the Commissioner of the Dock in 1753, built himself Hoe House in Hoe Lane in 1758, was Mayor

of Saltash in 1768 and succeeded his brother at Blachford and in the baronetcy in 1773. Two years later he retired on pension. He was followed as commissioner by Captain Paul Ourry, son of a naturalised Huguenot from Blois. Ourry was Captain Edgcumbe's lieutenant in a series of ships, became a captain in 1757 and fought a number of notable single-ship actions. No doubt

Left: *The gazebo in the South Yard of Devonport Dockyard, built to mark the visit of George III in 1789. His Majesty particularly admired the view from this vantage point.*

through the Edgcumbe connection he met the Treby family of Plympton and in 1749 married the daughter, Charity. When his brother-in-law died, Paul Ourry's wife inherited Plympton House and Paul became MP for Plympton in 1763, was given command of a guard-ship at Plymouth and in 1775 became Commissioner at Dock. There is a neat description of Captain Ourry entertaining Admiral Rodney in 1781 in the Commissioner's House in the yard, before Rodney sailed off to the Battle of the Saints: the two old men sitting on either side of the fire, both crippled with gout. Captain Ourry died in office just over a year later, but for him and Rogers it must have been a comfortable life, with authority in dock and large country houses not far away.

Seven years later, in 1789, came another commissioner with strong local links. Captain Robert Fanshawe's mother was a sister of Captain Sir Frederic Rogers, his father an admiral and his home at Stone Hall, the big house overlooking Stonehouse Pool. 'One of the finest seamen in the Navy', he became an Admiralty MP for Plymouth in 1784 and only resigned in 1790 on being appointed Commissioner of the Dockyard. He remained in that office until 1815, and was twice Mayor of Plymouth.

Thankes, just north of Torpoint, became the home of another naval officer, Thomas Graves, who in 1713 settled there with his new wife, Mary Warne, whose father had just bought the property and who ran the naval brewery at Southdown. Graves died a rear-admiral and his son, another Thomas, had a chequered naval career which finished gloriously with him the admiral commanding the van under Lord Howe at the Battle of the First of June in 1793. He was wounded and served no more, retiring to Thankes with a peerage and a pension of £1,000 a year. He had inherited the house in 1755, had two spells as Commander-in-Chief Plymouth after that time and died at Thankes in 1802. The family were there all through the nineteenth century but sold the house in the next century. It was rebuilt at Portwrinkle as the Whitsand Bay Hotel.

Admiral Sir Charles Morice Pole, younger brother of Pole-Carew at Antony, was born at Stoke Damerel in 1757 and was MP for Plymouth 1806–18. The great Edward Pellew gained his baronetcy for his gallantry at the wreck of the East Indiaman *Button* under the Citadel in 1796 (he had himself hauled out through the surf to the wreck and restored order with drawn sword). Pellew had been on his way to dine with Dr Hawker, the vicar of Charles, when he heard of the wreck. Lady Pellew bought Hampton House in Ebrington Street in 1804, and lived there until 1811. Her husband was made Viscount Exmouth in 1814 and was Commander-in-Chief at Plymouth 1829–32. Admiral Howe and his wife lived for a time in How Street. Collingwood, Nelson's second-in-command at Trafalgar, stayed with his family at the Fountain Inn at Dock and a letter of his gives a charming account of the family entertaining Nelson beside the fire.

Tobias Furneaux of Swilly was Wallis's second lieutenant in his 1766–68 voyage round the world and commanded the *Adventure*, Cook's second ship in his 1772 voyage. He was the first man to sail round the world in both directions. He died young, at Swilly, and was buried at Stoke Damerel.

James Hawker, of the Plymouth family of wine merchants, entered the Navy in 1744 and reached post rank. Three of his daughters married naval officers, one of them the one-armed Michael Seymour. Friary House was the Seymour home from 1798 until 1814, during which time Michael won much fame and a baronetcy in single-ship actions. His brother-in-law, Edward Hawker, became an admiral. His son, John Seymour, married Elizabeth Culme, whose family were neighbours at Tothill. When Elizabeth died in 1841, Sir John took the name of Culme-Seymour, to keep the Culme name alive, and both names survive as Mannamead street names on old Culme land.

Social and Intellectual Life

This mixture of county, naval and Plymouth families led to a considerable social life. In an advertisement of 1785:

The Nobility and Gentry are respectfully acquainted that the Long-Room, near Plymouth, will be opened for their reception with a CONCERT and ASSEMBLY on Thursday the 12th of May next...

The Long Room, with its tepid bath and 'a machine to bathe in the open Sea', had begun its fashionable life in 1766, on the Stonehouse shores of Millbay. It ended its social life in 1804 when a wooden-hutted barracks was built round it, but the Long Room itself survives, an elegant red-brick ballroom used by the Royal Marines as a gymnasium. Nelson in 1801 found he had 'given much offence' by not attending an assembly there. The Prince of Wales (later Prince Regent and then King George IV), the Duke of York and Prince William (later Duke of Clarence and eventually King William IV) gave a ball there in 1788. Prince William, captain of the frigate *Pegasus*, had been ordered to Plymouth to get him out of the clutches of a woman; his brothers visited him in defiance of their father, and Prince William further upset the family peace by falling in love with a local girl, Sally Winne. He was staying with her father, George Winne, a merchant who encouraged the affair because he hoped to become agent-victualler to the fleet. He had to be content with becoming Mayor of Plymouth in 1791–92. The Prince was packed off to sea again, out of harm's way. Prince William probably saw more of Plymouth than any other member of the royal family before or since. At one time he

Above: *The Long Room Stonehouse, about 1780. The flat ground in the foreground is now occupied by the Royal Marines Barracks and the sea at the foot of the hill (now quarried away) filled by West Wharf, Millbay Docks.* Below: *William Cookworthy, a portrait by Opie.*

lodged in Ordnance Street, between Morice Square and the gate of the Gun Wharf. He was a guest at dinner parties at many of the great town houses, and his name survives in street names and pub signs. As a young man he probably honoured, too, the assemblies at the Fountain in Fore Street, Devonport, the Old London Inn, Vauxhall Street – and, with his tastes in lechery, other less salubrious haunts.

In 1789, the year that William became Duke of Clarence, the king himself

visited Plymouth with the queen and his three eldest daughters. For them it was a round of Saltram and Mount Edgcumbe, a sham battle at sea and a trip up the Tamar. Saltram, where the royal party stayed, was the great centre of fashion, and from a diary in the Saltram archives a picture survives of the social round of the day, and the snobbery. In 1790 Lord Valletort (heir to the Earl of Mount Edgcumbe) and his wife were staying at Saltram for the Plympton Ball. 'The aldermen's wives do not like that the freemen's wives should go to the ball,' wrote 15-year-old Theresa Parker, and in 1796:

Government House and the Dock Ball, which amused us extremely. Such figures! such waists! such heads! as I never saw before... two of the best we discovered to be Stonehouse milliners and we saw them hard at work in their shop the next morning.

Lord and Lady George Lennox at Government House were of course great social figures; after all he was a great-grandson of Charles II, even if on the wrong side of the blanket. In 1798 Theresa Parker was at a 4p.m. dinner in a tent on Staddon Heights. 'Mrs

Bastard brought Lady Onslow and General Grenville; we met the Lennoxes and Lord Fortescue.'

The year before, Mrs Siddons, appearing at the Plymouth Theatre, was dined at Saltram, and Theresa found her 'very pompous'. Plymouth's first theatre in Hoegate Street had been replaced in 1758 by a building at the top of the newly developing George Street, which called itself the Theatre Royal after being honoured by George III and his family in 1789. All the great actors of the day played there and at the Dock Theatre.

It is a clue both to the social life and growing wealth of Plymouth that the corporation could in 1810 hold a competition for the design of a new theatre, hotel and assembly rooms, on a site at the bottom of George Street. The winner was an architect practising in Pall Mall, John Foulston. The massive block, with its two Ionic-pillared porticoes, was built in 1811–13 and cost £60,000. The hotel had over 50 bedrooms, the theatre could seat 1,192 people and the assembly room measured 80ft by 40ft. Foulston settled in Plymouth, building himself the long-vanished Athenian Cottage on the west side of Townsend Hill. With his new public and private buildings, and his planning of new streets, he created a neo-classical elegance in the Three Towns, as Plymouth, Stonehouse and Dock were beginning to be known.

So with balls, assemblies, theatres and dinners, Plymouth had its smart social life. There was also an artistic and intellectual life, often overlapping the social. Young Reynolds dining at Mount Edgcumbe was a fellow guest with Captain Keppel, the future

The pillared portico of the Royal Hotel, with Derry's Clock. The theatre at the other end of the block had a similar portico.

Admiral, who was bound for the Mediterranean. Keppel offered Reynolds a free passage and so enabled the painter to make his vital early visit to Italy. Reynolds, later established in London, became a close friend of Dr Johnson and brought him on holiday to Plymouth in 1762. They stayed with Dr John Mudge, fourth son of the vicar of St Andrew's. John, a little older than Reynolds, practised in Plymouth as a doctor all his life but was sufficiently distinguished in his profession and his other interests to be made a Fellow of the Royal Society in 1771. John's elder brother Zachariah II was a brilliant watchmaker who retired to Plymouth in 1771, became the king's watchmaker in 1776 and was eventually awarded £2,500 for his work on chronometers. Their father, the vicar, a great Hebrew scholar and preacher, so impressed Johnson that he wrote Mudge's obituary for the *London Chronicle*. Reynolds called him the wisest man he ever knew. Another friend of his learned circle was John Smeaton, the engineer and another FRS, who was in Plymouth from 1756 to 1759 building the third lighthouse to stand on the Eddystone Rock.

Smeaton lodged in Notte Street with William Cookworthy, the great Quaker chemist who dis- covered china clay in Cornwall and made the first true English porcelain. Captain Cook, who sailed from Plymouth on his three great voyages of discovery, was a frequent guest of Cookworthy's in his Notte Street house, and he brought the young scientist Joseph Banks with him in 1758. Banks, for so many years in later life the President of the Royal Society, was sailing with Cook on his first Pacific voyage. Another dinner guest and friend of Cookworthy's was Captain John Jervis, later the Admiral Lord St

Vincent, who built the fleet that Nelson was to lead. 'Whoever was in Mr Cookworthy's company', said Jervis, 'was always wiser and better for having been in it.' Jervis had met Cookworthy at Lord Edgcumbe's dinner table; how the social, intellectual and naval sides of eighteenth-century Plymouth life intertwined! Many of these men live still in the portraits of Reynolds, who had his first studio over the milliners' shop of his sisters in Dock and produced 30 portraits there and many landscapes. He was much in Plymouth 1744–49, but then moved to London and became the first President of the Royal Academy. He was followed to London by another famous Plymouth painter, James Northcote, who arrived with a letter of introduction from John Mudge.

The meetings of these men were not confined to private houses. John Mudge was a leading light of the Otter Club, which met for literary discussions at the Pope's Head at the top of Looe Street, in the building now fittingly enough the Plymouth Arts Centre. The odd name comes from the club's origin in a group of men who bathed under the Hoe together. Dr Mudge was also president of another club which met at the Bunch of Grapes in Kinterbury Street. In 1810 the Plymouth Proprietary Library was formed, and Foulston designed its original library, built in Cornwall Street in 1812. The organisation if not the building survives. So does the Plymouth Institution, founded by Henry Woollcoombe in 1812, which again had Foulston for the architect of its classical Athenaeum, built next to the Theatre Royal in 1818–19. The Library of Plymouth Law Society was founded in 1815. Plymouth Medical Society, again still flourishing, was founded in 1794 in the new Globe Hotel at the top of George Street. It too had its library. From its members came the foundation of Plymouth Public Dispensary in 1798, the first real source of medical aid for the poor. A legacy from Dr Charles Yonge of the Puslinch family paid in 1804 for the dispensary building in Catherine Street. In 1815 the Dock and Stonehouse Public Dispensary was built in Chapel Street.

Apart from the literary groups which began meeting in the leading inns, there were freemasons. The early records are unreliable but there seems to have been a lodge in Dock as early as 1734 and two more in Plymouth by 1748. St John and Fortitude were warranted in 1759, Friendship in 1761, Harmony and Brunswick in

Left: *Sir Joshua Reynolds, a self-portrait presented to Plympton to mark his year as mayor, 1773.*

131

An 1835 drawing by John Foulston of the lecture hall at the Athenaeum. The lecturer is at the far end of the hall, the chairman seated facing him. It must have been a special occasion because ladies are present.

The Old Chapel, Devonport, closed down in 1806 because it was so often threatened by protesting street mobs. Now the disturbances are from other sources.

1778 and Charity the next year. One lodge with clear records to the present day is Sincerity (No. 189), which was formed at the Three Crowns on the Parade in 1769 and, after using the Mitre and the Rose and Crown in Plymouth, moved to a succession of Dock inns before returning to Plymouth in 1829. There seems to have been a strong mercantile or naval background to the early lodges, for some were formed in other ports and later moved to Plymouth. The warrant of Fidelity (No. 230), for instance, founded in Rotherhithe in 1799, was used at Kingsand in 1810 and has been in Plymouth or Devonport since 1817. Prince William was initiated into Lodge No. 86 at the Prince George Inn in 1786, two months before the freedom of the town was presented to him 'at Mr Winne's'.

The Churches

The Church of England went along quietly enough in the eighteenth century, blessed by two powerful leaders. Mudge at St Andrew's was a strong high church man with no love for Nonconformists or Methodists, in spite of a dissenting youth. He only preached once a month. After his death in 1769 his curate, John Gandy, succeeded him and remained vicar until 1824 – two vicars covering 92 years. Gandy was 'a beautiful example of a Christian pastor' and a wit; John Wesley, visiting St Andrew's in 1775, was impressed by the 300 communicants. At Charles Church John Bedford, great-grandson of the first lecturer at Charles, was succeeded in 1784 by his curate Robert Hawker, who was vicar until his death in 1827. Hawker, originally a surgeon with the Royal Marines, was an evangelist who entertained John Wesley at his table and sympathised so much with the Methodists that he was reported to the bishop. A high Calvinist and a nationally popular preacher, he founded Plymouth's first Sunday school in 1787 and

built the Household of Faith in Vennel Street, near Charles, in 1798, to house his school. He ministered unflinchingly to the sick soldiers brought home in 1809 in the retreat from Corunna; 1,000 died of fever in a converted barn at he Friary and 3,000 Plymothians died in the same contagion. St Andrew's had an organ by 1735 but Charles had only an unsupported choir until 1821: organs until then were lumped with ornaments, a little Popish. The present stone spire was added in 1766.

To serve Dock's growing population Stoke Damerel Church was enlarged in 1750, though the Admiralty, asked for help, would only give masts for pillars and such-like supplies from the dockyard. But it was a long way from the town proper and two new churches were built in the town by public subscription, St Aubyn in 1771–72 and St John in 1797–99.

When Whitfield first came to the Three Towns in 1744 he found the Nonconformists 'low and afflicted'. They were split by endless schisms which were to continue on and off for the rest of the century. The Congregationalists in their Batter Street chapel were shaken by Unitarianism but they finally settled down with Christopher Mends, a Trinitarian, and the Unitarians moved to Treville Street. To fight the West Country's tendency to Arianism (the heresy which denies the full divinity of Christ), the London Congregational Fund Board moved their Western College from Ottery St Mary in 1766 to Radnor Place, Plymouth. It was rebuilt in 1861 on Townsend Hill and its buildings still form the northern side of Western College Road. The Baptists had a revival about mid-century and replaced their Pig Market chapel with one in How Lane in the 1780s, when Dock had its first Baptist chapel in Pembroke Street, with a daughter chapel in Morice Square.

A Tavistock convert of Whitfield's, Andrew Kinsman, moved to Plymouth in 1745 and married Ann Tiley, who gave the land on Bretonside where the 'Old Tabernacle' was built. A later split led to the 'New Tabernacle' being built in Norley Street in 1797; these two chapels became the ancestors of the present

Sherwell Congregational Church. The two Wesleys at first left the Three Towns to Whitfield. but began visiting in 1746 and were here many times before John's last call in 1789. They too found constant division which they worked hard to heal, but the first Methodist churches were Lower Street in Plymouth in 1779 and Ker Street in Dock in 1786, followed by Morice Square in 1811. The Lower Street building, which abuts on Exeter Street between the junctions with Sutton Road and Bretonside, is now in commercial hands. It is the only place in the city where there is evidence that John Wesley preached. It became a Baptist Mission Hall in 1849 and was partly rebuilt in 1882.

Methodism was stronger in Dock than Plymouth, but in both communities all the Nonconformists were not only constantly at loggerheads among themselves, but oppressed by the naval and military authorities, who regarded them as centres of disaffection. A Unitarian chapel built in George Street, Dock, so offended the dockyard authorities that it was closed in 1806; the building is still there as the Old Chapel public house. These were rowdy towns, and the mob, service and civilian, was happy to heave stones and start riots where they felt authority was on their side. The Nonconformist history of eighteenth-century Plymouth is not happy.

There were Roman Catholic priests in 1792, a building registered for worship in Dock in 1801 and a chapel built opposite the gates of the Naval Hospital in Stonehouse by 1807.

The growth of the Navy brought Jewish pedlars to Plymouth, and a small community had settled by 1740. Little Isaac, a Jewish pedlar, was murdered near Plymstock in 1760 (Jew's Wood is still there). The Jews were very much the butt of seamen, who accused them of cheating. But the Plymouth Synagogue, the oldest Ashkenazi foundation in Britain outside London, bought three gardens near the Citadel as a burial ground, and in 1762 built the synagogue which still stands behind the Guildhall. Many of the Jews had settled as shopkeepers or jewellers by the end of the century, and Abraham Joseph, the most important slopman in the Three Towns, held a royal appointment to Prince William.

Trade and Commerce

The business life of the Three Towns was greatly helped by the foundation of banks. John Baring of Exeter, who with his brother Francis was building up the great European banking firm of Baring Brothers in London, was a brother-in-law of the first Lord Boringdon. He launched the first bank in Plymouth in 1772, known as Baring, Lee, Sellons & Tingcombe and later as the Plymouth Bank. The year after came Harris, Harris, Tanner & Herbert, which became the Naval Bank. Dock's first bank was founded in 1788 by Elford, Elford & Hartwell. They were, apart from the Baring link, which did not last long, very local affairs based on the capital of the partners rather than the great national institutions we now know. The partners chopped and changed over the years, and there were several more private banks in both towns by the turn of the century. By making credit available and issuing bank notes, they facilitated business life very considerably.

The business life of Plymouth had changed very sharply under the pressure of the French wars, and nowhere is this better shown than in a book published in 1816 by William Burt, secretary of the new Chamber of Commerce. Over the centuries

French prizes sailing into the Hamoaze, a painting by Serres in 1796. An east wind enables them to sail through the Narrows under topsails.

Plymouth had grown on foreign trade. In 1814 Burt was writing that while Plymouth in the past year had imported coastwise 1,550 tons of sugar from other home ports, only 33 tons came direct from the West Indies, and this state of affairs applied to nearly every other commodity. Virtually all the coal came in non-Plymouth ships. The Cawsand and Kingsand pilchard fishery employed 50 men, the Plymouth trawlers 112 and the hookers about 50; the Newfoundland fishing was dead.

The port had, in fact 'become the greatest emporium for prize ships and goods, of which, during the war, many millions sterling have been sold here'. Another 1814 letter writer, remembered the Parade piled high with overseas imports, 'the property of merchants, particularly the great Mr Morshead'. The revival of the port's Newfoundland fishing in 1763, and all commercial enterprise in the port, was stopped by the outbreak of the American war in 1766. 'Wealth flowing in from the lucrative channel of prizes and prize goods without hazard... consequently all trade is stagnated.'

The prize business had reached large proportions much earlier. Advertisements in the *Sherborne Mercury* for 1757, during the Seven Years War, show ships and their cargoes being 'sold by the candle' almost daily, sometimes two a day, at Pinham's Coffee House on the Parade by Francis Fanning, the broker. 'A thousand barrels of fine French flour and a large quantity of biscuits, lately taken by His Majesty's Ship York' in mid-June; seven ships auctioned between 9 and 16 June the same year, including the 550-ton *Invincible*. In the eight and a half years ending 29 September 1801, 948 captured ships were brought into Plymouth. By 1813 there were 110 registered prize stores around Sutton Harbour, many specially built during the wars and still surviving, often dated. There was no point in normal trade, investing in ships, when the war brought enemy cargoes into port without risk to the merchant. The money involved was more than the Plymouth men could finance. Increasingly they became agents for the wealthier men of London, Bristol and Liverpool.

But if all normal trade was suspended for these 'speculative adventures', what was happening to the Plymouth ships? Vancouver, in his 1808 *General View of the Agriculture of Devon*, said that Plymouth had 245 ships totalling 15,574 tons and employing 1,105 men. In 1815 there were seven shipbuilders around Sutton Pool, six in the Cattewater and six adjacent to the Hamoaze, employing about 300 men and building 20–30 vessels a year. They were supported by 14 ropewalks and a dozen sail-makers. Even Bristol had a smaller fleet, though of much larger vessels. Some of the ships were coasting, but the bulk seem to have been privateering, private warships out for prizes. The Admiralty lists of privateers only gives the port of registration for the American War of Independence

but eight Plymouth ships appear. The first licence in 1777 went to the 70-ton *Swift* with a crew of 16, but by the end of the war bigger and stronger ships were engaged, with the *Plymouth* and the *Devonshire Hero* both having crews of 100. There are few local references, as if it were not a matter to be proud of, but 'many fortunes were made'.

Even the bigger craft in the smuggling fleet based at Cawsand had privateering licences from the times of the American war. The open boats, ostensibly seine net fishing for pilchards, were available with their six-man crews to meet ships at sea, but could also cross the Channel. They could carry six tons of brandy at a time, but the three-masted luggers and the bigger cutters could carry much more, 600–800 eight-gallon spirit casks, as well as tea and tobacco. In 1804 the Plymouth Collector of Customs estimated that 17,000 casks of spirits were smuggled into Cawsand every year. There were 50 craft in the trade by 1815. The Channel Islands were their main sources until 1767, and though Guernsey was still used until 1805, the main trade moved to Roscoff, which the French made a 'free port' in 1769 and which Napoleon later encouraged as a source of information as well as trade. There were some notorious battles in Cawsand Bay between smugglers and revenue men; in 1788 Henry Carter, the 'King of Prussia', barely escaped, though he lost his cutter, and in 1798 the men of the *Lottery* of Polperro opened fire on the revenue men and killed one.

Manufacturing in Plymouth had gone the way of commerce. The Shepherd family were out of the woollen business and just a small white serge business remained. The manufacture of fine porcelain by Cookworthy, which had employed up to 60 people, only lasted from 1768 to 1774 and was then moved to Bristol.

What is now a pub called the China House, but is the oldest waterside warehouse surviving in Britain, was used by Cookworthy as factory and store. In its time it has been a naval hospital, victualling store and shipyard.

By 1815 there were two earthenware potteries at Coxside, employing just over 50 people. The canvas makers and the tanners produced more than the town needed, but otherwise the little industry just supplied the local inhabitants and the shipping business. Sutton Harbour had been improved in the 1790s by the building of the two piers at the entrance, and after long disputes over harbour rights the local businessmen had formed the Sutton Harbour Company, which in 1812 leased the Pool from the Prince of Wales for £6,000.

Industrial Revolution

The real employer and source of wealth for all the Three Towns was the dockyard. Vancouver in 1808 reports 2,741 men employed in the yard, with a total wage bill of £191,153 a year. The actual 'take-home' pay of even the labourers was 16s. a week. No wonder it was hard to find labourers in the country districts around, for though they were busy feeding the ships and the Three Towns, their wage was only 7s. a week. Even dockyard pensioners – 380 in 1808 – had nearly 5s. a week, and to become an 'established' man in the yard, which meant a pension, was regarded as security indeed.

With the towns growing fast the major shore employers outside the yard were the housebuilders. Six or seven master builders in Plymouth alone employed some 350 craftsmen, and had built 500 houses in the ten years up to 1815.

Robert Bayly, who married the daughter of Captain Brabant of the Island House on the Barbican and inherited his business as a merchant and shipowner, started a timber company at Coxside in 1780 which long survived as Bayly-Bartlett.

The town was expanding slowly, eastwards with Brunswick Terrace and other houses along the new Exeter road and towards Coxside, northwards ('Charles Town') to Regent Street and north-westwards ('New Town') along Saltash Street towards Cobourg Street. The old Pig Market became Bedford Street, George Street was a residential area reaching down to the Royal Hotel and Theatre, and Lockyer Street, like much of the Hoe slopes and those north of the town, was dotted with middle-class villas. The old village of Stonehouse had its new Durnford Street gentility to the south.

Dock was virtually filled within the lines and, with the start of the Torpoint Ferry, development began at Morice Town, behind the ferry landing area. The first house was built there in 1796 and to bring in the needs of Dock three 'canals' were cut, lined with wharves by 1812 and soon backed by coal yards, breweries and a pottery. The ferry landing beach is still called Pottery Quay, and the southern 'canal', filled in, is under the hoarding-enclosed space between the two ferry roads. Dock had outgrown Plymouth by 1801, and increased its lead by 1811. The figures are:

	Plymouth	Stonehouse	Dock	Total
1801	16,378	3,807	23,787	43,972
1811	21,156	5,174	30,083	56,616

Plympton St Maurice had started the century worried about its trade; by the end it was prospering, mainly with wool and rope-laying. Commuting was already fashionable: a number of Plymouth professional and businessmen lived at Plympton and most of the houses on Fore Street have Georgian frontages. I n 1801 there were 604 residents. In Plympton St Mary the highway trade was bringing business to Ridgeway, which was developing fast: 1,562 people by 1801. Plymstock was even bigger by 1801, with 1,663 people: no doubt the villages beside the Plym,

Oreston, Hooe and Turnchapel, were growing with the maritime activity. There was much less growth to the north of Plymouth; in 1811 the Tamerton population was 747, Egg Buckland 711, St Budeaux 544 and Bickleigh 264.

But whereas the country districts had about six people to each house, old Plymouth had 9.2 and Stonehouse 9.5. In newer Dock the figure was 7.2; the towns were growing faster in population than houses could be built for them. By 1815 there was talk of uniting the Three Towns, and the new thoroughfare planned by Foulston which linked them all in 1815, across the old Sourpool marshes, was called Union Street.

The Three Towns, which had grown under the one impetus and formed one urban area, were now in effect the fifth largest provincial town in England; their previous ranking through the centuries had always been about twentieth. The only larger towns were Manchester, Liverpool, Birmingham and Bristol, in that order. Even Leeds was smaller. Plymouth, with its neighbours, was one of the new towns of the Industrial Revolution, with all the problems that entailed.

It was not always peaceful. In 1797 crews of the ships at Dock mutinied along with the men at Spithead and the Nore; the men of the *Powerful* set some officers adrift and came ashore with others to lock them up in the 'Black Hole' in Fore Street. Admiral Lord Keith put down the mutiny quickly and bravely; 14 ringleaders were hanged and many more flogged. Soon afterwards three marines were shot on the Hoe for seditious plotting. There were riots in the yard and the streets of Dock in 1780 and again in 1801 over systems of work and food shortages.

The *Grand Gazetteer* of 1759 nicely describes eighteenth-century Plymouth:

... in its most flourishing wicked time of what some call a good red-hot war with France, when indeed 'tis too much over-stocked with inhabitants newcome from Ireland, Cornwall and other parts, and gathered Flocks of Females, charitably inclined to solace money'd sailors in distress; and that they may do it honestly... marry them ex tempore, possibly half-a-dozen in as many months. The true Plymothians are in the main allowed to be as polite, genteel, religious and worthy a people as those enjoyed by any other place. [But in war] the vast resort of the necessitous, the rapacious, the lewd, by land, and of the half-mad Jack Addles from the sea, the scenes are altered much.

Against this there was the elegant, sophisticated society of the gentry and the professional classes. They all flocked to see Napoleon when he was brought into Plymouth Sound after Waterloo aboard the *Bellerophon*. It was the end of a near-century of war, and the dawn of a new era for the Three Towns.

CHAPTER 14

The Years of Expansion, 1815–1914

In the century from Waterloo to the outbreak of the Second World War the population of the Three Towns grew from 56,000 to 209,000, at about the same rate as the national growth. In spite of one of the highest mortality rates in the country, part of the growth was by natural increase, but in the main it was from immigration. In 1841–51 Plymouth showed an increase of 2,900 by a higher number of births than deaths, but an increase of 10,000 by immigration. With agricultural wages lower than wages in the Three Towns, so people were drawn in from west Devon and Cornwall, a process speeded up as the century went on, the Cornish mines closed, and the post-1870 farming depression began to bite. In 1861 13,652 inhabitants of the Three Towns had been born in Cornwall, 4,068 in Ireland and 3,079 in London. A quarter of these Irish people may have been servicemen, and many of the Londoners too, but there was a strong civilian Irish influx, able to reach Plymouth cheaply with deck passages on the coasting steamers. A random check of the 1861 census shows that only Liverpool among the ports had a bigger Irish population than the Three Towns.

The Spread of Devonport

When Devonport Guildhall was built it filled the last space left within the walls. A new working-class suburb was already growing at Morice Town, at the foot of Navy Row (now Albert Road) to serve the commercial area there. New villages were also developing at Lower Stoke, between the open 'killing area' in front of the walls (now Devonport Park and the Brickfields) and Stoke Damerel Church, and at Higher Stoke, where the turnpike to Tavistock crossed the ridge under the Blockhouse. Foulston had many commissions here, like Belmont House built in 1820 for John Norman, the Devonport banker, imposing terraces like Nelson Gardens and elegant villas as in St Michael's Terrace. Terraces of lesser houses, many slate-hung, grew up close by, dated by their names: Trafalgar Row, Wellington Street, Waterloo Street. Slowly over the years these villages spread until they joined up, and as the dockyard spread north so did the terraces creep along outside the dockyard wall, from Morice Town to Keyham and on to Weston Mill Lake, and up the old Keyham Creek as it was filled in to become St Levan Road.

The development of Devonport was plagued from the start not just by the St Aubyns sticking to the leasehold system, but by their working it on a 'three-lives' system with no right of renewal. People were reluctant to buy houses under such conditions and this, together with the rundown of the dockyard and the military forces after 1815, meant a static population until the beginning of the Steam Yard. The town did then increase between 1841 and 1861 from 35,820 to 50,440, and when one of the few pieces of freehold land in the borough came on the market in 1855, at Ford, the Devon & Cornwall Freehold Land Society bought it for working-class development. From 1861 to 1891 there was little change in the Devonport population, but then came a new spurt with the Keyham Extension Yard. From the 54,848 of 1891, Devonport grew to 83,678 in 1911. A Plymouth syndicate of builders bought the Keyham Barton site, north of St Levan Road, from the St Aubyn estate and covered the hillside with rows of small houses. They sold for £200 apiece; the area was nicknamed 'Klondike' as people rushed to buy, and Barton Avenue, in the heart of the area, commemorates the site of the old manor house ('barton') of Stoke, which was occupied almost up to that time. On the northern side of the hill Sir John Jackson was also building houses for his workmen, as well as two mission halls with two chaplains whose stipends he paid. So the reach northwards of Devonport was completed.

Eastwards the Higher Stoke tradition of villa development spread out across Molesworth Road, while the smaller houses between the dignified parts of Lower Stoke and the church began to grow on the northern side of Millbridge, and then spread steadily eastwards along Wilton Street towards Pennycomequick.

To the north the population was already beginning to spill over the Devonport border: St Budeaux grew from 1,096 in 1851 to 6,291 in 1901. Tamerton Foliot, beyond the reach of reasonable transport, went on living

Left: The last Devonport town crier.

on farming and market gardening (much of the latter to feed Devonport) and it stayed more or less level in these years, just falling from 1,147 to 1,102.

Stonehouse Fills Up

Stonehouse property was held on lease like Devonport, but the Mount Edgcumbes gave their tenants the perpetual right of renewal. It was a small area, hemmed in by Millbay, Stonehouse Creek and Plymouth. The Durnford Street elegance soon had working-class houses on either side, filling the peninsula, and from the ancient village on the east side of Stonehouse Bridge working-class streets spread eastwards so that the town was filled with houses by 1840. The population at the 1841 census was 9,712, and though it grew to a peak of 15,398 in 1891 there was little more room for houses, and the increase meant overcrowding.

The Sourpool marshes bisected by Union Street, from the town boundary where the Palace Theatre now is to Derry's Cross, were drying out enough for the Stonehouse building to cross the boundary and reach out to meet the Plymouth houses spreading westward. As early railway plans suggested that Eldad might become the heart of the Three Towns, so Wyndham Square was built, to Foulston designs, and North Road began to grow eastwards from the Naval Hospital wall. Again this was properly in Plymouth but, as lower down in Union Street, the development began at the Stonehouse end.

The Growth of Plymouth

The eighteenth-century spread northwards of old Plymouth into Charlestown, up to Regent Street, and Newtown, along Cobourg Street, was continued after 1815 with good-class houses and villas. They took the healthiest sites on the south-facing slopes on either side of Tavistock Road, and good houses spread westwards from Lockyer Street towards Millbay, Foulston's new town. The better-off moved out from the old town, leaving that to be packed with the poorer new people. The Bayly family presents a case history. From the Elizabethan Island House on the Barbican, still owned by them, they had moved to the Queen Anne red-brick house further along the Barbican, and then to the new (1811) Brunswick Terrace east of Exeter Street (only destroyed in 1978). As that became hemmed in by small houses various members of the family moved northwards to Seven Trees, north of Beaumont Park, and Bedford Park, off Tavistock Road. By 1822 Robert Bayly had rebuilt Torr House, right out of the town, and bought Elfordtown, Yelverton, where descendants live today.

Seven Trees still stands in its own grounds. South of it is Beaumont Park, the demesne of the Bewes at Beaumont House until 1890. Continuous with Beaumont Park on the eastern side was the 87-acre

The Barley House, seen across Stonehouse Lane which, when built up, became King Street.

estate of the Culme-Seymour family, which did not fall to development until nearly the end of the century. On the other side of the town, reaching from King Street (the renamed Stonehouse Lane) up to North Road, was the Barley House estate, home of the Elliot family until the 1860s and not developed until after then. So working-class housing development was confined by these estates. It spread west along King Street and north from King Street to North Road and Cobourg Street, up either side of the Barley estate. Fingers of speculative housing also began reaching up from Regent Street between the villas – Nelson, Wellington and Waterloo, again the street names date them – until they swamped the whole hill, incorporating the better-quality houses and terraces one by one. One can still distinguish the villas among the lesser houses; the district makes a fascinating study.

By 1881 the streets of Plymouth packed the whole area from the Hoe to what is now Victoria Park, and east of that to the main railway line. The only break was the western end of the Houndiscombe estate, where the Derry family lived, but that soon fell and Derry Avenue cuts through the centre. Tothill and Beaumont estates still held, but the first terraces of Mount Gould, the Seymour Terrace block and the Roseberrys, were built. North Hill was housed up to the crest and down the other side, to halfway down Alexandra Road (cut in 1863, the year of the royal wedding). There were houses along both sides of Mutley Plain, and Lisson Grove was the first street running eastwards.

But the railway line west of the Plain, the western pavement of the Plain itself, and the lane just north of Connaught Avenue were all on the town boundary, and houses had been growing fast enough outside that boundary, in Compton Gifford, where the rates were lower. The Culme-Seymours had sold the Mannamead fields in 1851 and the architect Damant, who with Wightwick was carrying on the Foulston practice, designed fine villas there. These spread down Townsend Hill to College Avenue and Hyde Park Road, all built up by 1880 and, between Ford Park and the railway, John Pethick had built five terraces of smaller houses. Compton, with less than 100 people in 1801, now had a population of over 6,000. There was a smaller group of working-class houses just outside the Plymouth boundary at Laira.

Further east Plympton St Mary and Plymstock both doubled in the first half of the century, but while Plymstock fell a little between 1851 and 1901, Plympton St Mary added 1,000, from 2,815 to 3,837. Little Plympton St Maurice with little room to spread just grew a little in this time, from 833 to 1,117.

By 1900 the Tothill estate had vanished under the massed terraces which ran to the end of Mount Gould Road, where a wall cut off Hockin's Farm – now the hospital – and right down across Beaumont Road and Prince Rock to join Cattedown. Close terraces ran from Mutley Plain to Lipson Farm. Peverell Park and its side avenues were built, and by 1914 the houses were reaching up to Beacon Park. Milehouse was still in the country but Devonport was reaching towards it slowly on the other side. The Three Towns were nearly solid, and overflowing their boundaries.

Overcrowding

There were in fact never enough houses. In the first half of the century Plymouth's population increased by 33,633 people, but the number of houses by only 1,396. In 1850 the Plymouth average was ten people to a house, when the national average was only five, and even in London and Liverpool it was only seven. Castle Dyke Lane, at the top of New Street, averaged 24 people to a house, and the worst house in the town had 90 inhabitants. Nor were the earlier speculative buildings of the King Street area any better; at the western end 825 people lived in 67 houses, and 57 had no water laid on; there were earth closets at best and drinking water fetched from a stream near No Place Inn. The 1902 Plymouth Medical Officer of Health's report said the town had 'practically a tenement population', by which he meant that most families shared a house; 604 in every thousand lived that way, and 86 people per thousand were living in one-room tenements. Even that was an improvement; in 1891 there had been 134 per thousand in single-room tenements, and 40 years before that a third of the population was in one-room tenements.

The towns were insanitary as well as overcrowded. In 1847 there were no drains in 27 Plymouth streets with a total of 3,300 inhabitants. In Nichols Court on Lambhay Hill there were 13 houses, 100 people and three privies. In the old town, houses built for the nobility now gave partial shelter to 'the improvident, the vagrant, the vicious and the unfortunate'. The new streets were little better. Claremont Street, off King Street, averaged one privy to 66 people. The Irish were in the worst houses; they flocked over because they were destitute, escaping the famines, and took houses that landlords would not repair. They were mainly in Stonehouse, not mixing with the English and living in ghettoes.

No one had any power to make landlords improve old houses, and there was little control over new building. In some streets and courts all the household refuse and nightsoil was collected in heaps until there were two or three cartloads to be removed. Two contractors were paid £500 a year to sweep the streets and collect refuse; they removed and sold 7,000 tons a year which, incidentally, went to manure the fields which fed the town. The worst slums of Plymouth in mid-century were around New Street and Bretonside, and in the new housing of King Street and Stonehouse. This area was still called 'the Marsh', and parts are still below sea level. In Devonport there were appalling hovels just behind Fore Street.

Smallpox, diphtheria, measles and scarlet fever were all regular killers. Epidemics of one or the other were common. In 1832 an outbreak of cholera killed 1,031 people in the Three Towns, 211 in one August week alone. In the 1849 outbreak the death-roll was 1894. These were the big outbreaks; Plymouth had 702 cholera deaths in 1839 and another 900 in 1850. There was a smallpox outbreak in 1872 with 448 fatalities out of 4,500 cases. The Three Towns were not alone, of course. The villages around suffered – 52 cholera deaths in Plympton St Maurice and Underwood in 1849, for instance – and all big towns were hit. But in 1832 Plymouth's mortality rate was the seventh highest in the kingdom. A government inquiry was ordered in 1850 because the annual mortality in Plymouth for the past seven years had been over 23 in every thousand. Yet in Stonehouse it was 27, in Devonport 29. Plymouth's average for 1869–72 was only down to 21 per thousand. By 1902 the Plymouth death rate of 16.52 per thousand was just below the national average, and in 1912 the

Left: *Old houses in High Street, showing how delapidated they had become before the late-Victorian slum clearances and street widening.*

Devonport figure of 11.9 per thousand was better than the national average of 13.3 per thousand. (The fairly constant death rate of the present day is 12 per thousand.)

Local Government and Voluntary Effort

It would be wrong to judge any other age, even the last century, by our own standards. The doctor's knowledge of sanitation and disease was limited, and only slowly did the idea die that poverty was a family's own fault, distress a natural punishment and self-help the only redemption. The doctors and clergy worked themselves nearly to death in the epidemics, and indeed the vicar of Charles, Dr Carne, and his wife, did die within four days of each other in the 1832 epidemic. It was a time of voluntary organisations or private enterprise doing the welfare work, with public money minimally employed. The doctors through their Plymouth Medical Society followed their dispensaries with an eye hospital at Millbay in 1821 – it became 'Royal' in 1828 under the Duke of Clarence's patronage – and the South Devon & East Cornwall Hospital in Notte Street in 1840, originally with 12 beds.

The Poor Law was reformed with the creation of elected guardians in 1835. Each of the Three Towns had its own board, while all the parishes from Tamarside to the Yealm were formed into the Plympton Union. Their major contribution to the needs of the age was to build new workhouses – Plymouth's on old charity Trust land at Greenbank in 1849, Devonport's at Ford in 1852–54, and Plympton's at Underwood. It could be cynically added that the town councils' contribution was new prisons, Plymouth's again at Greenbank in 1849 and Devonport's at Pennycomequick the same year. The Devonport prison officers' quarters still survive as private houses opposite the central sorting office. Private enterprise helped relieve the congested old churchyards when the Plymouth, Stonehouse & Devonport Cemetery Co. opened its 37-acre cemetery outside the town boundaries, between Pennycomequick and Ford Park, in 1849. In no time it was being called the best investment in the neighbourhood!

There was local concern about the state of things. The Liberal leader George Soltau had led the formation of a Plymouth branch of the Health of Towns Association in 1846, two years after its national inception. From this stemmed the notorious report by the Unitarian minister, the Revd W.J. Odgers, in 1847, which revealed the state of affairs in the slums. Odgers did manage to get bath-houses opened in Hoegate Street in 1850, with half-hearted corporation support spurred on by the 1849 epidemic. This also led to the formal government inquiry into the health of Plymouth in 1851, and three years later the corporation adopted the Public Health Act of 1848, under which it took over the work of the old Improvement Commissioners. A start was made on better drainage. The commissioners had widened a few streets during the century to let more light and air into the town, and more main streets were widened now. It did let in more air and light to congested areas, but it also removed a number of houses and so increased the overcrowding. Local authorities still had little power over new houses, and none to interfere with old houses; private property was still sacred. Devonport thought about the Health Act but did not adopt it until 1866.

Voluntary effort did open the South Devon & East Cornwall Blind Institution in Cobourg Street in 1860 (a blind man, James Gale, was the founder), and the Royal Albert Hospital at Devonport in 1862. Epidemics were still demanding temporary hutted hospitals from time to time, and from 1866 until 1929 there were one or two old naval hulks anchored in Jennycliffe Bay as isolation hospitals. There was an upsurge of interest in natural cures, and in 1870 a homoeopathic hospital started over a chemist's shop near Derry's Clock. It moved to Princess Square (so named in honour of Princess Victoria's visit in 1833, and now the site of the council chamber), where queues of patients caused obstructions, and then to Flora Place.

Public demand for better working-class housing had been growing since the mid-century, and though some Shaftesbury cottages had been built on North Hill in the 1850s there was no real activity until the

1880s. Then private enterprise took over, and people like Bulteel and Harris the bankers, Pethick the builder and Edward Bates the Plymouth MP began a number of blocks. Some survived until after 1945, looking a cross between a barracks and a prison, but they were a real contribution, and if this '5 per cent philanthropy' seems offensive to modern minds, it should be remembered that these men were taking a smaller return than they need on their money – though one can have reservations about the motives of 'Bully' Bates.

Left: Clare Buildings, Coxside, one of the 1880s private enterprise working-class housing blocks, which survived until the 1960s.

In 1884 the SD & EC Hospital was moved to its present site at Greenbank, a large, healthy building but making a trinity with the neighbouring prison and workhouse, known collectively to the poor as 'the Mutley Mansions'. An ear, nose and throat hospital was opened nearby. The Blind Institution had been moved to North Hill in 1876, the Homoeopathic Hospital was purpose-built in Lockyer Street in 1893 and the Royal Eye Infirmary moved to its present building in 1900.

Now local government proper began to be involved, and the old councils were given new powers. Plymouth and Devonport became county boroughs in 1888, and six years later Stonehouse and Compton were given urban district councils, and the Plympton Union area became Plympton Rural District Council. The Local Government Act of 1888 was supplemented by the Housing of the Working Class Act of 1890, which for the first time compelled local authorities to act, whereas before they could assume some powers if they wanted. So both Plymouth and Devonport now had their first Medical Officers of Health. In Plymouth the Liberal mayor, J.T. Bond, led a slumming tour and in 1893 the council set up a Housing of the Working Class Committee. By 1896 it had built the first council houses in Laira Bridge Road – the streets named after the committee members – and the next year, with the people rehoused, tore down the slums of How Street and rebuilt both sides with more council houses. In Devonport the editor of the *Independent*, Henry Whitfeld, launched a series of attacks on conditions there. A private Dockyard Dwelling Co. was formed, and Whitfeld was elected chairman of the council's new Housing Committee. It too began slum clearing. A number of streets, notably Fore Street, were also widened.

Nor were the two new county boroughs content to see large numbers of people enjoying the benefits of their towns while living outside their boundaries. The rates in Compton Urban District were only half those of Plymouth and the inhabitants fought bitterly at being brought into the town. But in 1896 Plymouth's extension Bill was successfully through Parliament and the old medieval boundaries changed for the first time, bringing in Laira, Compton and Peverell. Devonport followed suit in 1898, taking in St Budeaux. By 1901 the total population of the Three Towns was 192,755. Other conurbations had grown more rapidly, however, and this was now the eleventh largest in England and Wales, exceeded by Liverpool, Manchester, Birmingham, Leeds, Sheffield, Bristol, Hull, Nottingham, Newcastle and Leicester, in that order.

Water Supply

The growth of population had forced attention to be paid to water supplies. Iron distribution pipes had been laid in both Devonport (1816) and Plymouth (1826) and the old conduits removed, but there were still open leats blamed for much of the ill-health. The supply was still open along the west side of Mutley Plain in the 1890s. Plymouth steadily built storage reservoirs, first at Sherwell in Tavistock Road and in North Road (behind the high wall below Endsleigh Place) for the new Victualling Yard in the 1820s. Then came Crownhill reservoir (1851), Hartley (1859–62) and Roborough (1885); when the latter was constructed, 24in. iron pipes were laid from there to Crownhill. But the blizzards of 1881 and 1891 froze the leats across the moor from Weir Head and troops had to be sent to clear them while Plymothians queued for water at long-forgotten wells. A great reservoir controversy developed – nothing new – and eventually the Burrator site was agreed. By 1898 it was operating with a cross-country pipe carrying water to Roborough reservoir. Stonehouse since 1593 had lived on a leat from a stream at Torr. Storage reservoirs at Peverell – their skeletons can still be seen west of Peverell Park Road – helped the nineteenth-century town growth, but Stonehouse was glad to take Plymouth water from 1893 and its old system was abandoned. Devonport was not fed from Burrator until the Three Towns amalgamated in 1914. Its private water company watered the town from the leat which takes West Dart water through a tunnel under Nun's Cross Farm and so down the Meavy Valley, following the old Plymouth leat. It was inadequate for most of the nineteenth century, and dangerous after the prison at Princetown became a convict establishment because its sewage was flowing into the leat. Not until the late 1870s, ten years after the first alarms, were filter worksk built. Various storage reservoirs were built on the leat, at Stoke and Crownhill, and Devonport Corporation bought out the water company in 1902.

Parks

For centuries the Hoe has been the great lung of Plymouth, but even that was in danger of being lost early in the nineteenth century. The military claimed ownership of the eastern end and it took ten years of fighting before, in 1818, the rights of the townsmen were established. Soon after that Gill's quarries were removing the Hoe at the western end. For most of the century the Hoe stayed a rough clifftop playground. In 1887 the military surrendered the earthworks which surrounded the Citadel. The area was laid out as formal gardens, paths were made up and down the slopes, the Promenade was constructed and everything was neat and municipalised by 1888, the year of the Armada tercentenary celebrations, when the foundation stone of the Armada memorial was laid.

Plymouth had long paid no attention to its great Elizabethan seamen, but the immense national popu-

The Hoe and Promenade Pier in the 1920s, with bandstand and deck chairs, before the circular swimming pool was built at Tinside.

larity in the last decade of the history of the sixteenth century written by the Devonshire-born J.A. Froude had revived this interest. Froude made the Armada the climax of his work and applied the hero-worship of his master Carlyle; Plymouth loved it all and named Drake Circus to honour the hero, and new buildings in Tavistock Road imitated Elizabethan styles. On the Hoe the Boehm statue of Drake, a replica of that at Tavistock, had already been set up in 1884.

That year the Promenade Pier had also been completed. Its landward end rested on the Bullring, where so many political celebrations had taken place, but these were now banned. The Bullring too was formalised with a belvedere in 1891. The tower of the lighthouse which Smeaton had built on the Eddystone in 1756, and which was replaced by Douglas's Tower in 1890, was also rebuilt on the Hoe. Since then Plymouth Hoe has collected a plethora of war memorials, but it was established at that time much as we know it today.

It was a great time for parks. Freedom Park, where the greatest battle of the Civil War had been fought and Plymothians had long been accustomed to celebrate, became a formal enclosure, and the mounds of soil excavated from Hartley reservoir made another park. A little pleasure ground was made with the pillars from the Shambles, the old market, just below the Drake's Place reservoir at Sherwell. Beaumont House was bought in 1890 on the death of the Revd T.A. Bewes, and its demesne was made into another park. Plymouth joined with Stonehouse and Devonport in laying out Victoria Park (opened in 1891) in the old Mill Creek above Millbridge, at last filled in. Stonehouse's only open space was Devil's Point. Devonport as early as 1858 had obtained from the military the northern part of the glacis round the town and turned it into Devonport Park. So the Three Towns did have some open spaces, though they were well away from the areas that needed them most.

Left: *Drake's statue on Plymouth Hoe.*

Local Transport

As the Three Towns expanded so local transport was necessary to get men to their work and women to the shops. There were steamers on the Tamar from 1839 onwards, and John Gilbert of Saltash dominated the traffic by the end of the century with his Saltash & Three Towns Steamboat Co.'s mixed fleet of eight or nine paddlers and screw vessels. There were steamers supplementing the Torpoint Ferry from 1895 to 1932, a Millbrook-Mutton Cove-North Corner steamer, and steamers on the Cremyll Ferry by 1885. On the Cattewater Henry Elford of Oreston started the Oreston & Turnchapel service to the Barbican in 1871, moving to Phoenix Wharf when it was built in 1895.

There were ten horse-bus services surviving from coaching days, like Baskerville's bus from Roborough, but the great revolution came with tramways. The Plymouth Stonehouse & Devonport Tramways Co. Ltd was the first established under the 1870 Act and laid lines from Derry's Clock along Union Street to Cumberland Road by 1872, extending to Fore Street two years later. By 1881 it was carrying over a million passengers a year. These trams were horse drawn but in 1884 Plymouth Tramways Co. (local directors John Pethick and William Derry) ran steam trams for a couple of years on a route from which some of the very streets have now vanished, from Millbay through lower George Street, Lockyer Street, Princess Square, Westwell Street, Bedford Street, Russell Street, Richmond Street, James Street and Houndiscombe Road to Hyde Park Corner. This route avoided the climb of North Hill but the steam

engines – very noisy and smelly – were replaced by horses in 1889. The town bought this company out in 1892, and by the following year Plymouth Corporation Tramways had extended the line at each end to the Promenade Pier and Hender's Corner. By 1895 they had realigned the middle part of the route to climb North Hill using a third horse for the climb from Sherwell, as was done by the Devonport trams climbing from Stonehouse Bridge. PCT opened their second route, to Prince Rock in 1896. The corporation was building a power station there primarily to electrify the tramway system, but it also gave Plymouth its first electric street lights and eventually its whole power system. Devonport was building an electricity station at Newport Street, Stonehouse.

PCT first ran electric trams in 1899 and the PS&D electrified in 1901, replacing 250 horses. In 1901 the private Devonport & District Tramway Co. launched five routes reaching out from the town centre to the new suburbs. Plymouth too was opening new routes. Thus one urban area had three tramway systems – PCT in red and yellow livery, D&D in brown and the PS&D in green. Only the latter crossed borough boundaries; where Plymouth and Devonport met, as at Pennycomequick or Peverell Corner, people had to change trams. There was another hiatus; D&D built a line from Morice Square to Saltash Passage in 1901, but the old wooden bridge at Camel's Head could not carry trams, and so until the new embankment was finished in 1903 passengers had to walk over the bridge from one tram to the next.

Motor buses first appeared in 1900 with the short-lived Plymouth Motor Co.'s service from Derry's

Old Town Street in horse and cart days, with an early tram car.

Clock to Salisbury Road, and in 1904 the GW began bus services from Millbay station to Modbury and Yelverton. This killed off the Baskerville horse buses, just as in 1908 the first taxis began killing the horse cabs. There was another motor bus, from Fore Street Devonport to Tor Lane, run by the Peverell Road Car Co. from 1909 to 1911, but the vehicles were still not reliable enough for these companies to survive.

The LSW had started a local train service from St Budeaux to the dockyard as soon as the railway opened in 1890, and to the east the Turnchapel and Yealmpton lines started local services in 1897–98. One unusual link on the Yealmpton line was the steamer *Kitley Belle*, which from 1900 to 1929 took people from the Steer Point halt down the river to Newton and Noss. Then in 1904 the GW began running steam rail coaches on its main lines between Saltash and Plympton, opening a series of halts. The LSW followed suit and by 1914 the Three Towns had a tight and cheap local transport service, by train, tram and steamer, and all three served great recreational needs as well on summer evenings and at weekends. But it is noticeable that the transport services followed the spread of houses, rather than the other way round. The one exception is Yelverton, which was only a few scattered houses before the station opened in 1885.

The New Parishes

Spiritual health was not forgotten in the nineteenth-century expansion. St Andrew's built a chapel of ease, designed by Foulston and just across Lockyer Street from the Royal Hotel, in 1823. It later became St Catherine's though never a Parish Church, and no controversy touched it until its demolition in 1957 to make way for the Civic Centre car park. The next two Anglican chapels were built by disgruntled parishioners, St Luke's behind the Central Library in 1827 as a church for the curate of Charles, who was not elected vicar there, and Eldad because the curate of Stoke Damerel was similarly passed over in 1828.

But the new Bishop of Exeter, Henry Phillpotts, the Tory high churchman already unpopular in the Three Towns because of his opposition to the Reform Bill, would not consecrate Eldad, and John Hawker, the former Stoke curate, a son of Hawker of Charles and a true son of that Protestant church, continued to minister at Eldad as a Nonconformist. The battles in Plymouth Town Council over the appointments of two vicars of Charles (the ousted curate Courtney of 1827 was elected vicar when Dr Carne died in 1832) so upset the reformed corporation that

in 1842 it sold the advowsons of both St Andrew's and Charles to pay off the debts on the Royal Hotel and Theatre. After various people had made money on the trans- actions, both advowsons eventually ended in the hands of the evangelical Church Patronal Society.

The vicar of St Andrew's since 1824, John Hatchard, son of the Piccadilly bookseller and a strong low churchman, had long been at loggerheads with his bishop. Hatchard built Holy Trinity Church in Southside Street, and when Bishop Phillpotts came to consecrate it in 1842 the bitterness between the men flared into public battle. It was not eased in 1845 when Phillpotts ordered his clergy to wear the surplice, and Three Towns protests forced him to climb down. Equally at Stoke, the vicar, the Revd William St Aubyn, was fighting his parishioners over the graveyard and everything else.

Then Hawker of Eldad died, the Church of England bought the chapel and dedicated it to St Peter, and Phillpotts appointed a 30-year-old Looe man, the Revd George Prynne, to the new living. He was the first Puseyite – the forerunners of modern Anglo-Catholicism – in the diocese, and there was uproar, with Hatchard of St Andrew's and Isaac Latimer, the radical new editor of the *Plymouth and Devonport Weekly Journal*, leading the opposition. There were near-riots when Prynne donned the surplice for his 1848 induction, and this state of affairs lasted for years. Nor was it eased when in the same year the bishop invited Priscilla Seddon, a naval officer's daughter, to start work among the poor of Devonport. She did wonderful work there, but she too was a Puseyite. In the cholera outbreak of 1849 she and her Sisters of Mercy ran a temporary hospital on the site of the present St Dunstan's School, and there, for the first time in post-Reformation England, Prynne celebrated Holy Communion daily. In 1850 Miss Seddon started building St Dunstan's Abbey on the site and in 1856 became abbess of the first Anglican religious house since the Reformation. Since 1906 only the girl's school has survived at St Dunstan's. The disgraceful opposition of the evangelicals faded away slowly; Hatchard died in 1870 and when St Peter's was rebuilt in 1882 there were no disturbances. Prynne, who had married the admiral's daughter who paid for the 1848 conversion of the church, lived until

Left: *The Roman Catholic Cathedral, with St Peter's Church in the distance.*

1903. The green-capped 1898 tower of the church is his memorial, and he saw other high church strongholds established in Plymouth, notably St James-the-Less in Citadel Road and St John Sutton-on-Plym. Not that the evangelicals weakened: in Calvinistic Charles right up into this century there was no turning to the altar for the Creed and the priest would always doff his surplice – they did come to that – before preaching.

Oddly enough the establishment of the Roman Catholic Church created no such furore. Plymouth with its Irish population became in 1850 the centre of a diocese embracing Cornwall, Devon and Dorset. The first bishop, Dr George Errington, took the little chapel of St Mary in Stonehouse as his pro-cathedral and his successor, Dr William Vaughan, built the cathedral in Cecil Street in 1856–58. Hansom, who designed the cab named after him, was the architect; when half built the whole structure fell down. It was completed with schools nearby from which grew Notre Dame High School for Girls and St Boniface's College for Boys. The Stonehouse church was taken over by the Sisters of the Poor, who built St Joseph's Home in Torr Lane in 1883. By 1914 there were four Roman Catholic parish churches in the Three Towns.

Right through the century the Anglicans were also creating new parishes. When the Victualling Yard was built over the site of the ancient chapel of St Lawrence a new church, St Paul's, was built to Foulston's design in 1830 at the south end of Durnford Street. St George's at the other end continued to serve the Royal Marines and civilians, and St Peter's also took part of Stonehouse into its parish. With Robert Peel's New Parishes Act of 1843, which gave government grants to new churches and simplified the creation of parishes, there was a spate of building. In 1846 four new parishes were made in the cramped area of Devonport within the walls. Apart from Holy Trinity (from which a second parish of St Saviour, with a church on Lambhay Hill, was carved in 1870) the new Plymouth parishes were Christ Church, Eton Place, and St James-the-Less both 1847) and St John Sutton-on-Plym (1855). Then there was a lull until Frederick Temple, later Archbishop of Canterbury, arrived as Bishop of Exeter in 1869, on Phillpott's death. He founded the Three Towns Church Extension Society and before its translation to London in 1885 (he became Archbishop of Canterbury in 1899) another eight parishes had been created. There was a further spurt under the leadership of Bishop Robertson early in the twentieth century; the location of the new churches shows the pattern of urban growth. There was even the dream that Plymouth would become a separate diocese, and the Revd Gordon Ponsonby, vicar of Stoke, began a building in Collingwood Villas that was to be Devonport Cathedral. Crypt and Lady Chapel were built but war came. Bishop Robertson retired in 1916,

and the project languished. The crypt was used as a church hall until 1948 but was pulled down in 1969 and Stoke Damerel Primary School built on the site. Just the foundations of the cathedral have been preserved.

The Nonconformists

Dissent, which had reached a low ebb in the eighteenth century, came alive in the nineteenth in a revival led by the Methodists. Old habits die hard and the earliest new buildings were tucked away. The Wesleyans' 1817 Ebenezer Chapel in Saltash Street (rebuilt in 1939 as Plymouth Central Hall) sheltered behind high railings and a heavily-treed forecourt. The new Baptist Chapel of 1847 was buried behind George Street, approached by a narrow lane. For too many years they had had to hide from the mobs. Not until the Congregationalists moved out of the old town to build Sherwell Church in 1864 did they come boldly out on a main street, and then they shocked the old people with a gothic building and a tall spire; it even looked Anglican. When Mutley Plain became the heart of the expansion northwards the Baptists (1869) and the Wesleyans (1881) dominated the new thoroughfare with their churches.

There were many denominations; even the Methodists were split into Wesleyans, Primitive Methodists, Bible Christians and later United Methodists. The town gave its name to the Plymouth Brethren, though the movement was brought to the town by its founder, an Anglican curate from County Wicklow, in 1830. They had various meeting-places, and a number of schisms, but at first there was a strong following. Among them was George Soltau, twice mayor, whose wife cut up her drawing-room carpet to make rugs for the poor, and Samuel Tregelles, who became a famous Bible scholar.

But by 1851 there were more Free Church worshippers in Plymouth and Devonport than Anglicans; on Sunday, 30 March there were 23,761 at all the Anglican services and 30,900 in the Free Churches. It is interesting to see that as the old dissenters in both towns found their chapels getting cramped they moved out into the new areas. The one exception is King Street Chapel, which the Wesleyans planted in the heart of Plymouth's worst slum, just as St Andrew's established Holy Trinity and St Saviour's in the Barbican area. Parson Barnes, first vicar of Holy Trinity and creator of St Saviour's, was a hero of the battle against dirt, dissipation and ignorance.

Education

Apart from private schools for the children of the well-to-do, the Three Towns offered few facilities for education at the start of the nineteenth century. The headmaster of Plymouth's Elizabethan grammar school received just £20 to take a handful of sons of resident burgesses, and after that could take as many fee-paying pupils as he wished. Plymouth also had three charity schools, the Red and Blue (1658), founded out of the Hele and Lanyon charities, Greencoat (1714) and Lady Rogers (1764), founded under the will of the third baronet's wife, and two church schools, Batter Street (1785) and the Household of Faith, opened by Charles in 1787.

Then came the great dispute between the Lancastrians, who wanted undenominational teaching, and the National Society, which wanted Anglican principles taught. The Lancastrians took the lead locally with the Public Free Schools in Plymouth and Dock Public School, both in 1809, followed by Stoke Public School in 1819. Plymouth Public School moved to Cobourg Street in 1812 and its great years there began with the arrival of George Jago in 1842. He was headmaster for 43 years, making it the third biggest school in the country, with over 2,000 children. Stoke Public School's greatest days came later, under Alonzo Rider, who was there from 1863 until 1896, when he left to found Devonport High School for Boys.

Devonport, which had 40 private schools by 1830, had three national schools and one founded by dockyard artisans by that time. Then in 1832 the national schools won government grants and the churches, old and new, in all Three Towns, began to found their schools. Charles in Tavistock Place was the first in Plymouth, in 1838. Ragged schools started too in 1849, but the census required by the Education Act of 1870 showed that in Plymouth alone there were still 2,000 children receiving no education at all.

The Act required local authorities to establish elected, rate-levying school boards and provide schools for everyone, although attendance did not become compulsory until 1876 and education was not free until 1891. After fiercely fought elections, in which Plymouth voted against spending money on denominational education, the boards began to build. By 1903 Plymouth had built 18 schools and Devonport nine, in limestone and with a flamboyance of style which still excites in those which survive. When Bishop Temple arrived at Exeter he set out to encourage higher education and found a strong supporter in Professor the Revd F.E. Anthony of Western College, the Liberal chairman of Plymouth School Board for 23 years. A high school for girls was started in 1874 and one for boys in 1878. The boys' high school amalgamated with the 1854 Mannamead School in 1896 to become Plymouth College and remained independent. Plymouth High

Left: The Household of Faith, the school demolished to make way for Charles roundabout.

School for Girls was absorbed into the local education authority's plan for secondary education. Both towns, too, celebrated the Queen's Jubilee by incorporating existing art and science schools into technical colleges, with new buildings completed by Plymouth in 1892 and Devonport in 1899.

School boards disappeared in 1903 and the respective corporations became the local education authorities. In both county boroughs primary and secondary education were carved out of the old school system. Plymouth Corporation Grammar School, which had become almost completely a private school, was revived in this way in 1908 with C.W. Bracken, the local historian, as its first headmaster. At Plympton the grammar school was similarly revived as a county mixed grammar school.

Social and Intellectual Life

The free intellectual and social life of the eighteenth century formalised in the nineteenth, with the well-to-do enjoying the magnificence of the Plymouth Proprietory Library in Cornwall Street and the classical solemnity of the Athenaeum for meetings of the Plymouth Institution. This body fathered the Devonshire Association in 1862 and its scholarly ranks were swelled by scientists of the Marine Biological Association after their laboratory and aquarium were opened under the Citadel walls in 1885. For hoi polloi there were the mechanics' institutes started in 1825. The Plymouth institute had its own building in Princess Square in 1827 and the Devonport institute one in Duke Street in 1844. YMCAs opened in both towns in 1848, to become strong social and educational centres.

Plymouth built a new guildhall in 1870–73. It was at a time when the judges were in favour of holding the Cornish Assize in Plymouth instead of Bodmin, and the idea developed that if suitable modern accommodation could be provided that would be better than the archaic conditions in the Castle at Exeter, Plymouth could capture the Devon Assize as well. So at the western end of the new Guildhall were built the Western Law Courts with all possible facilities. In the end the Assizes did not move, but the Plymouth courts were well provided for. The building also included a central police and fire station. With the municipal buildings across a square, flanked by St Andrew's Tower to the east and eventually a new Post Office to the west, it all made

Guildhall Square. The ruins of the Municipal Buildings (with Alderman Rooker's statue in front) were demolished after being burnt out in the Blitz to make way for Royal Parade.

a new focal point for the town. In the same way its great hall became the major centre for social events and meetings of every kind. The old guildhall in Whimple Street became a free library in 1876, and in 1882 Devonport bought out the Mechanics' Institute to make its Duke Street premises their free library and museum. (The Plymouth Mechanics' Institute merged with the Athenaeum in 1899.) Plymouth started its museum in Beaumont House in 1897, but by 1910, with Carnegie aid, had built the present library and museum in Tavistock Road.

Of the philanthropic work in the century the great innovation was that of Agnes Weston, whose mother was one of the Plymouth Baylys. She came to Devonport in 1873 working for the temperance movement among sailors and three years later opened the first Sailors' Rest; Queen Victoria later gave it the 'Royal' prefix and made Miss Weston a Dame, but to the Navy it was always 'Aggie Weston's'. She set out to create 'a public house without the drink', and gave the men comfort, bright colours, mirrors and gilding. It was right outside the dockyard gates, in Fore Street, and its cabins could house 900 men.

For the gentlemen there was the Plymouth Club at the top of Lockyer Street, and the yacht clubs, led by the Royal Western, which was formed in 1827 and grew out of the first Plymouth regatta. Its earliest club house overlooked Millbay. From 1880 it had a splendid block alongside the Grand Hotel, a social establishment of the first order with the finest yachts in the world racing under its burgee.

This was all gentlemanly yachting. At the other end of the scale were the regattas, which every water-side community, from Saltash Passage and Morice Town round to Sutton Harbour and the Cattewater villages, held each summer. Then there were Plymouth Races, held every August on Chelson Meadow from 1828, which matched with their showmen and sideshows the great Plymouth November Fair held in and round the market. The sport was provided at the races by the hunting frater-nity, and chief among them for years was Charles Trelawny, who lived in Bedford Street. He was master and owner of the Dartmoor Foxhounds from 1843 until 1873, when, at the age of 74, he gave up, but for all those years was a familiar sight in his pink coat, mounting his horse outside his house – where the Dingle's Royal Parade entrance was – to ride to the kennels at Ivybridge. Very often

Left: *Winter Villa, replaced in postwar years by an old people's home.*

J.R. Newcombe, the famous lessee of the Theatre Royal from 1845 to 1887, would hack off with him. With the growing naval and military establishments in the Three Towns there was strong service support for hunting and the associated point-to-point meetings.

Though there were undoubtedly social meetings between the businessmen, the county families and the service officers, there was a greater division than in the previous century. The Earls of Morley continued to be presidents of Plymouth Chamber of Commerce, and the Earl of Mount Edgcumbe built Winter Villa at Stonehouse in 1856 because his countess could not stand the winters at Mount Edgcumbe. The Duke of Edinburgh, Queen Victoria's second son, when Commander-in-Chief Plymouth from 1890 to 1893, played his violin in the concerts of Plymouth Orchestral Society. The queen's son at Mount Wise, with his wife a daughter of the Tsar of Russia, brought a glitter to high life not known since the Lennox days, and before they left their eldest daughter, Princess Marie, had married the Crown Prince of Romania. But social life polarised, with county and services standing apart from the tradesmen of the town.

Above: *The Hustings of 1868 outside the Theatre Royal. The Mayor is presiding and the candidates are Collier, Morrison and Lane.*

Politics

Devonport remained a staunchly Liberal constituency for most of the century. 'Bully' Ferrand with prodigious work broke through in 1863 for the Conservatives, boasting that Devonport was no longer a government pocket borough, and in 1865 he hauled his gentle partner Fleming in as well. Both were unseated on petition for bribery – they gave half a day's wages to each dockyardee who voted for them. There was such argument about the dockyard officers controlling voting in the government interest that Disraeli moved in the House that dockyardsmen should be disfranchised. That was enough to get both seats back for the Liberals, until economies in the dockyard put the Tories in from 1874 until 1892. Then, after Gladstone's great 1891 tour of the west, the Liberals were back. H.E. Kearley, founder of International Stores, was one member from 1892 until 1910, when he became Lord Devonport. In that year Sir John Jackson and Sir Clement Kinloch-Cooke won the seats for the Conservatives.

Plymouth had a similarly stormy period. Robert Collier, son of Plymouth's first Reform MP and a distinguished lawyer, was the most important of the two Liberal members until 1871, when he became a judge. There was some acrimony over Collier's judgeship; the Liberal candidate was Alderman Rooker, who was held to have split the Liberal vote on a previous occasion, and Edward Bates from Liverpool took the seat for the Conservatives. Bates, one of the richest, biggest, hardest and most hated shipping owners in the world, was never known to

give to any philanthropic cause in Liverpool, but in Plymouth was lavish in his presents. Just before the 1880 general election he put enough capital into the ailing sugar refinery in Mill Lane to keep it in business. That everlasting firebrand Isaac Latimer petitioned; Bates was unseated for bribery to much local indignation, and the lawyer brought down to defend him, Edward Clarke, took the seat again for the Tories. Bates was back as MP in 1885, was made a baronet in 1886 and retired in 1892. Apart from the Liberal landslide election of 1906 the Conservatives held Plymouth from 1874 onwards. H.E. Duke from Merrivale, another distinguished lawyer, was one of the members from 1900 until 1906. The members who put out the Liberals at the second general election of 1910 bore names familiar to modern Plymothians: Sir Arthur Shirley-Benn and Waldorf Astor.

Local Politics

In the political philosophy of the times, too much government was regarded as a bad thing. The Conservatives were the arch-apostles of this doctrine of *laissez-faire* and the Liberals the more inclined to want to do things. Whatever happened, the great thing for both parties was to keep the rates as low as possible. When the guardians built the new workhouse in 1849 the corporation bought the old site and adjacent property to build a guildhall. The Liberal Alfred Rooker (he was also a deacon of Sherwell Church) was the great advocate of the scheme, but not until 1873 did he see the Prince of Wales open it.

Derry's Clock before the First World War, with hansom cabs and people waiting for the tram just rounding the corner from Lockyer Street,

A statue was put up to Rooker's honour – Drake is the only other mayor so honoured – but not all the Liberals loved him by that time, and the Tories certainly did not. So the statue finished up at the side of the municipal buildings overlooking the public lavatories, even though public subscription paid for it. The German bombs which destroyed the municipal buildings in 1941 blew the statue off its plinth and the sledge-hammer of an American demolition worker finally destroyed it. The only other piece of pure ornament in the Plymouth of those days was Derry's Clock, and though the corporation built it in 1863, most of the money was given by the mayor, William Derry, another Liberal and the son of a Sherwell deacon. (He held the contract for all local horse transport for the GW.)

For most of the century the mayors were leading members of the strongest party on the council. Generally the Liberals seem predominant, though the Conservatives had their spells. But the mayors were also men of substance, industrialists, bankers, professional men, merchants. They were the leaders of the town in the fullest sense, and very different from some of the odd choices of the previous century. The Liberals were dominant when the 1888 reforms gave the council more powers, and they set about using them. In J.H. Ellis the corporation had its first professional town clerk, and he provided the driving force. The market was rebuilt, Old Town and Ebrington Streets widened, the Hoe laid out, parks opened, a tram company bought, new sewage works and the workmen's dwellings at Prince Rock built. Burrator reservoir was in use. Compton had been dragged expensively into the town. The Plymouth rates went up to 1s. in the pound. The Liberals lost their majority, the Conservatives demanded control of the main spending committees, the retiring mayor, J.T. Bond, could not find a successor and the Conservatives refused to try. After some horse-

trading over committee chairmanships the Tory Alderman Pethick – 'Honest John', the major building contractor – became mayor. Is it significant that the following year saw the house-building boom in Plymouth back in full swing? From this time emerged the pattern of electing mayors from each party on the council in annual turn.

The Labour Party was not yet in existence. There had been Chartists in Plymouth in the 1840s and George Odger, the shoemaker born at Roborough, had worked in Plymouth before he moved to London and became from 1860 one of the first trade union leaders. In the 1880s unions and the associated political parties began to develop in the Three Towns. A Trades Council was formed in 1892, broke up over the idea of running candidates in local elections, reformed in 1897 and in 1899 entertained the Trades Union Congress. The Plymouth Congress passed the resolution to seek political representation – the birth of the modern Labour Party. The Plymouth Social Democratic Federation in 1900 formed the Three Towns Housing Association, pressing the local authorities for more council houses. By 1913 they were petitioning for amalgamation of the Three Towns.

The galaxy of local governments in an area where different sides of a street were under different control – Mutley Plain was so split, for instance – produced many anomalies. The Plymouth borough police of a Saturday night would push a drunk over into Stonehouse for the county police to cope with, and the county police would push him back. When Stonehouse was only a sanitary district certain contagious disease laws did not apply there as in the towns proper. So all the prostitutes flocked to Stonehouse to live.

With such close neighbours there were of course petty jealousies and rivalries between the three neighbouring authorities, particularly between Plymouth and Devonport. They came to a head when Admiral Sir Lewis Beaumont arrived as commander-in-chief and steadily snubbed the Mayor of Devonport, W.J. Moon, a naval outfitter. When the king and queen visited the town in 1907 the Mayor of Plymouth was invited to lunch in the Admiralty yacht, but not Mr Moon. The Mayor of Plymouth, Sir Charles Radford was only a draper too, but he was head of Popham's, which catered for the best people, and he had a big house at Yelverton. So Mr and Mrs Moon boycotted the royal visit, and his townsmen pointedly kept off the streets for the royal processions.

The idea of amalgamation had been mooted in 1835 and 1888 (when Plymouth also asked to become the capital of a South Devon county), and Sir Joseph Bellamy had promoted a conference on the subject in 1902 in Stonehouse Town Hall. But the 1913 ballots in Plymouth and Devonport which came from this new pressure encouraged Plymouth to make a formal representation to the Local Government Board for the amalgamation of the Three Towns.

The inquiry opened in Plymouth Guildhall on Wednesday, 28 January 1914. Plymouth put up as first witness its town clerk, J.H. Ellis. Then an impressive figure appeared in the hall, Major-General A.P. Penton, CVO, CB, Officer in Command South West Coast Defences. He was in residence at Government House, Mount Wise, in effect the successor to centuries of Governors of Plymouth. Ellis stood down and General Penton took the stand as Plymouth's witness. His vital testimony was:

In peacetime the organisation of the Three Towns into three distinct bodies does not affect us much... In wartime it is an entirely different question. You would have the fortress commander having to go to three different bodies... In fact if I was fortress commander here in wartime I should have to go to the three chief civil magistrates and say 'One of you must represent the civil community...'

Counsel for Devonport, the chief opponent, made heavy weather of a short cross-questioning. Ellis went back in the box, and the inquiry lasted another four days. But it was 1914. The German threat had been clear for years. War did break out six months after the inquiry ended, and from October 1914 General Penton had only one authority to deal with.

CHAPTER 15

War and Peace, 1914–45

August 1914 came to Plymouth as so many wars before had done. The fleet was already at battle stations and the reserves mobilised. The battalions of the 8th Infantry Brigade at Crownhill and Raglan marched to the railway stations with their commanders riding at their head, to be caught almost at once in the retreat from Mons. The Territorials mobilised. Millbay Drill Hall was full, schools like Prince Rock became temporary barracks as later on other schools, like Salisbury Road and Hyde Park Road, became hospitals. The dockyard built up its labour force. As the war in France settled down to its man-eating trench warfare, so the civilians volunteered for the Army, or were called to the colours, if they had not found work in the yard.

The dockyard employed just over 10,000 men at the outbreak of war; before the end it had nearly 19,000. There were war bonuses which doubled the men's wages, and much overtime: no danger and no departure from home comforts. For the men who went into the services there was poor pay, huge casualty lists, discomfort and little home leave. It was to leave a bitter taste in many mouths long after the end of the war.

The Fleet Reservists, who had been the first called up, were men who had done their full service and retired to live with wives and families in the ports on whose strength they had been borne. Many of these men went into the older ships also called out of reserve – the most vulnerable – and every one lost produced a large Plymouth casualty list. The Battle of Jutland at the end of May 1916, in which the Royal Navy lost 14 ships and 6,274 men, hit the port desperately, for five of the lost ships, and at least four of those badly damaged, were Devonport-manned. There were crowds outside the newspaper offices for hours awaiting casualty lists and, for weeks after, the streets seemed full of black widows' weeds. Every battle in France too, with its infinitely larger casualty lists, hit the town, but none like the Battle of the Bois de Buttes in May 1918. The 2nd Devons, long since robbed by the long war of their regular soldiers and largely made up of wartime soldiers, went down to hopeless odds with Colonel Anderson-Morshead of the old Plymouth merchant family dying with them, revolver in one hand and hunting crop in the other.

For Plymouth itself, far from the battle and out of air range, with only the sea-facing lights kept dim, there was little but the numbing wait for casualty lists. The Canadian Expeditionary Force, diverted unexpectedly into the port in October 1914 to avoid U-boats in the Channel, provided the spectacle of 33 liners steaming through the Sound into the dockyard to disembark 25,000 men. After the Battle of Coronel, when hundreds of reservists went down with the Devonport-manned *Monmouth* and the *Cape of Good Hope*, the dockyard had secret orders to prepare the squadron which was to avenge them at the Battle of the Falkland Islands. If the yardees had not finished the work in time, ordered Churchill, they were to sail with the ships, but as with so many Churchill orders there is a veil over the outcome.

Apart from repair and maintenance work, and fitting out the Q-ships in the latter campaign against the U-boats, the dockyard built the battleship *Royal Oak*, the cruiser *Cleopatra* and two of the weird and ill-fated K-class submarines. They were designed to steam at the same speed as the battle fleet and actually had two funnels. They were always in trouble. K-6, on trials in the basin at Keyham, submerged and sat on the bottom for two hours, refusing to come up. The defect was repaired by an inspector of engine fitters aboard, but yard men refused to dive in her again. Perhaps the major dockyard excitement of the whole war was generated by the large numbers of women employed to make up the manpower shortages. Even outside the yard there were women tram conductors.

The war penetrated the Cattewater. Submarines sailed up to Turnchapel Wharves, which the Admiralty had bought in 1905 together with the quarries behind for oil storage, to refuel. When the Americans came into the war they took over Victoria

Mount Batten, with the Royal Air Force in occupation.

Wharves as a naval base in June 1917. Within weeks two destroyers and over 60 submarine chasers were based there, with over 3,000 men working from the port and headquarters in Elliot Terrace.

The biggest new development was at Mount Batten. The peninsula was closed to the public in 1916 and the Royal Naval Air Service set up a base. At first the little Castle Inn was the officers' mess, the petty officers were in the coastguard cottages facing the Sound, men were ferried across each day in the Oreston & Turnchapel Company's *Rapid* and a hangar housed the first Short seaplanes. A rail track was laid along Batten Breakwater to enable a crane to hoist the planes in and out of the water. Hangars and living quarters were built, with slipways for the planes and motor launches attached. When on 1 April 1918 the RNAS and the Royal Flying Corps were merged, Mount Batten became an RAF station. With the end of the war and the anti-U-boat patrols, Mount Batten went into 'care and maintenance'.

Greater Plymouth

Under the stress of war the Three Towns had merged themselves into one Corporation of Plymouth without much public concern. The mass referendum in 1914 had shown the people of all Three Towns in favour of amalgamation. Devonport Corporation had spent thousands of pounds in fighting the proposal in spite of that, and with its members the old rancour died hard. They found themselves as they feared in a minority on the new council; of the aldermen Plymouth had 11 seats, Devonport seven and Stonehouse two; of the councillors Plymouth had 33, Devonport 21 and Stonehouse six. The 1913 Mayor of Plymouth, Thomas Baker, became the first mayor of the new borough and continued under the pressure of war for two years; he was a Liberal who was to be knighted in 1920. Baker's successor as mayor was Colonel J.P. Goldsmith of Devonport, to keep the balance. The first town clerk was J.H. Ellis of Plymouth. R.J. Fittall of Devonport was his deputy and took over in 1917, a robust extrovert quite capable of digging committee chairmen in the ribs and demanding: 'How can you be so stupid?' The war, and the problems of amalgamating three councils and all their undertakings occupied their energies. With the end of the war a burst of energy was released, an outward-looking period under Conservative control which matched the Liberal developments of the 1890s. J.Y. Woollcombe, descendant of that Reform leader of a century earlier, had been the Tory leader since 1913, exercising what the *Western Morning News* called 'a benevolent dictatorship'.

The first need was housing, for the soldiers coming home looking for 'houses fit for heroes' found a greater shortage of accommodation than even before the war. Under the 1919 Addison Housing Act, Plymouth was recommended to clear 19 insanitary areas covering 1,017 houses and 9,685 people. Houses had to be built for them first. When the Prince of Wales came to Plymouth that year to accept office as Lord High Steward, he cut the first turf at North Prospect for a new council housing estate. The Swilly estate had also been bought. The first two houses were occupied by the end of 1920, 264 more by the end of 1921 and 402 in 1922. By the end of 1924 802 houses had been built by the corporation, compared with 215 by private enterprise in the same period. The new council houses were used partly to accommodate ex-servicemen with families nd unsatisfactory housing, but above all to clear the worst slum areas of the Three Towns. The housing programme went on steadily through the 1920s and 1930s – Swilly houses in 1929 were being built for £400. By 1939 Plymouth had 5,000 council houses and flats. There were patches of private house-building – a 1930s house in Stangray Avenue sold new for £850. The Great Western Railway also built an estate for its workmen at Peverell, and the Astors another estate, complete with an Institute, at the end of Mount Gould. The Admiralty built 174 houses in 1927 at Pemros Street, St Budeaux, to house men displaced by the closure of Pembroke and Rosyth Yards – hence the ugly street name.

The tramway system had been linked up in 1915 when Plymouth bought out the Devonport company (though the PS&D went on until 1922). In that year, when the Bath and West Agricultural Show was held in what is now Central Park (the idea of buying this large open space which was becoming locked in by houses generated from the show). Alma Road was widened and tramlines were laid from Pennycomequick to Milehouse. But the corporation was still paying an annual sum for its trams to cross Stonehouse Bridge, and the ha'penny gate was a nuisance to every other user.

The tolls had survived from turnpike days. Some fell into disuse when the cost of collecting became greater than the amount yielded, but not until the end of the 1850s did the gates go from Milehouse, Cattedown Corner, and the Plymouth end of Mutley Plain ('Lewis Jones's gate'). Plymouth bought the Iron Bridge and the Embankment in 1897 but kept the tolls on to recoup the cost. The tolls at Mill Bridge (which had caused an uproar when they were imposed in 1807) and Stonehouse Bridge had been sold by the Edgcumbes to a private company, but now they too were bought out, and on 1 April 1924 the mayor, Solomon Stephens, toured all four toll points and declared them free.

The Rise of the Labour Party

All this had been done in typical postwar depression years. Once again men were flocking out of the Forces, and the dockyard was cutting back. From the wartime peak of nearly 19,000 the labour force was back to 15,837 and still falling: 1925, 11,436; 1927, 10,854, and then 800 sacked in a few weeks. In the early postwar years it had been the wartime temporaries going out, but by 1924 men who had regarded the dockyard as their career were being discharged. There were strikes in civilian industry: a dockers' strike in 1919 which halted coal supplies and nearly left the town without gas; a builders' strike which lasted six weeks – the men wanted an extra half-penny an hour. In 1926 came the General Strike, which hit Plymouth as hard as the rest of the country. Though the strikers played a football match against the police the trams were rumbling through the streets shrouded in wire netting to stop the stones being thrown at them.

Against this background the Labour Party grew to strength in local affairs. The pioneer was J.J.H. Moses, born in Dartmouth, leader of the Shipwrights' Union in the dockyard, a Methodist local preacher, large, shambling, sanctimonious, able to use tears to win an argument. He was a member of Devonport Town Council by 1914 and came over to Plymouth with the amalgamation. He was a guardian too – the separate Plymouth and Devonport boards remained until 1926, when their work was taken over by local authority Public Health Committees. The guardians were Labour's first target and six were elected to the Devonport board in 1919, led by H.M. Medland. He was an Okehampton boy, the leader of the Engineers' Union in the dockyard and their full-time secretary by 1921. Bert Medland fought Jimmy Moses over work allocations in the yard, refused to 'humbly petition' the Lords Commissioners when he was fighting for wage increases, and walked into the Admiral Superintendent's office smoking a cigarette. From guardians the attack moved to the town council; by the end of 1923 Jimmy Moses was an alderman and had been joined by Medland, R.R. Oke, a railway-man, J. Churchward, chairman of Plymouth Trades Council, and H.G. Mason, another dockyardee. Two years later another half-dozen socialists were elected, and they became a real force. In 1926 Jimmy Moses became Plymouth's first Labour mayor and Medland leader of the party, living up to his 'Stormy' nickname. They demanded their share of committee chairmanships, and got them, four to the 22. Medland had Public Health. He had declared war on the Poor Law when he became a guardian; now he could act. His great achievement was to convert Plymouth Workhouse into the City Hospital. From now on the mayoralty went in turn around the three parties.

The council was changing in many ways. The Liberal leader, Sir Thomas Baker, who died in 1926, did much to teach and encourage the new Labour members. But the Liberals were a dwindling force, the radical torch had passed to the new men, and the Conservatives were firmly in power. In face of the Labour challenge the Tories and Liberals agreed not to oppose each other in ward elections. The Liberals suffered the fate of all minor parties in coalition.

The Tory leader, Woollcombe, had died in 1923. Very soon Lovell Dunstan took over. He was a ship chandler and from the little room behind the shop in Southside Street he ran Plymouth. Callers would find him there with one or more of his cabal, all businessmen – G.P. Holmes, W.J.W. Modley, F.D. Baxter, W.H.J. Priest – all chairmen of the major committees. In the expansive years after the war rates had soared (each of the Three Towns had a separate rate until 1930, while the liabilities were ironed out) from about 8s. to 14s. Now the aim was to bring them down; by 1930 a 10s. rate had been achieved, and holding it at that level was to be Lovell Dunstan's policy, watch-word, guiding principle. It was good for businessmen but it was not good for Plymouth. Much that should have been done was left on one side. When in 1924 the Housing Committee approached those 1919 slum clearance areas they cut the cost to a quarter by reconditioning instead of rebuilding, and only put blocks of flats in where areas had to be cleared. It was to preserve the historic features, they said, but they still destroyed many old buildings, and even the Elizabethan House, No. 32 New Street, was only saved by A.S. Parker, the architect and founder of the Old Plymouth Society, after the roof had gone.

Town Developments

Not everything stood still, of course. The capacity of Burrator was increased 50 per cent in 1928 after the dam had been heightened by 10ft (the road was carried by a suspension bridge for two years). The polo field at Roborough – the George Hotel was the club headquarters and Lord Louis Mountbatten one of the naval members – was bought as a municipal aerodrome. As early as 1923 the *Western Independent* and the *Western Morning News* were pushing the idea of an airmail service to pick up the incoming ocean mail at Plymouth. They promoted trial flights, and the Air Ministry tried running an experimental service with Alan Cobham piloting the first flight in

Roborough Airport seen from the air, with the College of St Mark and St John to the right and the Nuffield Hospital in the foreground.

1923. There were rival sites at Chelston Meadow and Staddon Heights, but Roborough won; the town council took an option on the ground in 1924 but the Chamber of Commerce hung back, there was no government aid, and it was seven years before Plymouth's aerodrome finally came into being.

In 1931 Central Park was opened; it was aimed to keep it as a piece of countryside with green fields and lanes between hedges, but the idea has been largely forgotten over the years. Stanley Leatherby, a Conservative councillor out to make his name, began promoting Plymouth as a holiday resort. Bathing houses had been built at Tinside in 1913 and there were small bathing pools for men, women and children. In 1928–33 the large circular pool was built there with new changing rooms, sun terraces and other facilities, and various advertising schemes were launched. Madeira Road, until 1933, ended at Fisher's Nose: pedestrians could only reach the Barbican by going up steps and along a passage enclosed by corrugated iron. Now the road was driven through to join Commercial Road and the last warehouses of the old Victualling Yard were destroyed to open the view.

This was no loss, but the removal of the eighteenth-century pillared watch house opposite the Admiral MacBride was strongly but unsuccessfully opposed. The old Greenbank Prison, which had long been the responsibility of the Prison Commissioners, was demolished in 1935 and the council converted it into magistrates' courts, a central police station and a fire station, to replace the now inadequate arrangements behind the Guildhall.

Plympton and Plymstock

On the eastern and northern side the town had grown to its boundaries. With the advent of the motor car and buses it became easier to live further afield. Plymouth was encircled by Plympton Rural District Council land; their rates were lower than those of Plymouth, and their powerful clerk, Percy Loosemore, supported every possible development

The housing sprawl of Plymstock and Pomphlett, seen in this pre-1960 photograph, was mostly built between the wars. Now most of the empty spaces are filled.

in his area that would encourage housing and so push up the rateable value of the district. The RDC began providing electricity in 1926, and improved its water supply in 1928. Not only were areas like the Torr estate – old Bayly land and contiguous with the Plymouth boundary on the north – being built up, but Plympton and above all Plymstock were growing fast. The population of Greater Plymouth, static from 1911 to 1921, had fallen by 1931 from 209,857 to 208,166. The central areas of the old Three Towns showed a decrease in density of population, and the nineteenth-century suburbs were static. The city population owed its decrease to migration, while Plympton RDC showed an increase of 19.3 per cent by migration alone. Plympton and Plymstock grew from 7,032 in 1901 to 12,134 in 1931 and 17,840 in 1949. The whole dormitory area was growing from Wembury to Dousland.

So when Fittall retired as town clerk in 1935, Colin Campbell was appointed from Burnley, partly because he had experience of boundary extensions. He was set to work on this at once, but life was difficult. Percy Loosemore played bridge every Friday night at the Plympton home of the father of the two Leatherbys on Plymouth Council; Lovell Dunstan was another player. The editor of the *Western Evening Herald*, W.O. Mills, was in the magic circle, and his Saturday 'Citizen's Diary', which could flow to eight or ten columns, was the most influential local journalism of the day. Loosemore thus had his allies in the Plymouth camp, but Dunstan, against extension, was overruled (and sometimes purposely kept in ignorance). Plymouth won its boundary application in 1938, growing from 5,711 acres to 9,595. It was still hemmed in by the rivers, and the Plymstock-Plympton suburbs, as they had really become, were still outside. However, Plymouth had become a city in 1928 and its chief citizen lord mayor in 1935.

Members of Parliament

Under the parliamentary reorganisation of 1918 Plymouth was reduced to three Members of Parliament, cut into the constituencies of Devonport, Drake and Sutton. Waldorf Astor, son of the naturalised American millionaire, had been a Plymouth MP since 1910. He succeeded to his father's title in 1919 and his wife Nancy fought and won the Sutton Division. She was the first woman to take her seat in Parliament and held Sutton for 25 years. In 1923 Leslie Hore-Belisha won Devonport for the Liberals. He too sat until 1945, surviving the landslides of 1919 and 1931, becoming a chairman of the National Liberal Party and a minister in each successive 1930s government. As Minister of Transport he made many reforms and Belisha beacons are a memorial; then he went on the War Ministry and did more to reform the Army than any man since Haldane. But his impatience, his showmanship and the necessary speed of his changes upset the generals, and they forced his resignation in January 1940. Jimmy Moses won Drake for Labour in 1929, Plymouth's first Labour MP, and survived a petition to unseat him. The allegation was that A.C. Ballard, a rich eccentric who gave weekly pocket money to every member of his vast boys' club at Millbay, had spent unexplained monies on Jimmy Moses's behalf. But he was swept out of the House in the 1931 National Government landslide.

Harbour Work

After the war the work of the port went on much the same: wheat, fertiliser, timber, coal and sugar came in; china clay went out. In the 1920s the port handled between £2½, and £3 million worth of goods each year, falling away in the Depression to a low in 1932 both in imports and exports, and then climbing again, although by 1938 it was still not back to the 1920 figure. The one major increase was in petroleum imports, the 10 million gallons of 1920 climbing to 55 million gallons in 1939. New ships based on the port were the cable-layers of Cable & Wireless, which took over Turnchapel Wharf in 1922.

Fish stocks had grown in the under-fishing of the war years and the market was busy for the next ten years. There was also a winter glut of herrings that brought the Cornish boats and the east coast drifters

Herring drifters pack the Fish Quay in the early 1930s.

in; from 1926 to 1936 there were up to 100 east coast drifters and even more Cornish boats working out of Sutton Harbour. The peak year was 1930, but yields fell away after that. There were only three east coast drifters in 1938, and then they were seen no more. But in those boom years Plymouth became again the major West Country fish port, taking the title which Newlyn had regained at the turn of the century. By 1938 there were 13 steam trawlers in the port but only one sailing trawler.

The inter-war years were the zenith of the liner trade. Though the United States Navy's flying boat

NC4 reached Plymouth in 1919 after the first-ever Atlantic flight, there were to be no trans-Atlantic passenger flights until 1939. The ocean liner was still the last word in luxurious, prestigious travel. The New York-Europe route was the most glamorous of all, with the biggest ships in the world racing to establish the fastest times. Plymouth was the nearest European liner port to New York; Cunard moved into the Channel in 1919 and all their ships, from the old *Aquitania* and *Mauritania* to the first *Queen Mary*, were anchoring in Cawsand Bay, as were the famous French, German and American ships. So too were the less renowned liners, from every corner the globe,

The American seaplane NC4, the first aircraft to fly the Atlantic, at Mount Batten.

and there could be times with five liners having to be handled at once. Plymouth had four tenders capable of carrying 2,460 passengers, and often all had to be in service. The peak year was 1930: 788 liners called, 41,130 passengers and 307,000 bags of mail passed through the port. After 1926 it was only the two depression years of 1932 and 1933 that saw fewer than 30,000 passengers. Among them were the most famous people in the world: politicians, film stars, writers, sportsmen. It was the fast, smart, elegant way to cross the Atlantic.

The Services

Plymouth was still very much a service town: four battalions of infantry with brigaded corps troops, the Artillery in the Citadel, the Royal Marines at Stonehouse, the shore-based sailors at Keyham, and all still in uniform when out of barracks. In 1934 the naval supremacy was marked by the commander-in-chief moving into Government House and renaming it Admiralty House, and the senior soldier moving back to the smaller house at Mount Wise. There were still enough ships for whole fleets to be anchored in the Sound, to entertain with searchlight displays. Between 1921 and 1930 the yard converted Fisher's three giant 'light cruisers', *Furious*, *Courageous* and *Glorious*, into aircraft carriers and achieved the expertise that has made Devonport pre-eminent in such work for as long as aircraft carriers survived. In 1927 there was an echo of the K6 story, but without a happy ending, when the submarine H29 sank in dock at Devonport and seven men died. There had been two disasters before the war, A8 sinking just outside the Breakwater in 1905 with the loss of 15 men and A7 lost in Whitsand Bay in 1914 with 11 dead. In 1927 the first Washington treaty cruiser *Cornwall* was laid down, followed by *Devonshire* and *Exeter*, among others. With the accelerated naval programme after 1937 the old battleship *Valiant* was modernised.

But the major change was at Mount Batten, which came out of 'care and maintenance' in 1928 to become the home of two flying-boat squadrons of the RAF and, during 1935–37, two flights of the Fleet Air Arm. In addition to liners, cargo ships, fishing boats and warships, the Sound was enlivened by these flying boats taking off and landing. The most renowned airman ever to serve there was Aircraftman Shaw, hiding the identity of Lawrence of Arabia in his job as the station commander's runner. His experience in three fatal plane crashes in the Sound, and his experiments with his own high-speed launch, led him to bully the RAF into developing the rescue launch service which was to be so important when war came.

Employment

Census tabulations do not make much sense in a city like Plymouth, where some 25 per cent of the working population were in the dockyard in the inter-war years, and 14 per cent in the Armed Forces. The 1931 returns, for instance, show a high figure in industry, but much of that was in the yard or in industries serving local needs. Biscuit manufacture had ceased, but a baker in Exeter Street, E.E. Farley, had been making rusks for babies from the recipe of a local doctor. In 1921 Farley's Infant Food Ltd was formed by the Trahair family, who had bought the recipe; in 1931 they built a modern factory at Torr Lane, and in 1938 they doubled it; Farley's rusks became nationally known. The soap works had closed, but the American scientist Acheson had chosen Prince Rock in 1911 as the site of his only British factory making industrial colloids – the first American factory in Plymouth. Of the pre-1914 factories serving national needs there really only remained the fertilisers and the Reckitt starch works. Their factory also did all the printing for the group, and Plymouth still had its book printing firms of national repute.

In 1931 building employed 4,700 people, but there was little major work being done. After the first council house building in the early 1920s slum clearance became a patchy affair. The oldest streets in Devonport (Cornwall Street) and Stonehouse (High Street) were cleared and flats built, and Plymouth's ancient High Street (now foolishly called Buckwell Street) was partially treated so. A new bank, several motor showrooms, three super-cinemas and a newspaper office represented the only 1930s developments in Plymouth, and these point to the city's second strength. The second largest employer was the distributive trade, employing 21 per cent of the workforce compared with the dockyard's 25 per cent. But it was not a wealthy city by any means. The average percentage of unemployment in Plymouth for the years 1929–38 was 16.3, 1.5 per cent higher than the national figure.

Shopping and Entertainment

The city of a quarter of a million people was the shopping and entertainment centre for three-quarters of a million. Many people living within 20 miles came in for weekly shopping. Others would come 50–60 miles for special shopping – a dress 'bought in Plymouth' had a cachet none of the country towns could give. Day-out shopping, taking in a meal and a show as well, had a hinterland west of the line from Bude to Kingsbridge.

A fortnightly 5s. return excursion train from Penzance, run to coincide with Plymouth Argyle's home games, would on average bring 2,500–3,000 people to Plymouth. On those days the Fifty Shilling Tailors in Union Street sold an extra 200 suits.

The heart of the shopping area stretched from Drake Circus to Derry's Clock. George Street had the expensive shops and was the fashionable place; Genoni's Swiss Restaurant had world-famous customers and Nicholson's Long Bar (no women allowed on its sawdust floor) was a legend among naval officers. The smell of Goodboy's coffee (they were southern Irish Quaker immigrants of the mid-nineteenth century) still haunts old Plymothians. Bedford Street had the four great department stores. Joseph Spooner in 1858 opened a draper's shop in Bedford Street which grew to dominate half Old Town Street as well. It was an ebullient family, with Mr Spooner's Harriers and Kenneth Spooner's amateur dramatic society, but the business was taken over by Clarence Hatry's Drapery Trust in 1927. The trust merged with Debenham's later that year, and after Hatry's crash in 1929 Debenham's took full control, although keeping the Spooner name. Next down Bedford Street was Popham's, with brass plates on the front so polished over the years that 'Popham Radford' could hardly be read. The business had been founded in the 1820s by Elizabeth Radford of Plympton; Alderman Sir Charles Radford, who died in 1916, was the most distinguished member of the family. Popham's was expensive, for the best people: it did not open on Saturday afternoons. John Yeo's, next door, was very different. The original John Yeo came from north Devon, learnt his trade in London and Paris, and as a good Methodist and Liberal ran the business he began in 1871 on

Spooner's Corner in the 1930s, said to be the busiest corner in the country outside London. The area is now under St Andrew's roundabout.

'cash only' lines, attracting considerable country trade. His nephew, John Beckley, joined him in 1893; he and his heirs maintained the family style. For the smart and fashionable there was Dingle's, run by Jack Baker and Frank Dingle, whose fathers had founded the firm in the 1880s, already expanding by taking in first Underwood's the grocers and then Vickery's the outfitters. In Frankfort Street was Coster's, run by the Leatherby family and very much down the price scale. At the bottom of Frankfort Street was the vast Plymouth Co-operative Society's 1894 headquarters with its clock tower, assembly hall and educational operations over the shop. Founded in 1859 by nine working men, the Co-op had another large building at Drake Circus and by 1936 it had 140 branches, eight farms, 78,000 members and 2,300 workers. At Devonport there were the shops of Tozer's, Boold's and Love – later Garratt's – but none had the gloss of the Plymouth stores. The eclipse was showing even in the 1920s.

While the women shopped on Saturdays, the men watched Plymouth Argyle, the city's one professional association football club. It had been started by old boys of Launceston College and their first match was against the school in 1885 (Argyle lost 2–0). Their treasurer lived in Argyle Terrace and green and black, still club colours, were thought to be the Scottish Argyle clan's colours. The club entered the Southern League in 1903; their first professional was Bob Jack, who became their first manager and built up the famous 1920s team which was for six years runner-up in the Third Division, and reached the Second Division in 1930. A crowd of 20,000 at Home Park was normal, and big fixtures would attract 40,000. Argyle had taken over Home Park in 1901 from Devonport Albion, a rugby football club which had grown out of the Dockyard Technical College, started in the South Yard in 1846 to train marine engineers. In time the club became Plymouth Albion; Devonport Services drew on all service establishments and the RNEC produced a third first-class side. But rugby never drew crowds like Argyle.

Theatres and Cinemas

After Argyle and shopping, there was the Palace Theatre of Varieties on Saturday night to make it a real day out. Opened in 1898, it mixed crimson plush and gilt with art nouveau, and after 1911 had the flamboyant Tommy Hoyle as owner. His widow kept this music hall going right into the Second World War with Jack Fitchett as manager for many years, and every major variety act played there season after season.

For straight theatre there were the imposing Royal and the 1889 Grand Theatre, built by Henry Reed when he failed to get the lease of the Royal on the death of J.R. Newcombe, his father-in-law. By the 1920s, however, they were losing out to the cinemas. The Grand was converted in 1930 and the Royal finally succumbed a few years later, playing its last pantomime in 1936. The repertory company in the old Mechanics' Institute, launched by George S. King in 1914, bravely kept going until 1934, but by then the organiser of its supporters' club had started the Tamaritans, the amateur theatre group, and the 'Rep' died with its last prop removed. The story was the same in Devonport; the Hippodrome at the top of Fore Street switched to moving pictures, and the down-at-heel Alhambra around the corner collapsed in the late 1930s after a run of very fourth-rate touring companies.

The cinemas swamped the theatre; in the 1930s there were 250,000 picture-house seats a week and the *Western Evening Herald* was reviewing 16 houses every Tuesday. They began to swarm from 1906–07 but by 1910 these penny gaffs were eclipsed by the picture house built in Union Street by Horace Andrews, the last manager of the great Victorian centre of entertainment, St James's Hall, which had been bought out and shut when the Palace opened. Billy Lindsell, Andrews's assistant, then established the Cinedrome in Ebrington Street and cinemas were opening further afield, the Ford Palladium before 1917 and the Belgrave (on the site of the mews which hired out tram horses) soon after. In 1918 Reuben Eady turned a skating rink in Ebrington Street into the New Palladium, a monster seating 3,500 under a corrugated iron roof which resounded like thunder in heavy rain.

Various public halls were rebuilt as cinemas in 1921, like the Electric at Devonport and the Savoy in Union Street on the site of the St James's Hall. The Savoy was the elegant place in the 1920s, and the first converted for talking pictures in 1928. The other houses rapidly followed, and the wave of excitement brought new mammoth houses. In 1931 two local men, Guy Prance and William Mumford, head of the major motor firm in the town, built the 3,254-seater Regent in Frankfort Street and Gaumont-British built its 2,232-seater Gaumont Palace on the site of Andrews's picture house. The Royal Theatre was replaced by a 2,400-seater cinema in 1938 by the ABC Company, who put Tom Purdie in as the first manager; he was to stay for 30 years. There was much wheeling and dealing by the big companies: the Odeon was negotiating for a Union Street site for another super-cinema but bought the Regent instead and changed its name; since 1945 that has been pulled down, the old Gaumont became the Odeon and then a night club and the Royal has changed its name with every change of owner.

Country Buses

The public for Argyle and the shops, the Palace, the pictures and the pubs now had a new form of transport. Plymouth Corporation bought its first 20 buses through Mumford's in 1920 to serve places like Laira and Mount Gould not reached by trams; between 1930 and 1939 it replaced all trams with buses except on the Peverell route, which survived until 1945. But in the post-1918 era there were Army lorries for cheap sale and ex-Army drivers needing work. The garage firms of A.C. Turner and Mumford's began building charabancs on the lorry chassis; one-man outfits began operating excursions with Princess Square as the base, and the Co-operative Society and Mumford's Purple Tours established touring fleets. Local services began as well, though the one-man outfits were gradually absorbed by the Embankment Motor Co.

Then in 1923 Commander E.T. Hare and his ex-service drivers moved into Plymouth with their Devon Motor Transport Co. and for nearly ten years they battled to win the country bus routes. There was fare cutting – 'Plympton 4d.' – racing, timetable juggling and complete anarchy, with DMT from St Andrew's Cross winning the ascendancy. In 1927 it was bought out by the National Bus Co., which brought in the first covered double-deck buses, and in 1929 it amalgamated with the GW, which had bus interests in other parts of Devon and Cornwall, to form the Western National.

A number of the smaller companies joined Hopper & Berryman, a Mumford concern; the 1930 Road Traffic Act brought rationalisation to the services, and within three years Western National had absorbed all its local rivals. Embankment reverted to tours only.

Apart from the local service battles, there had been much in-fighting for the new long-distance road transport, with 14 companies running into the south-west by 1930. Fare-cutting reduced the London-Plymouth return fare at one point to 12s.6d. (62^1/₂p). Plymouth was mainly served by the Royal Blue coaches from Bournemouth, which in 1934 joined a pool called Associated Motorways, so that co-ordination replaced competition. It made no difference when the Western National became owners with Southern National of the Royal Blue fleet.

Newspapers and Radio

Plymouth also saw newspaper competition removed in these years. There had been any number of short-lived weekly papers since the early-eighteenth century, but the *Plymouth and Devonport Weekly Journal* eventually became pre-eminent, particularly after the arrival of Isaac Latimer in 1844, first as editor and eventually as proprietor. A Cornishman with national experience and a friend of Charles Dickens, he had established himself as a power in Plymouth and a leader of Liberal thought when in 1860 two Bath businessmen, William Saunders and Edmund Spender, in Plymouth considering another enterprise, decided to launch a daily paper. The establishment of the railway and the telegraph, and the imminent repeal of the tax on newspapers, all made the timing right. The *Western Morning News* appeared from a George Street office, opposite the Theatre Royal, in January 1860. Within six months Latimer launched the rival *Western Daily Mercury* from Frankfort Street, and the weekly *Journal* soon disappeared. The *Mercury* was a Liberal paper as against the politically independent *Morning News*. Both fought for local causes and were served by distinguished journalists; if the *Morning News* could claim the first 'London Letter' and the first weather forecast in journalism, and a major part in the founding of the Press Association news agency, the *Mercury*, under Latimer's direction for 30 years, showed more dynamism. Albert Groser, editor of the *Morning News* from 1878 until his death in 1895, was a master of timetables and organisation and carried his newspaper into every corner of Devon and Cornwall.

In 1895 the young R.A.J. Walling, son of the *Mercury* editor, was invited by the new owner of that paper, Thomas Owen, to start an evening paper. It was done in great secrecy and the *Western Evening Herald* took Plymouth by surprise when it first appeared in April 1895. R.A.J. Walling was the first editor; when he moved into the *Mercury* chair his friend and colleague J.J. Judge took his place. The *Morning News* launched its own *Western Evening News* in reply but this lasted only a few months, and a revival in the Boer War lasted just a year. If there was no room in the Three Towns for two evening papers, equally the West Country could not support two morning papers. In 1921 Sir Leicester Harmsworth, brother of the press lords Northcliffe and Rothermere, bought the *Morning News* and a few months later the *Mercury*, which was running at a heavy loss, and the *Evening Herald*. The two mornings were amalgamated and published with the evening paper from the old *Mercury* office; the *Morning News* premises in New George Street were a 1936 rebuilding on the same site. Walling refused the editorship of the new *Morning News*, which James L. Palmer, the first news editor of the combined papers, rapidly assumed, and when a year later Lord Astor bought the *Western Independent*, the last surviving weekly (and still one of the only two provincial Sunday papers in England), Walling became its editor. Judge quickly left the *Herald* to join him in a partnership that lasted until 1949. During 1920, when Harmsworth was negotiating for the *Morning News*, Lord Astor considered buying the *Mercury* as he thought a Harmsworth *Morning News* would be 'politically very undependable'. After all, Leicester Harmsworth had been a Liberal MP for many years. However, his papers, though still in theory independent, became strongly Conservative and the Liberals never got over the loss of the *Mercury*. As late as 1936 Isaac Foot, doyen of West Country Liberals, thundered against 'the Harmsworth press' in Plymouth Guildhall; 'Devon is my washpot, and over Cornwall have I cast my shoe', he accused them of thinking, in his parody of Psalm 60. But in their news columns these papers accepted their monopoly position in the region, and gave all sides a fair share of space.

Within three years of the amalgamation Plymouth had a new channel of communication with the opening of the BBC's radio station, 5PY. Its first broadcast was a concert given in Plymouth Guildhall by the Royal Marines Band on 28 March 1924. The studio proper was an upstairs room in Athenaeum Lane, a pedestrians-only link between George Street and Union Street, and the transmitting aerial was stretched between the two chimney stacks of the old sugar refinery in Mill Lane. Its children's hour made the greatest local impact, with amateur actors performing as uncles and aunts. Several of the men were in the dockyard and a taxi waited each day at 5p.m. to rush them from the Fore Street gates.

Church and Education

The dream of Plymouth as the centre of a new diocese was revived in 1922 and a popular lecturer and writer, Dr J.H.B. Masterman, was actually offered the new bishopric and exchanged livings with Mr Ponsonby at Stoke. But Lord William Cecil, Bishop of Exeter since 1916, either changed his mind or forgot (his bad memory was a by-word), and Dr Masterman had to be content with becoming the first suffragan Bishop of Plymouth in 1923. On his death in 1933 he was succeeded as bishop by the Revd F. Whitfield Daukes, vicar of St Andrew's since 1924. The Revd T. Wilkinson Riddle was not far away at George Street Baptist Church; both were big, stately men and celebrated preachers who could fill their churches; their Sunday evening sermons were almost rival attractions.

Dr Masterman was also chairman of the Plymouth Committee of the University College of the South West. The aim was to create a full regional university with colleges at Exeter, Plymouth and Redruth. Lord and Lady Astor tried to force the pace by creating a hall of residence at Devonport and brought Bernard Shaw down to open it in 1929. But it was to be over 20 years before UCSW became a full university, and then it was concentrated at Exeter.

Under the impetus of Chandler Cook, the Secretary for Education, Plymouth made radical changes in its schools in the 1920s, creating junior and senior elementary schools, raising the school-leaving age to 15 ahead of the nation, and ending secondary school fees. Much of this was negated by the 1931 depression and subsequent economies, and in 1937 the Education Committee marred its record by closing the Corporation Grammar School, the city's only co-educational establishment and descendant of the Elizabethan foundation of 1561. The last headmaster of the school, Frank Sandon, so badgered the committee about the inadequate premises that they accepted his view and closed the school.

The Approach of War

But sterner issues were at hand. Under the threat of Nazi Germany the dockyard was building up again with the rearmament programme. That, and falling world prices, brought a renewal of prosperity. The city had its taste of fascism with the creation in Plymouth of a strong branch of Oswald Mosley's Fascist Party. Their demonstrations brought the Plymouth Communists on the streets too; meetings broke up in brawls, and there were police baton charges outside Fascist headquarters in Lockyer Street. Thugs imported to beat up opponents finally disgraced the Fascists in local eyes and the organisation disappeared. The Munich crisis brought a scurry of activity with the mobilisation of the naval reservists. Within a few minutes of Chamberlain's broadcast on the morning of Sunday, 3 September 1939, air-raid sirens wailed over the city. The all-clear soon followed, but those sirens had signalled the death knell of the old city.

Destruction and Reconstruction

Blackout, gas masks on shoulders, rumours, the City Museum a services recruiting centre: the war had an eerie start. Within two weeks rumour became reality. The aircraft carrier *Courageous*, Devonport-manned and with many reservists in her crew, was torpedoed at the mouth of the Channel. It made hundreds of widows in Plymouth.

The council set up a War Emergency Committee of the three party leaders, Dunstan, Churchward and Solomon Stephens. The town clerk, Colin Campbell, took over as Air Raid Precautions Officer and found little prepared, shortages all round and little money: the danger areas were supposed to be in the south-east. It was agreed that the next lord mayor should serve for the duration of the war and Lord Astor was persuaded to accept office. Alderman Modley became his deputy, and was to hold the fort loyally and modestly in Astor's absences.

Early in 1940 first *Ajax* and then *Exeter*, victors in the *Graf Spee* battle, limped into port to heroes' welcomes, with the First Lord of the Admiralty, Winston Churchill himself, down to greet *Exeter*, Devonport-built and manned. 'A flash of colour,' Winston said, but there were desperate days to come. Germany overran western Europe and Churchill became Prime Minister. As the shattered armies came out of Dunkirk nearly 80,000 French troops were brought to Plymouth and shipped back to western France to continue the struggle. Before the last had gone the civilian refugees from western France were crowding into the Sound in all shapes and sizes of craft.

The 1st Division of the Canadian Army was embarked at Millbay for France, and disembarked, and a fresh wave of refugees poured in from St Nazaire and the Biscay ports – French and British civilians and units of the British Expeditionary Force. The greatest test for the Plymouth emergency services were the thousands of survivors of the liner *Lancastria*, sunk from the air off St Nazaire with an estimated 3,000 killed – nearly the worst marine disaster of all time.

France surrendered on 25 June, and the German Air Force was now just across the Channel. Within a fortnight the first bombs fell on Plymouth, killing three people at Swilly. The raids went on all that summer, while the Battle of Britain raged to the east. Mount Batten, which had been taken over by No. 10 Squadron of the Royal Australian Air Force on 1 April, was among the targets. Men flocked to join the new Home Guard and an Invasion Committee began planning resistance.

Plymouth had 21 raids by the end of October and then the Luftwaffe switched its main offensive from London to the munition towns and ports. The pattern was set at Coventry; the raids on Plymouth grew heavier and at the end of the month the oil tanks at Turnchapel were hit and burned for days, marking the city by day with a vast pillar of smoke and floodlighting it with flames at night. Hospitals were hit, gas supplies cut, electricity intermittent; hardly an area was free from damage. The death-roll was mounting. The city was already so stricken that the king and queen came down on 20 March, and there was an alert before they had left.

That night, and the next night, the heart of Plymouth was wiped out; 336 civilians were killed. High explosives cut the water mains and incendiaries completed the damage. The ARP control had to abandon their headquarters in the cells under the Guildhall when the building above them was burnt out. From Drake Circus to the Octagon just a few modern buildings were left in the devastation – 20,000 properties were destroyed or damaged.

For a month Plymouth struggled to recover. Only the shopping centres of Devonport and Mutley Plain survived, and every kind of administration had to find a new home. There were a few raids to keep nerves on edge, and every night people who had no duty in the city made their way out into the countryside around. Then for five nights out of nine at the end of April the bombers were back in force, completing the destruction of central Plymouth, flattening the heart of Devonport, severely damaging the South Yard of the dockyard and the Naval Barracks, wrecking whole blocks in every residential suburb. Some 590 civilians were killed, even more injured, and an unknown number lost without trace; 1,500 dwellings were destroyed or damaged beyond repair, and another 15,000 damaged.

How much death and damage the services suffered had remained hidden. In his war history Churchill said that the dockyard was saved by false fires, at the expense of the city. Mass Observation, a survey group working for the government, upset the Cabinet by reporting that at Plymouth, where the civil and domestic devastation and the dislocation of everyday life exceeded anything they had seen elsewhere, panic lay close behind the surface of local confidence. It was the chaotic and primitive flight of evacuees (to use their words) that most upset these observers. Yet in these raids there was a warden service alone of 2,500, nearly all part-time, and a normal 90 per cent turn-out in raids. The untrained were better out of the city; for those who stayed it was a time of terror, and much heroism.

The French writer André Savignon, winner of the *Prix Goncourt*, went through the Plymouth Blitz. Even before the March raids he wrote of 'the almost physical impression that a city is slipping away from under one's very feet'. Of dawn on 21 March he wrote, 'in this town that was wasting away in reddish trails of smoke, only a few citizens wandered: the others were still in hiding; or lay, all distress ended, under the ruins'. That evening: 'The silence returned, but not to last. A great breath of fear soughed through the town: "they" were coming.' Later: 'Ashes, mud, dust... this poignant acrid smell... this effluvia of death.' As night fell in Plymouth in those Blitz days it was unnerving to walk the narrow path between the shattered buildings of once fine streets, frightening in their emptiness. Those who were staying were snatching sleep before the bombers came; those who could were walking, or waiting silently for lorries, on the main roads out of town. Stanley Goodman has written of leaving the burning YMCA on the night of 20 March:

Nobody wanted to move much because the noise outside was hellish, but we did file out through the broken front... to find that the whole of Spooner's on the opposite side of the road was alight. It was burning steadily and evenly like the wide wick of an oil lamp with a great

The Blitz. Shops burn in Old Town Street.

crackle and roar, and the heat was so great that we could not look at it... it was lighter than day and great bombs were falling every few seconds.

He then went off to look for his bicycle! On 1 May it was decided to evacuate the children: whole schools were moved. On 2 May Winston Churchill came down to cheer the people. Air-raid victims were buried at Efford cemetery in a common grave. Dancing was started every evening on the Hoe. A fighter airfield was constructed at Yelverton, the rubble of destroyed Plymouth the foundation for its runways, and opened by 15 August. As a direct result of the Plymouth experience, where fire brigades from other towns stood by helpless because their equipment would not fit that of Plymouth, or anywhere else, the National Fire Service was set up. Plymouth's balloon barrage and the gun defences

1941: lorries at the top of Alexandra Road, Mutley, taking people out into the countryside to escape the night's bombing.

were strengthened, the ARP strength built up to 3,500. ARP control, burnt out again, found a third base at Pounds House, as did the town clerk's office. The administration found homes in many queer places, and the big shops were spread from Drake Circus to Hyde Park Corner. Raids continued for the rest of the year, on a lesser scale, and then for 1942 the city was left in comparative peace. It was needed.

Not until February 1943 did Germany change its tactics again and resume night bombing, but now defences were stronger, and a number of times the citizens saw enemy planes shot down. That spring 29 Division of the United States Army was garrisoned in Plymouth and the American Navy established a Cattewater base from Sutton Pool to Laira Bridge. They increased the polyglot population of wartime Plymouth, which already had Free French, Dutch, Norwegian and Polish servicemen – even Spanish refugees from the Civil War. The Americans set up their own anti-aircraft guns around the city and on city bomb sites, and constructed camps and embarkation hards on every waterfront. The Second Front, the way back, was imminent.

With the new confidence the children were coming back, to the embarrassment of the education authority. By midsummer 8,000 of the evacuated 12,000 were home again. There were still air raids, some of them sharp, but the last – though Plymouth could not know it then – came on 30 April 1944. The waterfront and railway lines were the main targets. Nine people were killed in Plymouth, 18 at Oreston.

The fleet for the invasion of Europe was already building up, and V and VII Corps of General Omar Bradley's 1st US Army embarked at Plymouth for the bloody landings on Tuesday, 6 June, at Omaha and Utah beaches. After the initial bombardments some of the American battleships came into the dockyard for repair, including the *Arkansas*, which had been in the Sound only a few years earlier on a courtesy visit. By the beginning of August the armies were breaking out of Normandy, by the end they were over the Seine and the war was moving eastwards. In September Plymouth relaxed the blackout, in November the Home Guard stood down, and on 8 May 1945 Plymouth joined in the celebrations of Victory in Europe. It was time to count the cost.

There had been 602 air-raid alerts, 59 actual bombing attacks, 1,172 civilians killed and altogether 4,448 civilian casualties. Apart from the two main shopping centres, two guildhalls, a theatre, six hotels, eight cinemas, 26 schools, 41 churches and 100 public houses, 3,754 houses had gone and another 18,389 were in need of major repair. All told the houses damaged – not counting just broken windows – were 72,102, more than the number of houses in the city because many had been damaged more than once. So many people had been forced to find homes out of the city that the population was down from 208,000 to 127,000.